Art of the Kwakiutl Indians

AND OTHER NORTHWEST COAST TRIBES

Art of the Kwakiutl Indians

AND OTHER NORTHWEST COAST TRIBES

By Audrey Hawthorn

THE UNIVERSITY OF BRITISH COLUMBIA   Vancouver

UNIVERSITY OF WASHINGTON PRESS   Seattle and London

To Harry Hawthorn

Preface

This volume is an attempt to make accessible for scholars, artists, and others the wide array of material culture manufactured by some of the most imaginative, industrious, and skillful craftsmen of the tribal world: the Indians of the Northwest Coast of North America. Their material culture is here illustrated by photographs of the complete collection of objects made for ceremonial use and now in the Museum of Anthropology of the University of British Columbia.

This collection is an unusually rich and full one, especially of the masks and other items of the ceremonial life of the Kwakiutl Indians, one of the seven major tribal groups inhabiting the Northwest Coast; in addition it contains comparable materials from other tribal groups: the Tlingit, Tsimshian, Haida, Bella Coola, Nootka, and Salish Indians.

The years after the Second World War were years of social change in this coastal region, and a large number of Indian families chose to discontinue their family participation in some aspects of traditional ceremonial life. In 1950 Mungo Martin, Chief Nakapenkem of Fort Rupert of the Ma'mtagila clan, was brought to the University of British Columbia to repair some old totem poles in the university collection and to carve some new ones. While he was at the university, Mungo became intensely interested in the concept of a museum as a place in which to preserve and interpret material culture, and he was influential in directing to the museum many of the Kwakiutl people who were at a point of culture change where they wished to abandon their places in the potlatch system and had no wish to hold onto the materials of the potlatch, which had lost its importance.

Money was made available by Dr. H. R. MacMillan, who had been purchasing collections for the museum since 1947. Others also added their support, among them Dr. Walter C. Koerner and the Leon and Thea Koerner Foundation, which made considerable grants to support special purchases. Several pioneer missionaries had spent their lives collecting objects in the region of their special endeavors and had amassed outstanding collections. Among these were the Reverend G. R. Raley of the United Church, the first missionary at Kitamaat; Dr. G. H. Darby of Bella Bella; and the Reverend W. E. Collison of Skidegate. They desired permanent housing for their collections, which were purchased for the museum. In addition, many fine gifts were made by families and individuals whose lives were intertwined with the history of this region.

Already in his seventies, Mungo Martin was keenly aware of the great changes brought by the years, and was anxious to record what he knew of the culture in which he had grown up, and in which he had seen the changes come. While he was at the museum he helped to identify and describe the materials as they came in. Once the machinery of purchasing was established, many Kwakiutl people traveling to Vancouver on their own concerns began to come to the university. Some were careful informants, and all gave some assistance in identifying the owners, area of provenience, and uses of the various objects, and helped in other ways to sort out the materials and their meanings. Meanwhile, various faculty members got to know the families of several tribal groups of the coastal areas and extended the interpretations.

During the days when Mungo and his wife, Abayah, were at the university, Mungo visited the museum frequently to see what had arrived during the week. At the height of the flow of materials, wooden crates, old trunks, sea chests, and cardboard boxes came in by every ship from the north. Addressed to the university, to Mungo Martin himself, and to a number of other addresses, these reached their destination with the help of the wonderfully understanding post office. Mungo awaited the unpacking with keen interest. Being a full participant in the ceremonial system, he recognized many individual pieces and identified almost all of them with assurance. He gave both the Kwakiutl name and a translation, based on his clear comprehension of the use and background of the piece. He was concerned that his words should not be wasted. "Write that down, now," he often said, and then, "Say it back," until he was satisfied that the transcription was reasonably correct. He himself had some command of an orthographic system introduced by a missionary.

Sometimes Mungo would counsel against buying a mask because the owner had no right to it and was selling someone else's property, or because it did not belong in the inherited myth but had simply been "invented" by somebody. Should "people see it here, they would laugh" and say that the museum had bought a mask that was not genuine. Abayah also recognized old pieces with pleasure and would often be moved to communicate anecdotes about the time she had seen them used. Unfortunately, Mungo could not stay with the museum forever, and the carving program he was engaged in moved to Victoria. Over the years he returned from time to time, and the major new acquisitions were always brought for his inspection. Dan Cranmer, Pelnagwela Wakas of the Nimpkish band at Alert Bay, who was married to Mrs. Martin's daughter, also came a few times and gave the same sort of guidance in the naming and identification of materials.

Many other Kwakiutl showed an interest when they came to Vancouver on their own business. They came out to see what was new or to see the collection for the first time. Those who came were those who cared most about the ceremonial art, and usually they were able to add information, perhaps about the pieces they had been associated with in their own lives. Sometimes in the trunks and boxes there would be a letter from an old person making the effort to communicate some of the knowledge that should go with the pieces sent down. Others had prevailed on a child or grandchild to write for them.

We had facilities for making tea and coffee in the workrooms, and on many afternoons an old couple sat with their grandchildren in the midst of the bustle and turmoil of work going on around them, drinking tea and looking at the things still on the storeroom shelves, and then offering reminiscences and anecdotes with the humor and wistfulness a time now distant evoked for them.

With the achievement of greater prosperity and the return of open potlatching, materials came in from the southern Kwakiutl less frequently. There were no longer any men who had the depth of knowledge of Mungo Martin and Dan Cranmer. In order to obtain additional identifications and other information that was still needed, Gloria Webster, oldest daughter of Dan Cranmer, agreed to work in Alert Bay for a time. Mrs. Webster is a graduate in anthropology who has successfully lived in both worlds and has maintained her bonds with young and old. She was initiated as a Tokwit dancer in 1949, and some of the materials used on that occasion are illustrated in this book.

Mrs. Webster's mother, actively interested and hospitable, made her house available as a headquarters where those who wished to visit and assist in the project could come and talk. Gloria took the file of photographs from the museum and worked systematically through them. She also traveled into Fort Rupert at a time when a number of people from various islands were visiting there. The many comments and interpretations she recorded, some of them following lengthy discussions among the old people, have been preserved in detail in the files of the museum.

As the collections accumulated, limitations of space in the museum made it increasingly difficult to make all of the material available for study. Through the illustrations and text of this volume we have therefore attempted to construct a true "museum without walls," in which the masks, blankets and other costumes, feast dishes, spoons, rattles, and drums can be seen side by side and in their whole range.

Only the objects associated with ceremonial life have been selected for illustration. Articles of daily and domestic life, not designed for use in the potlatch or the dancing orders and not decorated with family crest designs, are not included, although they remain in the museum as an important demonstration of the variety of technological inventions developed by the Indians of the Northwest Coast.

It is apparent that there are no duplicates in the carvings and paintings shown here. While it has long been appreciated that this region was outstanding among the tribal cultures of the world in material artistry, little attention has been directed toward comparisons of individual productions. The full illustration of the pieces, organized in their categories so that a type of mask, feast dish, or carved spoon can be seen within a total range, shows clearly that not all craftsmen were equally skilled or imaginative.

The greatest proportion of material represented is Kwakiutl. It would, however, be less useful to include only the materials of this tribe since there was frequent interchange of ideas, materials, forms, and institutions with neighboring tribal friends and rivals. Through copying, buying, marrying, or wresting possessions by force, there was a constant new inflow of items and ideas. Materials purchased by the museum from Kwakiutl owners then living in their own territory have been labeled Kwakiutl unless the facts of origin in another locality were clearly established; in such cases the foreign origin is noted. When no place of origin is mentioned, it is unknown. The following place names, which will be found in the captions, do not appear on the maps: West Saanich and Patricia Bay, near Victoria, and Klemklemalitz, on the Cowichan River, all on Vancouver Island; Musqueam Reserve and North Vancouver Reserve, both in Vancouver; Khutzeymatleen Inlet, north of Prince Rupert at the mouth of the Nass River.

The orthography used in this volume is based on the modifications by Wilson Duff and Bill Holm—two ethnographers who have a direct knowledge of the spoken Kwakiutl language—of the transcriptions of Boas, Curtis, and others. Where Boas and Curtis are cited, their own orthography is, of course, retained.

Acknowledgments

I am indebted to Helen Codere for encouragement and helpful comment; to Wilson Duff for permission to use three of his original maps as the basis for the maps in this book, for his special information on Kwakiutl geography and place names, and for his help with the transcription of various Kwakiutl orthographies into a standard and pronounceable form; and to Edward Malin for careful and constructive criticism and advice.

I am especially indebted to Bill Holm, the foremost contemporary scholar on Kwakiutl ceremonial life, and an active participant in the dancing system, who has given much time and thought to the correct orthography and to the details of the whole of the ceremonial procedure, especially the Hamatsa ritual and its paraphernalia. Any mistakes are mine, not his.

I wish to acknowledge the special assistance of Gloria Webster, who undertook to find answers to some tangled questions among her friends and relatives of Alert Bay and adjacent islands; Jill Willmott, who helped to supervise the photography and arrange the data for more than two thousand items, and who helped in many other ways to further this project; and Margaret Stott, who patiently and skillfully kept the records up to date, collated and compiled the many versions, and contributed some special knowledge and assistance. Eric Waterton supervised and guided much of the photography through the many stages needed for final completion, and helped with many points of library research. I wish especially to acknowledge the skilled and watchful expertise of Alice Bownick, who typed and retyped the many versions, with all of the difficult phonetic spellings, through five long years.

Other students who devoted much time and attention to the many details of this project over the years are Thora Hawkey, Chris Rose, Peter McNair, Tony de Jong, and Ingeborg Ruus.

The color photographs are by Johsel Namkung, senior medical science photographer at the University of Washington. All black-and-white photographs are by Arthur P. Holborne, Photography Supervisor of the University of British Columbia Extension Department.

The collection of Indian material in the Museum of Anthropology is owed largely to the generous support (1948-65) of Dr. H. R. MacMillan through a series of annual and special grants to the museum. The museum is also indebted to Dr. Walter C. Koerner for his unfailing interest and helpful support, both for the museum and for the general carving program undertaken by the University of British Columbia. The Leon and Thea Koerner Foundation has made many special grants over the years for special purchases.

Finally, publication of this book was made possible by special grants from the Canada Council and the University of British Columbia Board of Publications. The Leon and Thea Koerner Foundation made special grants to the museum for the preparation of photographs, and an additional grant to help in the publication.

AUDREY HAWTHORN

August, 1967
Vancouver, B.C.

Contents

Part I: THE SETTING

The Northwest Coast   3

Craft and Technology of the Artist   8

Kwakiutl Religion and Mythology   19

Inheritance   21

The Potlatch   25

The Copper Complex   30

The Ceremonial Year   33

The Klasila   34

The Tsetseka Season   36

Staging the Tsetseka   39

Hereditary Officials and Their Ceremonial Roles   43

Kwakiutl Dancing Societies   46

Dancing Societies of Other Northwest Coast Tribes   49

Hamatsa Ritual   50

Ritual of Winalagilis, the War Spirit   54

Atlakim Dancing   57

Dluwalakha Dancing and Masks   58

Part II: CEREMONIAL ART

Ceremonial Curtains   67

Supernatural Treasures   72

Batons, Whistles, Clappers, and Rattles   77

Mourning Masks   90

Masks of Gakhula, the Intruder   92

Hamatsa Bird-Monster Masks   95

Hamatsa Cedar Bark Head and Neck Rings   116

Noohlmahl Masks   123

Tanis Masks   127

Ceremonial Skulls   129

Sisiutl Headdresses and Ceremonial Objects   133

Atlakim Masks   138

Tsonokwa Masks   152

Coppers   158

Ceremonial Weapons   163

Ceremonial Cedar Bark   168

Ceremonial Clothing   173

Hats   184

Chiefs' Headdresses or Dancing Hats   191

Helmet Headdresses   197

Jewelry and Cosmetics   202

Ceremonial Staffs   207

Feast Dishes   215

Feast Ladles and Spoons   226

Baskets and Mats   234

Potlatch Properties   236

Komokwa Masks   239

Fish, Pugwis, and Killer Whale Masks   247

Animal Masks   253

Bird Masks   270

Insect Masks   280

Natural Element Masks   283

Bookwus Masks   291

Kwekwe Masks   297

Speaker Masks   302

Human Face Masks   309

Complex Masks   319

Kerfed Boxes, Dishes, and Cradles   325

Canoes and Paddles   336

Totem Poles, House Posts, and Mortuary Poles   343

Human and Animal Carvings   354

Soul Catchers   367

Stonework   369

Part III: APPENDIXES, GLOSSARY,
        BIBLIOGRAPHY, INDEX

Appendix I: Style and Attributions   377

Appendix II: A Potlatch at Alert Bay in 1966   384

Appendix III: An Eye-Witness Account
        of the Hamatsa Ritual   387

Appendix IV: Northwest Coast Collections
        in the Museum of Anthropology,
        University of British Columbia   391

Glossary   394

Bibliography   399

Index   406

Illustrations

MAPS

1. Indians of British Columbia, Linguistic Subdivisions   2
2. The Southern Kwakiutl, Tribal Boundaries and Village Settlements   6
3. The Northern Kwakiutl and Adjacent Tribes   7

COLOR PLATES *(following page 34)*

      I.   Rattle with bear design, probably Haida
     II.   Haida, Kwakiutl, and Bella Coola bird rattles
    III.   Kwakiutl Hamatsa raven and Hokhokw masks
    IV.   Kwakiutl Hamatsa Crooked-Beak and multiple masks
     V.   Kwakiutl Hamatsa multiple masks
    VI.   Kwakiutl Tsonokwa mask
   VII.   Kwakiutl button cloaks
  VIII.   Kwakiutl and Haida button cloaks
    IX.   Kwakiutl and Tlingit Chilkat cloaks
     X.   Kwakiutl speaker's staff and Tsimshian dance shirt
    XI.   Kwakiutl chiefs' headdresses
   XII.   Kwakiutl and Tsimshian chiefs' headdresses
  XIII.   Kwakiutl heron and duck helmet headdress
  XIV.   Haida frog bowl, Nootka duck, Kwakiutl loon helmet headdress
   XV.   Kwakiutl eagle feast dishes
  XVI.   Tsimshian spoon, Haida hat, Haida drum, Tlingit killer whale crest basket
 XVII.   Kwakiutl killer whale masks
XVIII.   Tsimshian killer whale masks
  XIX.   Kwakiutl wolf masks
   XX.   Kwakiutl Komokwa mask
  XXI.   Kwakiutl moon mask
 XXII.   Kwakiutl moon mask
XXIII.   Kwakiutl sun mask
XXIV.   Bella Coola moon and cod masks

XXV.   Kwakiutl eagle mask
XXVI.   Kwakiutl complex echo mask with eight mouthpieces
XXVII.   Tsimshian mask of woman's face, Haida bird and
    human face mask, Bella Coola human face mask,
    Haida mask of woman's face
XXVIII.   Kwakiutl woman's face and fish masks
XXIX.   Kwakiutl and Haida kerfed boxes
XXX.   Haida kerfed oil dish and Tsimshian kerfed food dish
XXXI.   Nootka Kwekwe masks
XXXII.   Kwakiutl and Haida model canoes, Tsimshian and Haida canoe paddles

FIGURES

1. Bone, wood, and antler wedges   15
2. Greenstone blades   15
3. Stone hammers   15
4. Stone mauls   16
5. Stone "elbow" adzes   16
6. D-adzes   17
7. Curved knives   17
8. Paints and brushes   18
9. Leather templates   18
10. Kwakiutl ceremonial curtain   69
11. Kwakiutl ceremonial curtain   70
12. Kwakiutl ceremonial curtain   70
13. Kwakiutl ceremonial curtain   71
14. Kwakiutl ceremonial curtain   71
15. Kwakiutl Tokwit puppets   74
16. Kwakiutl Tokwit puppets   74
17. Kwakiutl Tokwit puppets   75
18. Kwakiutl Tokwit box   75
19. Kwakiutl Tokwit cradle   75
20. Kwakiutl Tokwit frog   76
21. Kwakiutl Tokwit raven   76
22. Kwakiutl Tokwit crab   76
23. Kwakiutl Tokwit crab   76
24. Kwakiutl batons   80
25. Kwakiutl whistles   80
26. Kwakiutl whistles   81
27. Kwakiutl whistles   81
28. Nootka and Kwakiutl whistles   82
29. Tsimshian, Kwakiutl, and Nootka whistles   82
30. Salish, Kwakiutl, and Nootka bird rattles   83
31. Kwakiutl, Tsimshian, Haida, and Bella Coola bird rattles   84
32. Kwakiutl rattles   85
33. Kwakiutl and Tsimshian rattles   86
34. Tsimshian rattles   87
35. Tsimshian and Kwakiutl copper rattles   87
36. Haida and Kwakiutl rattles   87
37. Two rattles   88
38. Kwakiutl Solatlala rattles   88

39. Three rattles   88
40. Various rattles   89
41. Kwakiutl killer whale rattles   89
42. Kwakiutl clappers   89
43. Kwakiutl mourning masks   91
44. Kwakiutl Gakhula (Intruder) masks   93
45. Kwakiutl Gakhula (Intruder) masks   94
46. Kwakiutl Hamatsa Raven masks   97
47. Kwakiutl Hamatsa Raven mask   98
48. Kwakiutl Hamatsa Raven mask   98
49. Kwakiutl Hamatsa Raven mask   98
50. Kwakiutl Hamatsa Raven mask   99
51. Kwakiutl Hamatsa Raven mask   99
52. Kwakiutl Hamatsa Raven mask   99
53. Kwakiutl Hamatsa Raven mask   99
54. Kwakiutl Hamatsa Raven mask   100
55. Kwakiutl Hamatsa Raven mask   100
56. Kwakiutl Hamatsa Raven mask   100
57. Kwakiutl Hamatsa Raven mask   100
58. Kwakiutl Hamatsa Raven mask   101
59. Kwakiutl Hamatsa Raven mask   101
60. Kwakiutl Hamatsa Raven mask   101
61. Kwakiutl Hamatsa Raven mask   101
62. Kwakiutl Hamatsa Raven mask   101
63. Kwakiutl Hamatsa Raven mask   102
64. Kwakiutl Hamatsa Raven mask   102
65. Kwakiutl Hamatsa Raven mask   102
66. Kwakiutl Hamatsa Raven mask   102
67. Kwakiutl Hamatsa Raven mask   102
68. Kwakiutl Hamatsa Raven mask   103
69. Kwakiutl Hamatsa Raven mask   103
70. Kwakiutl Hamatsa Raven mask   103
71. Kwakiutl Hamatsa Raven mask   103
72. Kwakiutl Hamatsa Raven mask   103
73. Kwakiutl Hokhokw mask   104
74. Kwakiutl Hokhokw mask   104
75. Kwakiutl Hokhokw mask   104
76. Kwakiutl Hokhokw mask   104
77. Kwakiutl Hokhokw mask   105
78. Kwakiutl Hokhokw mask   105
79. Kwakiutl Hokhokw mask   105
80. Kwakiutl Crooked-Beak mask   106
81. Kwakiutl Crooked-Beak mask   106
82. Kwakiutl Crooked-Beak mask   106
83. Kwakiutl Crooked-Beak mask   107
84. Kwakiutl Crooked-Beak mask   107
85. Kwakiutl Crooked-Beak mask   107
86. Kwakiutl Crooked-Beak mask   108
87. Kwakiutl Crooked-Beak mask   108
88. Kwakiutl Crooked-Beak mask   108

89. Kwakiutl Crooked-Beak mask   109
90. Kwakiutl Crooked-Beak mask   109
91. Kwakiutl Crooked-Beak mask   109
92. Kwakiutl Crooked-Beak mask   110
93. Kwakiutl Crooked-Beak mask   110
94. Kwakiutl Crooked-Beak mask   110
95. Kwakiutl Crooked-Beak mask   111
96. Kwakiutl Crooked-Beak mask   111
97. Kwakiutl Crooked-Beak mask   111
98. Kwakiutl Crooked-Beak mask   112
99. Kwakiutl Crooked-Beak mask   112
100. Kwakiutl Crooked-Beak mask   112
101. Kwakiutl Crooked-Beak mask   113
102. Kwakiutl Crooked-Beak mask   113
103. Kwakiutl Crooked-Beak mask   113
104. Kwakiutl Crooked-Beak mask   114
105. Kwakiutl Crooked-Beak mask   114
106. Kwakiutl Crooked-Beak mask   114
107. Kwakiutl Crooked-Beak mask   114
108. Kwakiutl Crooked-Beak mask   115
109. Bella Coola Crooked-Beak mask   115
110. Kwakiutl Hamatsa multiple mask   115
111. Kwakiutl Hamatsa head rings and Crooked-Beak headpiece   118
112. Kwakiutl Hamatsa head rings and headpiece   119
113. Kwakiutl Hamatsa neck rings   120
114. Kwakiutl and Haida Hamatsa neck rings   121
115. Kwakiutl Hamatsa neck rings   122
116. Kwakiutl Hamatsa neck rings   122
117. Kwakiutl Noohlmahl mask   125
118. Kwakiutl Noohlmahl masks   125
119. Kwakiutl Noohlmahl masks   126
120. Kwakiutl Noohlmahl masks   126
121. Kwakiutl Tanis masks   128
122. Kwakiutl ceremonial skulls   130
123. Kwakiutl ceremonial skull and ghost dancer's mask   131
124. Kwakiutl ghost dancers' masks and headdress   131
125. Kwakiutl Hamatsa head ring and robe   132
126. Kwakiutl Sisiutl headdresses   134
127. Kwakiutl Sisiutl ceremonial board   134
128. Kwakiutl ceremonial belts with Sisiutl design and Sisiutl baton   135
129. Kwakiutl Sisiutl batons and ceremonial belt with Sisiutl design   136
130. Kwakiutl power boards with Sisiutl designs   137
131. Kwakiutl Atlakim buffoon mask   140
132. Kwakiutl Atlakim mask   141
133. Kwakiutl Atlakim masks   142
134. Kwakiutl Atlakim masks   143
135. Kwakiutl Atlakim mask   144
136. Kwakiutl Atlakim mask   145
137. Kwakiutl Atlakim mask   145
138. Kwakiutl Atlakim mask   146

139. Kwakiutl Atlakim mask   146
140. Kwakiutl Atlakim masks   147
141. Kwakiutl Atlakim "door" mask   148
142. Kwakiutl Atlakim masks   149
143. Kwakiutl Atlakim masks   150
144. Kwakiutl Atlakim masks   151
145. Kwakiutl Tsonokwa mask (Geekumhl)   154
146. Kwakiutl Tsonokwa masks (Geekumhl)   155
147. Kwakiutl Tsonokwa masks (Geekumhl)   155
148. Kwakiutl Tsonokwa masks   156
149. Kwakiutl Tsonokwa masks   156
150. Kwakiutl Tsonokwa masks   157
151. Kwakiutl Tsonokwa head and mask   157
152. Kwakiutl copper   159
153. Kwakiutl copper   160
154. Haida copper   160
155. Kwakiutl copper   161
156. Kwakiutl copper   161
157. Kwakiutl coppers   162
158. Kwakiutl ceremonial cradle   162
159. Kwakiutl ceremonial harpoon   164
160. Kwakiutl ceremonial harpoon   165
161. Kwakiutl ceremonial spear   166
162. Kwakiutl Tsonokwa wedges   166
163. Kwakiutl ceremonial bow with Sisiutl design   166
164. Kwakiutl Tsonokwa wedge and ceremonial daggers   167
165. Bella Coola and Kwakiutl ceremonial daggers   167
166. Kwakiutl copper-cutting stand   167
167. Kwakiutl head rings   169
168. Kwakiutl head rings   169
169. Kwakiutl and Haida head rings   169
170. Coast Salish headdress   170
171. Kwakiutl and Haida head rings   170
172. Coast Salish head rings   170
173. Bella Coola head ring   171
174. Kwakiutl Klasila neck ring   171
175. Coast Salish headdress   171
176. Coast Salish headdress   171
177. Coast Salish headdress   171
178. Tsimshian neck rings   172
179. Coast Salish new dancer's harness   172
180. Kwakiutl cedar bark skirt   172
181. Haida Chilkat cloak   175
182. Haida Chilkat cloak   175
183. Tlingit Chilkat cloak   176
184. Tsimshian Chilkat pattern board   176
185. Kwakiutl Chilkat pattern board   176
186. Kwakiutl button cloaks   177
187. Kwakiutl and Tahltan button cloaks   178
188. Tsimshian button cloak   179

189. Salish blanket 179
190. Kwakiutl dance apron 179
191. Kwakiutl dance apron 179
192. Kwakiutl dance and Chilkat aprons 180
193. Kwakiutl Chilkat apron 181
194. Tlingit Chilkat apron 181
195. Haida Chilkat shirt 181
196. Tsimshian Chilkat headpiece 181
197. Haida Chilkat leggings 182
198. Tsimshian cloak 182
199. Tsimshian dance apron 183
200. Coast Salish spirit dance costume 183
201. Tsimshian dance apron 183
202. Coast Salish headdress 183
203. Kwakiutl hat 186
204. Haida hat 186
205. Haida hat 187
206. Haida hat 187
207. Haida hat 188
208. Haida hat 188
209. Kwakiutl hat 188
210. Haida hat 189
211. Haida hat 189
212. Haida hat 189
213. Haida, Nootka, Salish, and Kwakiutl hats 190
214. Kwakiutl chief's headdress 192
215. Kwakiutl chief's headdress 193
216. Kwakiutl chief's headdress 193
217. Kwakiutl chief's headdress 193
218. Kwakiutl chief's headdress 193
219. Kwakiutl and Bella Coola chiefs' headdresses 194
220. Kwakiutl chief's headdress 195
221. Kwakiutl chief's headdress 195
222. Kwakiutl chief's headdress 195
223. Kwakiutl chief's headdress 195
224. Tsimshian chief's headdress 196
225. Bella Coola chief's headdress 196
226. Tsimshian chief's headdress 196
227. Tsimshian chief's headdress 196
228. Kwakiutl loon or swan headdress 198
229. Kwakiutl loon headdress 198
230. Kwakiutl double loon headdress with coppers 199
231. Kwakiutl double raven headdress 199
232. Kwakiutl raven headdress 199
233. Kwakiutl Thunderbird hat 199
234. Kwakiutl Thunderbird headdress 200
235. Kwakiutl hawk, killer whale, and bear headdresses 200
236. Nootka hawk headdress 201
237. Nootka hawk headdress 201
238. Nootka grouse headdress 201

239. Nootka grouse headdress   201
240. Kwakiutl and Haida bracelets   204
241. Kwakiutl and Haida bracelets   205
242. Assorted jewelry   206
243. Pair of Haida walking sticks   208
244. Tsimshian shaman's staff   209
245. Kwakiutl speakers' staffs   210
246. Tsimshian speaker's staff   211
247. Haida shaman's staff   212
248. Haida speaker's staff   213
249. Kwakiutl speaker's staff   213
250. Kwakiutl ceremonial staffs, Salish and Kwakiutl batons   214
251. Kwakiutl Sisiutl feast dish   217
252. Kwakiutl Sisiutl feast dish   217
253. Kwakiutl Sisiutl feast dish   217
254. Kwakiutl feast dish   217
255. Salish bear-shaped feast dish   218
256. Tsimshian bear-shaped oil dish   218
257. Kwakiutl wolf-shaped feast dish   218
258. Kwakiutl wolf-shaped feast dish   218
259. Kwakiutl wolf-shaped feast dish   219
260. Kwakiutl wolf-shaped feast dish   219
261. Kwakiutl wolf-shaped feast dish   219
262. Kwakiutl wolf-shaped feast dish   219
263. Kwakiutl feast dish   219
264. Pair of Kwakiutl feast dishes   220
265. Kwakiutl whale-shaped feast dish   220
266. Kwakiutl fish-shaped oil dish   220
267. Tlingit oil dish   220
268. Kwakiutl seal-shaped oil dish   221
269. Kwakiutl seal-shaped feast dish   221
270. Kwakiutl seal-shaped feast dish   221
271. Kwakiutl seal-shaped dish   221
272. Kwakiutl seal-shaped feast dish   221
273. Kwakiutl otter-shaped and beaver-shaped oil dishes   222
274. Haida frog-shaped bowl and oil dish   222
275. Kwakiutl frog-shaped oil dishes   222
276. Tsimshian frog-shaped feast dish   223
277. Kwakiutl duck-shaped feast dish and Tlingit bird-shaped dish   223
278. Haida food dish   223
279. Kwakiutl feast dish   223
280. Kwakiutl canoe-shaped oil and feast dishes, Nootka
     canoe-shaped festival dish, Haida dish   224
281. Kwakiutl canoe-shaped feast dish   225
282. Tsimshian food dish   225
283. Salish food dish   225
284. Kwakiutl canoe-shaped food dish   225
285. Kwakiutl canoe-shaped feast dish   225
286. Salish feast dish   225
287. Salish feast dish   225

288. Haida and Kwakiutl horn spoons   227
289. Haida, Kwakiutl, and Tsimshian horn spoons   227
290. Kwakiutl and Tsimshian ladles   228
291. Kwakiutl ladles   229
292. Kwakiutl ladles   230
293. Kwakiutl ladles   230
294. Haida and Kwakiutl spoons, Kwakiutl ladle   231
295. Kwakiutl ladle   231
296. Haida and Kwakiutl ladles   231
297. Salish, Tsimshian, and Kwakiutl ladles   232
298. Tsimshian, Haida, and Kwakiutl ladles   232
299. Kwakiutl spoon, Tsimshian ladle, Kwakiutl ladle, soapberry spoon   233
300. Soapberry spoons   233
301. Haida basket   235
302. Haida basket   235
303. Kwakiutl mat   235
304. Kwakiutl potlatch bird   237
305. Nootka headpiece   237
306. Kwakiutl ceremonial box lid   237
307. Kwakiutl chiefs' ceremonial seats and ceremonial plaque   238
308. Kwakiutl Komokwa mask   241
309. Kwakiutl Komokwa masks   242
310. Kwakiutl Komokwa mask   242
311. Kwakiutl Komokwa mask   242
312. Kwakiutl Komokwa mask   243
313. Kwakiutl Komokwa mask   243
314. Kwakiutl Komokwa masks   244
315. Kwakiutl Komokwa masks   244
316. Kwakiutl Komokwa masks   245
317. Kwakiutl Komokwa masks   245
318. Kwakiutl Komokwa masks   246
319. Kwakiutl Komokwa masks   246
320. Kwakiutl halibut masks   249
321. Kwakiutl Atlakim fish masks   249
322. Kwakiutl fish masks   250
323. Kwakiutl fish masks   250
324. Kwakiutl fish and killer whale masks   251
325. Kwakiutl Pugwis mask   252
326. Kwakiutl Pugwis mask   252
327. Kwakiutl land otter mask   256
328. Kwakiutl land otter mask   256
329. Kwakiutl dog mask   256
330. Kwakiutl deer masks   257
331. Kwakiutl bear masks   257
332. Kwakiutl bear masks   257
333. Kwakiutl bear mask   258
334. Kwakiutl grizzly bear mask   258
335. Kwakiutl bear mask   258
336. Kwakiutl bear mask   259
337. Kwakiutl bear masks   259

338. Bella Coola bear claw   259
339. Kwakiutl wolf mask   260
340. Kwakiutl wolf mask   260
341. Kwakiutl wolf mask   260
342. Kwakiutl wolf mask   261
343. Kwakiutl wolf mask   261
344. Kwakiutl wolf mask   261
345. Kwakiutl wolf mask   262
346. Kwakiutl wolf mask   262
347. Kwakiutl wolf mask   262
348. Kwakiutl wolf mask   263
349. Kwakiutl wolf mask   263
350. Kwakiutl wolf mask   263
351. Kwakiutl wolf mask   264
352. Kwakiutl wolf mask   264
353. Kwakiutl wolf mask   264
354. Kwakiutl wolf mask   264
355. Kwakiutl wolf mask   265
356. Kwakiutl wolf mask   265
357. Kwakiutl wolf mask   265
358. Kwakiutl wolf mask   266
359. Kwakiutl wolf mask   266
360. Kwakiutl wolf mask   266
361. Kwakiutl wolf mask   266
362. Nootka wolf mask   267
363. Nootka wolf mask   267
364. Nootka wolf mask   267
365. Nootka wolf masks   268
366. Kwakiutl frog mask   268
367. Mountain goat, rabbit, and frog masks   269
368. Kwakiutl seal and squirrel or mouse masks   269
369. Kwakiutl Thunderbird mask   272
370. Kwakiutl Kolus mask   272
371. Kwakiutl Thunderbird mask   273
372. Kwakiutl Thunderbird mask   273
373. Kwakiutl Kolus mask   273
374. Kwakiutl Kolus mask   274
375. Kwakiutl eagle mask   274
376. Kwakiutl eagle mask   274
377. Kwakiutl eagle mask   274
378. Kwakiutl eagle mask   275
379. Kwakiutl eagle mask   275
380. Tsimshian eagle mask   275
381. Kwakiutl and Bella Coola hawk masks   276
382. Kwakiutl eagle and Khenkho masks   276
383. Kwakiutl Khenkho mask   276
384. Kwakiutl raven mask   277
385. Kwakiutl raven mask   277
386. Kwakiutl raven mask   277
387. Nootka raven mask   277

388. Nootka raven mask and Bella Coola raven headdress — 278
389. Kwakiutl raven mask — 278
390. Kwakiutl grouse and raven masks — 278
391. Haida raven headdress — 279
392. Kwakiutl Atlakim bird masks — 279
393. Kwakiutl bumblebee mask — 281
394. Kwakiutl mosquito mask — 281
395. Kwakiutl bumblebee mask — 281
396. Kwakiutl bumblebee masks — 282
397. Kwakiutl sun mask — 284
398. Kwakiutl raven in the sun mask — 285
399. Bella Coola sun mask — 285
400. Kwakiutl sun mask — 285
401. Kwakiutl human face and moon mask — 286
402. Kwakiutl weather headdress — 287
403. Kwakiutl weather headdress — 287
404. Kwakiutl weather headdress — 288
405. Kwakiutl weather headdress — 288
406. Kwakiutl earthquake mask — 288
407. Kwakiutl echo mask with interchangeable mouthpieces — 289
408. Kwakiutl echo mask with interchangeable mouthpieces — 289
409. Kwakiutl echo mask — 290
410. Kwakiutl echo mask with interchangeable mouthpieces — 290
411. Kwakiutl Bookwus mask — 292
412. Kwakiutl Bookwus mask — 292
413. Kwakiutl Bookwus masks — 293
414. Kwakiutl Bookwus masks — 293
415. Kwakiutl Bookwus masks — 294
416. Kwakiutl Bookwus masks — 294
417. Kwakiutl Bookwus masks — 295
418. Kwakiutl Bookwus masks — 295
419. Tsimshian and Kwakiutl Bookwus masks — 296
420. Tsimshian, Bella Coola, and Kwakiutl Bookwus masks — 296
421. Kwakiutl Kwekwe mask — 299
422. Kwakiutl Kwekwe mask — 299
423. Coast Salish and Kwakiutl Kwekwe masks — 300
424. Coast Salish Kwekwe masks — 300
425. Coast Salish Kwekwe masks — 301
426. Coast Salish Kwekwe masks — 301
427. Kwakiutl speaker mask — 303
428. Kwakiutl speaker mask — 303
429. Kwakiutl speaker masks — 304
430. Kwakiutl speaker masks — 304
431. Kwakiutl speaker masks — 305
432. Kwakiutl speaker masks — 305
433. Kwakiutl speaker mask — 306
434. Kwakiutl speaker masks — 306
435. Kwakiutl speaker masks — 307
436. Kwakiutl speaker masks — 307
437. Kwakiutl speaker masks — 308

438. Kwakiutl speaker masks   308
439. Kwakiutl human face "ridicule" mask   311
440. Nootka human face mask   312
441. Tsimshian human face masks   312
442. Bella Coola and Kwakiutl human face masks   313
443. Kwakiutl and Haida human face masks   313
444. Tsimshian and Bella Coola human face masks   314
445. Tsimshian and Nootka human face masks   314
446. Kwakiutl and Bella Coola human face masks   315
447. Kwakiutl human face masks   315
448. Kwakiutl twin human face masks   316
449. Kwakiutl and Nootka human face masks   316
450. Tsimshian and Bella Coola human face masks   317
451. Nootka human face masks   317
452. Nootka human face masks   318
453. Nootka human face masks   318
454. Kwakiutl complex wolf-man mask   321
455. Kwakiutl complex raven-man mask   322
456. Kwakiutl complex raven-Kolus mask   323
457. Kwakiutl complex raven-man mask   324
458. Nootka complex wolf-eagle mask   324
459. Tsimshian and Kwakiutl storage boxes   327
460. Haida and Kwakiutl storage boxes   327
461. Haida and Kwakiutl storage boxes   328
462. Tsimshian and Tlingit storage boxes   328
463. Kwakiutl storage boxes   329
464. Tsimshian storage boxes   329
465. Tsimshian and Kwakiutl storage boxes   330
466. Tsimshian and Haida storage boxes   330
467. Kwakiutl storage boxes   331
468. Kwakiutl storage boxes   331
469. Kwakiutl storage boxes   332
470. Kwakiutl food box   332
471. Kwakiutl oil box   333
472. Haida oil boxes and Tsimshian food box   333
473. Kwakiutl grease box and Tlingit food storage box   334
474. Kwakiutl oil box and Haida dishes   334
475. Tsimshian food dish   335
476. Kwakiutl cradle   335
477. Kwakiutl cradle   335
478. Bella Coola model canoe   338
479. Kwakiutl model canoe   338
480. Haida model canoe   338
481. Haida model canoe   338
482. Haida model canoe   338
483. Kwakiutl canoe paddles   339
484. Haida and Tsimshian canoe paddles   340
485. Haida and Tsimshian canoe paddles   341
486. Haida, Tsimshian, and Coast Salish canoe paddles   342
487. Kwakiutl totem pole   345

488. Haida model totem poles   346
489. Haida model totem pole   347
490. Haida model totem pole   347
491. Haida model totem poles and Tsimshian totem pole   348
492. Kwakiutl human figure house post   349
493. Kwakiutl human figure house post   350
494. Kwakiutl bear house post   351
495. Kwakiutl house posts and Haida memorial pole   352
496. Tsimshian house front boards   353
497. Salish house post with otters   353
498. Coast Salish grave figures   356
499. Kwakiutl ancestor figure and grave effigy   357
500. Kwakiutl grave effigy and Tsimshian ceremonial carving   358
501. Kwakiutl human head carving and Haida carving of seated chief   358
502. Bella Coola carving of man and Kwakiutl grave effigy   359
503. Coast Salish carving of Indian   360
504. Coast Salish carving of Indian agent   360
505. Tsimshian carved angel and Kwakiutl carved bear   361
506. Salish bear head and Haida sea bear carvings   361
507. Kwakiutl wolf and hawk carvings   362
508. Kwakiutl crane's head and Salish duck carvings   362
509. Kwakiutl killer whale carving   362
510. Kwakiutl fish-man charm   363
511. Tsimshian carved fish   363
512. Prehistoric club   364
513. Kwakiutl and Tsimshian clubs   364
514. Kwakiutl clubs and net float   364
515. Coast Salish mat creaser and Kwakiutl net float   364
516. Tsimshian canoe bailer and Kwakiutl carving of man and animal   365
517. Prehistoric spear thrower and Haida halibut hook   365
518. Kwakiutl and Haida halibut hooks   365
519. Coast Salish spindle whorl   366
520. Tsimshian bow, Haida musket, and Tsimshian carving   366
521. Kwakiutl soul catcher   368
522. Nootka soul catcher   368
523. Kwakiutl soul catcher   368
524. Kwakiutl, Salish, and Haida stone carvings   370
525. Salish stone carving and Kwakiutl pile driver   370
526. Haida stone carving and Salish soapstone bowl   371
527. Kwakiutl stone carving and Bella Coola stone bowl   371
528. Haida stone mortar bowls   371
529. Kwakiutl stone bowls   372
530. Kwakiutl stone hammer   372
531. Kwakiutl stone mortar dish   373
532. Haida stone carving and Tsimshian pile driver   373
533. Bella Coola stone pile drivers   373
534. Haida stone killer whale club   374
535. Haida stone fish carving   374
536. Tsimshian stone killer whale carving   374
537. Kwakiutl stone club   374

PART I
The Setting

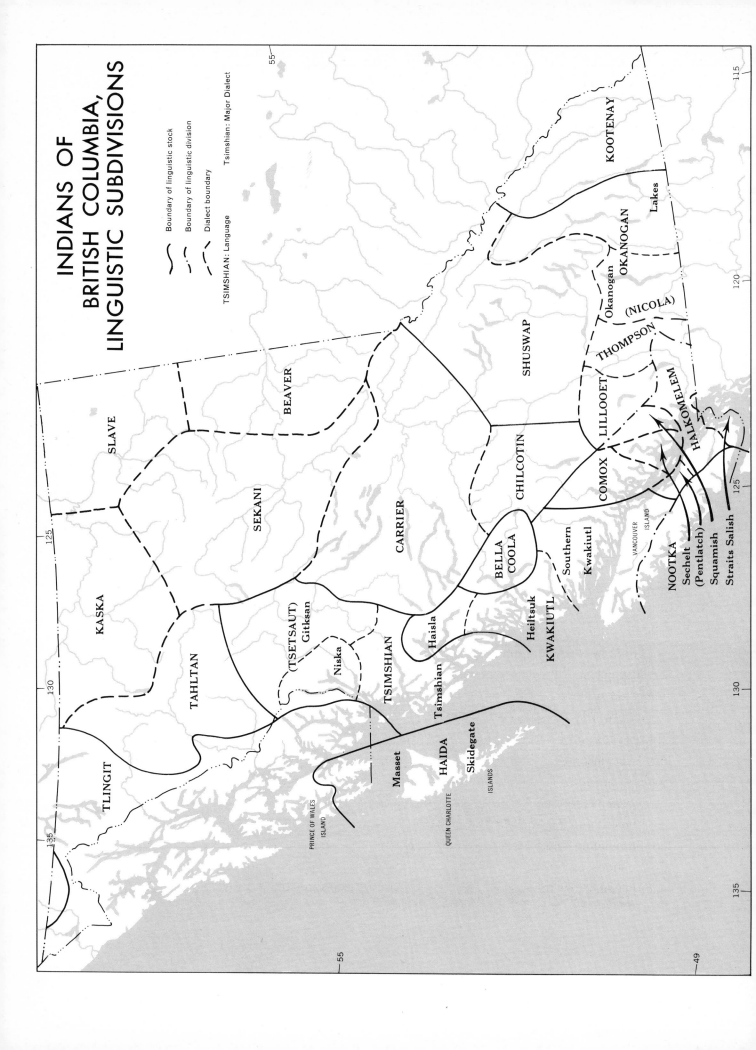

INDIANS OF BRITISH COLUMBIA, LINGUISTIC SUBDIVISIONS

Boundary of linguistic stock

Boundary of linguistic division

Dialect boundary

TSIMSHIAN: Language

Tsimshian: Major Dialect

TLINGIT

KASKA

SLAVE

BEAVER

SEKANI

TAHLTAN

(TSETSAUT) Gitksan

Niska

TSIMSHIAN

Tsimshian

HAIDA

Masset

Skidegate

PRINCE OF WALES ISLAND

QUEEN CHARLOTTE ISLANDS

CARRIER

Haisla

Heiltsuk

KWAKIUTL

BELLA COOLA

Southern Kwakiutl

CHILCOTIN

SHUSWAP

COMOX

LILLOOET

THOMPSON

(NICOLA)

Okanogan

OKANOGAN

Lakes

KOOTENAY

HALKOMELEM

VANCOUVER ISLAND

NOOTKA

Sechelt (Pentlatch)

Squamish

Straits Salish

55

55

49

115

120

125

130

135

125

130

135

The Northwest Coast

The Indians of the Northwest Coast inhabited the long, narrow strip of shore-line that stretches from Puget Sound up to the Alaskan panhandle—thirteen hundred miles long, deeply indented by fiords and rivers, and studded with islands heavily forested by the dark green conifers of the temperate rain forest.

The lives of these people were oriented toward the sea. Their villages of large plank houses were built facing the sea, and upon its waters they traveled in beautifully made canoes, both large and small. Parties of skilled seamen, setting out to trade, hunt, fish, wage warfare, or make social visits —all used the sea as their familiar path.

From the sea, the men harvested a rich profusion of sea mammals and fish, of which salmon was the preferred kind. An elaborate fishing technology supported a standard of living unrivaled among tribal cultures having no agriculture. The Indians preserved this abundance of fish by smoking, drying, and processing it for its oil, and sometimes built up a huge surplus which they used in ceremonial hospitality. Freed during the long winter months from the quest for food, they had leisure time to devote to their ceremonial life and to its material manifestations in painting, carving, and weaving.

The red cedar of the rain forest, with its straight, soft grain, made possi-ble the building of their large permanent houses and the production of the great canoes, totem poles and house carvings, boxes and masks, and other materials of social and domestic life. The cedar tree also supported a variety

3

of textile arts carried out by the women, who used fibers split from the narrow rootlets and bark stripped from the green living trunk to weave fine baskets, hats, mats, blankets, and the clothing of everyday use.

This propitious environment, with its abundance of food and of material for carving, made possible the elaborate social and ceremonial structure about which life on the Northwest Coast was centered.

Seven different linguistic groups shared a culture that was essentially common to all in the region, although, from north to south, the particular emphasis varied, and there were gradations of practice and custom. In the north lived the Tlingit and Tsimshian tribes. The Haida inhabited the Queen Charlotte Islands. On the west coast of Vancouver Island lived the Nootka, while the Kwakiutl shared the north region of Vancouver Island and the mainland directly opposite. The Salish occupied the delta of the Fraser River and some southern parts of Vancouver Island, and were distributed southward down the Washington coast; one of the groups of Salish people occupied territory to the north, near the Bella Coola River. There were an estimated 70,000 people living within these tribal boundaries at the end of the eighteenth century when the Europeans first arrived (Duff 1964:39).

Sharing a common environment and similar technologies, these tribes also shared a number of beliefs. Their mythologies involved legends in which primal ancestors had been given special privileges by the myth people, the supernaturally endowed beings of earth, sea, and sky. Such myths and privileges were valued property to be handed down to their descendants. In the three northern groups property was inherited through the maternal line; in the south, mainly through the paternal line; and in the central group, both maternal and paternal inheritance were the practice. All of the tribal groups organized their society according to social rank; those belonging to the most important inherited social ranks graded step by step into the larger number of those who had inherited positions of little importance—or none at all. Slaves taken in warfare were outside of the social system, but all took part as contributors in some way—donors, recipients, actors, or audience—in the elaborate social life of the potlatch, which was centered around the establishment of social claims and was marked by the ceremonial distribution of hospitality and gifts. On these occasions totem poles and heraldic carvings might be erected to mark the special cause of the celebration.

Dances, songs, and theatrical performance demonstrated special inherited privileges, and the performances were witnessed by invited guests, often from other tribal areas.

The intensity and the emphasis of these ceremonies and the activities centered around them varied with the tribal group. This presentation centers about the social life and ceremony of the Kwakiutl, who borrowed, adapted, and elaborated many themes into complex series of dances, ceremonies, and theatrical performances employing an equally complex series of items of related material equipment. The Kwakiutl are the focus of this study, and it is their art that is most profusely illustrated.

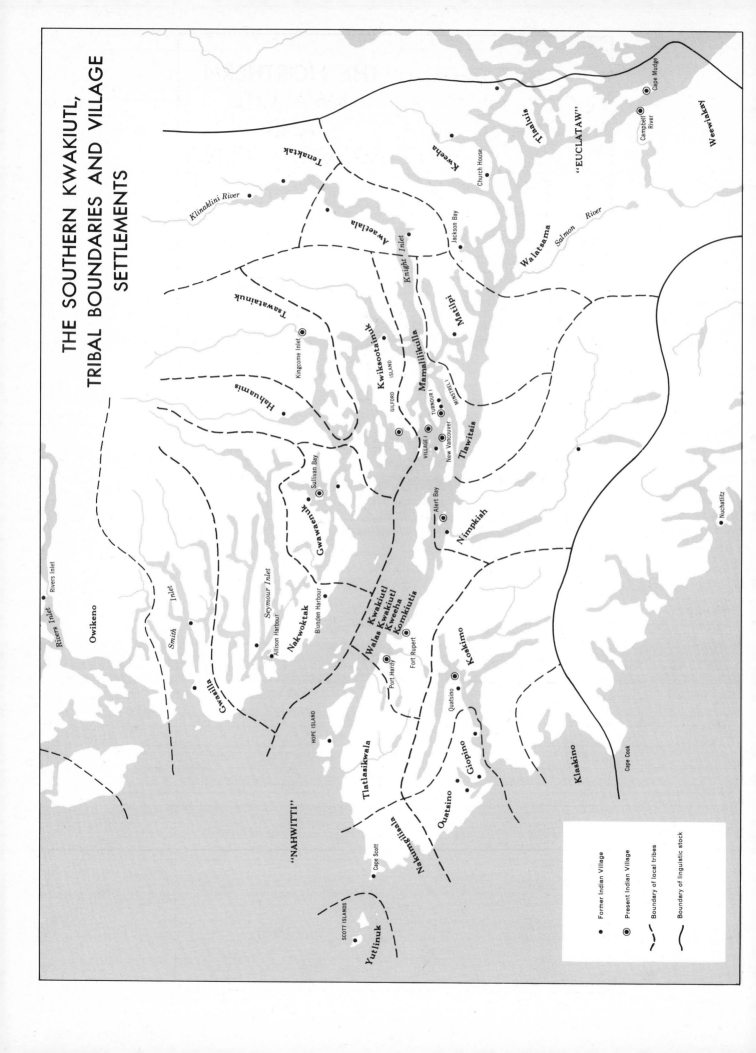

THE SOUTHERN KWAKIUTL,
TRIBAL BOUNDARIES AND VILLAGE
SETTLEMENTS

Rivers Inlet

Owikeno

Smith Inlet

Seymour Inlet

Allison Harbour

Nakwoktak

Blunden Harbour

Gwasilla

SCOTT ISLANDS

Yutlinuk

"NAHWITTI"

Cape Scott

HOPE ISLAND

Tlatlasikwala

Nakumgilisala

Quatsino

Giopino

Koskimo

Quatsino

Port Hardy

Fort Rupert

Walas Kwakiutl
Kwakiutl
Kweeha
Komkiutis

Klaskino

Cape Cook

Gwawaenuk

Sullivan Bay

Hahuamis

Tsawatainuk

Kingcome Inlet

Kwiksootainuk

GILFORD ISLAND

VILLAGE I

Mamalilikulla

TURNOUR I

MINSTREL I

New Vancouver

Alert Bay

Nimpkish

Tlawitsis

Matilpi

Awaetlala

Knight Inlet

Jackson Bay

Tenaktak

Klinaklini River

Walatsama   Salmon   River

Kweeha

Church House

Tlaaluis

"EUCLATAW"

Cape Mudge

Campbell
River

Weewiakay

Nuchatlitz

Former Indian Village
Present Indian Village
Boundary of local tribes
Boundary of linguistic stock

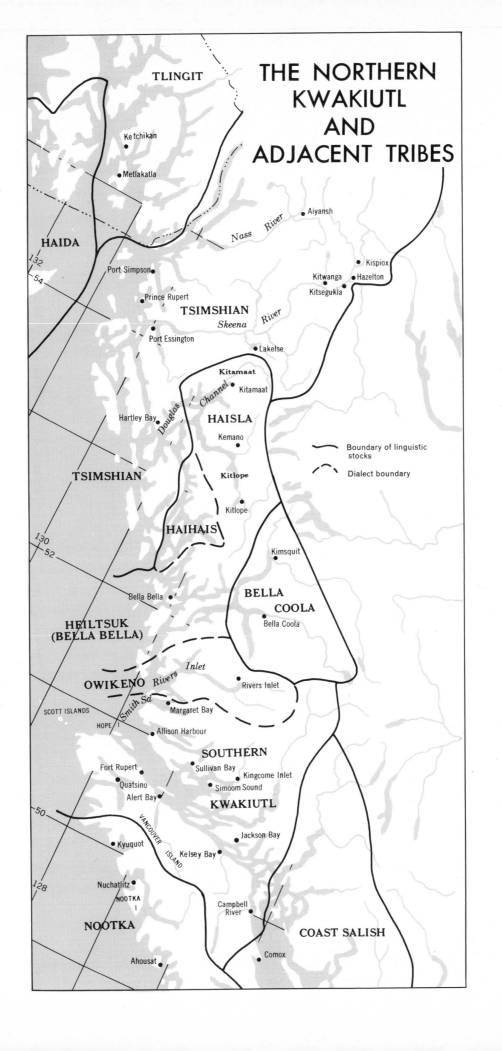

THE NORTHERN
KWAKIUTL
AND
ADJACENT TRIBES

TLINGIT

Ketchikan

Metlakatla

HAIDA

132
54

Port Simpson

Prince Rupert

Port Essington

Aiyansh

Nass River

Kispiox

Kitwanga   Hazelton

Kitsegukla

TSIMSHIAN

Skeena   River

Lakelse

Kitamaat

Kitamaat

HAISLA

Kemano

Hartley Bay

Douglas   Channel

TSIMSHIAN

Kitlope

Kitlope

HAIHAIS

Kimsquit

130
52

Bella Bella

BELLA
COOLA

Bella Coola

HEILTSUK
(BELLA BELLA)

Boundary of linguistic
stocks

Dialect boundary

Inlet

OWIKENO   Rivers

Rivers Inlet

SCOTT ISLANDS   Smith Sd.

Margaret Bay

HOPE

Allison Harbour

SOUTHERN

Fort Rupert   Sullivan Bay

Kingcome Inlet

Quatsino   Simoom Sound

Alert Bay   KWAKIUTL

50

Jackson Bay

Kyuquot   Kelsey Bay

VANCOUVER   ISLAND

128

Nuchatlitz

NOOTKA I

Campbell
River

NOOTKA

COAST SALISH

Comox

Ahousat

Craft and Technology of the Artist

Among the Kwakiutl, labor was divided according to sex. Fishing and hunting, the manufacture and repair of gear, woodworking, carving, and painting were the tasks of men. To the women were left the gathering and cooking of foodstuffs, housekeeping, and the weaving of baskets, blankets, nets, mats, and clothing. Not all people were equally adept at all things. A particularly experienced man would become known in the community for his special skill in constructing a house or burning and steaming a dugout canoe. The carver was a specialist who was commissioned and well paid to make the various crests and masks for ceremonial occasions and who paid others to hunt for him and perform other routine duties.

The education of all young Kwakiutl consisted primarily of the imitation and perfection of the tasks and techniques executed by their elders for the maintenance of daily living. Young boys who showed artistic promise were encouraged to develop their skills, and underwent a period of apprenticeship which combined magical practices with the observation and imitation of expert craftsmen.

It should be noted, however, that not all ceremonial equipment was produced by skilled specialists. This can be seen in the range of concept and execution of masks, rattles, and other objects. Whether because of poverty or indifference, unskilled individuals sometimes chose to make their own. Several contemporary participants in dancing ceremonials have told of repainting a basic mask form for various different occasions, and an exam-

8

ination of photographs and of older objects collected in museums shows that even in the earliest times these were not always made by especially gifted craftsmen.

The tools and techniques used by Kwakiutl carvers and painters were the same as those of other Northwest Coast craftsmen. Prehistoric artifacts in bone, ivory, and wood bear witness to an early establishment of a tradition of woodworking technology that reached a level of breathtaking range and virtuosity. The Northwest Coast collections in the major museums of the world offer some idea of the tremendous productivity of these craftsmen, and of the apparently endless variations within the traditional forms of representing the family crest themes.

The forests provided abundant wood for the carver's craft. Red cedar (Thuya plicata), a soft-grained, easily split pink wood, was used for such massive carvings as totem poles, house posts, memorial poles, large figure carvings, masks, feast bowls, and ladles. It was also used for split boards, as in house walls and roof planks; for the one-piece boards that were kerfed and bent into shape by steam; and for canoes, which were burnt out and steamed, and polished to a glassy finish. Yellow cedar (Chamaecyparis nootkaensis) was used for small totem poles, the frontal pieces of headdresses, some masks, kerfed boxes, chests, and canoe paddles. Alderwood (Alnus rubra), a light white wood with a slight fragrance, relatively fine-textured and nonabsorbent, was favored for small dishes and spoons as well as for rattles, headdresses, and masks. Yew (Taxus brevifolia), a very hard, close-grained wood, was used mainly for making bows, carpenters' wedges, and canoe paddles. Maple (Acer macrophyllum) was used for rattles, headdresses, frontlets, and skewer hairpins. Hemlock (Tsuga heterophylla) was used for making spoons.

A tree was cut down with a heavy-bladed chopping adze. To obtain planks for a house or a box, a log was split by inserting wedges of bone or antler, of graded sizes, into a small cut, and pounding with a heavy maul. These wedges were moved successively to produce a widening split on both sides of the log. The completed board was separated, trimmed evenly at each end, and smoothed with an adze.

A number of efficient, adaptable tools were used (Figs. 1-7). These included the hammer; the chisel; the curved knife; the elbow adze, for the first rough hewing of forms from the log; and the D-adze, whose blade could also be used as a chisel, for the fine, rippled finish strokes. Whether these tools had stone blades, polished to a fine, sharp edge; shell blades; or blades of steel, they were very adaptable and provided all the precision and flexibility needed for the wide variety of strokes employed by the artist.

Simple drills—short cutting bits fastened to handles which were rotated between the palms—and pump drills were used to make holes. It is not certain if a pump drill was used aboriginally, but there is one in the museum in which an early iron drill is hafted into a twenty-eight-inch shaft and rotated by thongs attached to a crosspiece. A neat, smooth finish was given to the article through the use of fine sandstone and sharkskin abrasives.

All tools were made by the craftsmen themselves, and, although there appears to have been no prohibition against using another man's implements, it is said that each set was so fitted to individual work habits that it was difficult for even the most skilled carvers to achieve the same effect with tools made by anyone else. This expectancy that each man would make his own gear, tools, and weapons gave all the men a broad base of technological competence and familiarity.

The rewards offered by the culture to the specialist were sufficient to induce the development of special skills in woodworking. Canoes, for example, were highly valued, their standards of smooth and functional form extremely important, their lines much admired, and so it was with every class of carving. Thus, in addition to the artist's kinesthetic pleasure in the rhythmic, recurring motion of carving, he enjoyed the reward of having the appreciation of the social group for his fine mask, rattle, or house carving. Especially honored was the "supernaturally" inspired artist who was unusually gifted. This close integration of the artist with his society was a notable characteristic of the Northwest Coast culture.

Certain similarities in all Northwest Coast carving gave it its characteristic style. The basic patterns of house building and canoe building varied from north to south, but the technology was everywhere similar. The carving of totem poles, house poles, boxes, dishes, rattles, masks, and similar gear also employed the same basic technology throughout the region.

Local tribal styles of rendering these objects were distinctive, as artistic tradition varied from area to area. However, the object carved and decorated was likely to be similar in all groups in general function and design. What was portrayed was most commonly the major theme of the Northwest Coast: the family crest and the heraldic figures, the family myth of the owner. These represented the ancestor and his special supernatural visitations or relations with the myth people, in their forms as birds, animals, and other beings. The basic iconography was understood and used by all tribal groups.

The planes of sculpture are plastic, curving and swelling freely into concavities and convexities, with rigid sharp lines used only for deliberate effect. In the masks, curves are emphasized on nostrils, eyes, and lips by deeply incised carvings, contrasting color, or both. Nearly all lines, whether incised or painted, have the tendency to run parallel and taper to a terminal point at each end.

Within the basic and characteristic style of the Northwest Coast, distinctions can be made among the rather flat, delicate, refined carving of the Tsimshian; the well-modulated, subtle carving of the Haida; and the strong, clear carving of the Kwakiutl. A highly distinctive style which apparently had a great influence on the Kwakiutl was that of the Bella Coola, who are regarded as late arrivals on the Northwest Coast. Theirs was a strongly sculptural form, characterized by deep planes of many levels of depth, each important in building up the whole. Most Bella Coola masks were of natural elements: echo, moon, sun, and birds and flowers.

In addition to the massive, heavy, highly sculptured planes, Bella Coola carving can be recognized by the upthrust of chin and jaw, the three-dimensional sculptural treatment of each individual feature, and the fact that the head is usually surrounded by a round plaque. Many such masks have been found in Kwakiutl areas and have been labeled as Kwakiutl when there is no proof of provenience, but stylistically they are unmistakably Bella Coola.

The masks in Plates XX (Komokwa), XXVIII A (Komokwa's wife), XXVI (echo), and XIX A (wolf) are undoubtedly from the hand of the same carver and are carved in the Bella Coola style, although they come from Sullivan Bay. They are beautifully painted in a combination of colors not found in any other examples: dark and light green, blue, orange, red, and black. It seems likely that the two fine feast dishes representing the eagle (Pl. XV), also from Sullivan Bay, are the works of the same artist.

The Nootka varied from other stylistic traditions by a certain massive simplicity, less elaborated and with fewer planes of decoration, and less delicate painting.

The Salish carvings are still simpler and less elaborately carved, except in the case of their characteristic and unique mask, that of the Kwekwe, which is strongly and crisply formed with very careful and precise elaboration (see Figs. 423-26).

Painting was usually regarded as an adjunct to carving, and was used to enhance, emphasize, or embellish the basic forms. Precommercial paints included red earth ocher; white from burnt clamshells; blue from copper oxide or blue clay; and black from mud and charcoal ground up in small stone dishes or mortars and mixed with salmon eggs to provide an oily base (Fig. 8). Powdered graphite was sometimes used to produce a shiny, highlighted gray-black. Ground cinnabar mixed with oils gave a bright vermilion coloring. In the use of colors, the traditional Kwakiutl choices were dark red, black, and white. Sometimes a dark green was used, obtained from copper sulphide. The Bella Coola used an intense pale blue, plus white, red, and black. The Haida, Tsimshian, and Tlingit tended to leave more unpainted wood surface, limiting painting to decorative touches of black and red.

The brush was made by binding porcupine or other hair onto a stick and cutting the tips at an angle, so that they tapered to a narrow point (Fig. 8). For regular design forms, such as the symbols on a painted box front, tracing patterns or templates were cut out of leather or bark (Fig. 9).

Special characteristics of Northwest Coast painting are:

1. The use of salient recognition features, such as beaks, claws, or fins, as a representation of the bird or animal portrayed.

2. Frequent use of a highly stylized symbol for the whole animal.

3. The use of "X-ray" painting to establish the design form of a whole animal, disposed over the area to be covered.

4. The establishment of a number of stylized design units such as sockets, joints, and eye forms, used interchangeably. The context reveals which anatomical feature they actually represent.

5. The avoidance of empty space where a design form or line will add to the interest of complexity. This embellishment is, however, done with sufficient restraint to maintain a proper integral balance of line, form, and carving. Bill Holm (1965:35) points out that the formline, usually established by the use of black paint, is the most characteristic element of the design.

6. The use of tapered and swelling lines to break the monotony of geometric form. A circle, rectangle, or oval, a feather or a claw, is depicted in such a way that it is a complete and pleasing design symbol in itself.

7. The use of texture to supply variation in design. The carved cross-hatching of a beaver tail or a wing feather is echoed by the use of painted cross-hatching—small parallel lines or shading. One or two colors are sufficient to add these important textural variations.

8. The acceptance of the form of the area to be treated. On columnar poles, the cylindrical form is the basic space determinant, and the figures rise one above another in relation to this shape, although occasionally a piece is mortised to the pole to form a bill, wings, arms, or hands. On a round crest hat, the painted design is constructed and placed quite differently.

One other important characteristic of Northwest Coast art that should be noted is the device of visual "punning," sometimes called "kenning" (Rowe 1962:15). A natural space in the carving or painting is used for the introduction of a new form with an independent meaning. See, for example, the house post from Kitamaat (Fig. 494), where there is a face in the ear of the bear and another in its paw, and the faces in the tails of the killer whales (Pl. XVIII A; Fig. 324 [A 1973]).

The subjects of both the carving and the painting were the animals and mythological beings claimed as family and clan ancestors by their descendants. The endless variations on the family crest theme are illustrated throughout this book. There were two basic approaches. The first was through realistic, naturalistic, three-dimensional carving with painting as an adjunct decoration, as illustrated in totem and house poles, masks, rattles, speakers' staffs, and headgear. The second was a highly stylized, symbolic representation, as in most canoe and paddle paintings, house fronts, storage boxes, stage screens and curtains, crest hats, cloaks, mats, and some baskets.

The iconography of the culture—the family crests and certain traditional forms of representing them—offered a framework to the artist within which he was free to embellish, to add details, and to explore. The gifted artist emerged as an individual, and even without written records it is still possible to discern the basic styles of certain individual craftsmen. A more detailed discussion of attributions will be found in Appendix I.

Finally, a word should be said about the adaptation of materials. To denounce the craftsmen's use of store paint or factory-made buttons as degenerate or unauthentic is to miss the main point: that the mind of the craftsman concentrated on invention and improvement and was quick to seize on any material that added to the effect he was striving to create. It is precisely this eagerness to add, to experiment, and to improve that resulted in the rich proliferation and inventiveness of Kwakiutl art. It is probable that borrowing, adaptation, and invention went on throughout the development of Northwest Coast style.

Iron and steel blades, more effective carving tools than stone, led to an immense increase in output. A money economy aided the staging of huge potlatches and the further development of ceremonial life. Trade copper sheeting was used for the "copper," that most important symbol of wealth, which may have been previously made in a smaller form out of naturally occurring copper beaten flat. Store paint replaced earth ochers, but did not change the style of painting in any significant way, and traditional color choices tended to be continued. Blankets were turned into ceremonial robes of great brilliance by the addition of red flannel appliqués and cut shell buttons. Abalone was traded up from California because its brilliant dark blue-green color outshone the relatively colorless local product. Silver and gold coins from the Russians in Alaska gave the Indian craftsman a chance to reproduce his crest art in the portable and conspicuous form of jewelry, which was coveted by women of rank. String twine was substituted for cedar bark rope and was used in exactly the same way—dyed red for the head and neck rings of the winter ceremonies. Muslin cloth was used for the ceremonial curtain, replacing earlier cedar planks, and was similarly adorned with a painting of the house spirit.

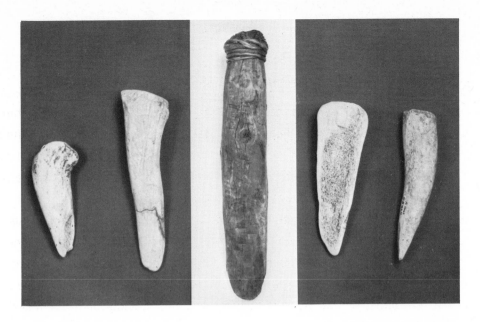

Fig. 1. Bone, wood, and antler wedges. (*Left to right*) A8379, A1085, A6480, A115030, A1063

Fig. 2. Greenstone blades. (*Left to right, top*) Finished: A8191 (Lytton), A8887 (no data), A8549 (Fraser River); (*bottom*) unfinished: A6074 (Lytton), A8192 (Lytton), A6053 (Lytton)

Fig. 3. Stone hammers. (*Left to right, back*) A7321 (no data), A7364 (Yale), A1646 (Kitlope), A3055 (no data), A6471 (no data); (*front*) A6510 (no data), A1802 (Lytton), A4491 (no data)

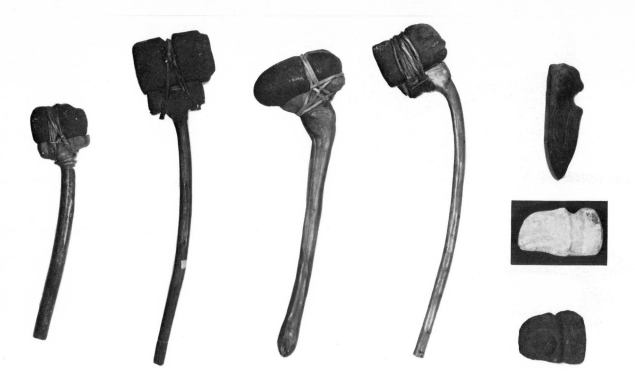

Fig. 4. Stone mauls. (*Left to right*) A108 (Rivers Inlet), A8749 (Kitlope), A8813 (Kitamaat), A1104 (Bella Bella); (*top to bottom*) A7157 (Queen Charlotte Islands), A7155 (Queen Charlotte Islands), A7322 (Skeena River)

Fig. 5. Stone "elbow" adzes. (*Left to right*) A1639 (Kitamaat), A8711 (Kitamaat), A8710 (Kitamaat), A6436 (Kispiox)

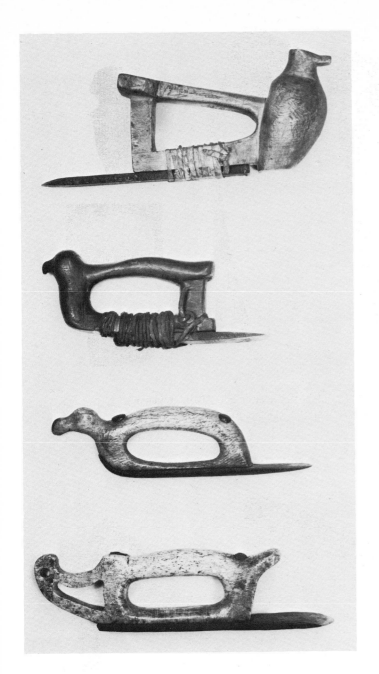

Fig. 6. D-adzes. (*Top to bottom*) A2052 (Bella Coola), A7365 (no data), A6575 (Vancouver Island), A3518 (Vancouver Island)

Fig. 7. Curved knives used by various carvers. (*Top to bottom, left*) A7038 (Skidegate), A7040 (Skidegate), A1627 (Kitamaat), A3493 (no data), A1626 (Kitamaat); (*right*) A3433 (Lytton), A149 (Port Essington), A7238 (no data), A6894 (no data)

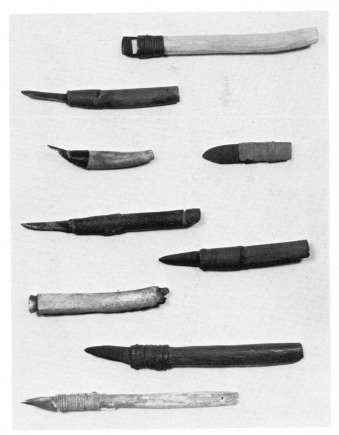

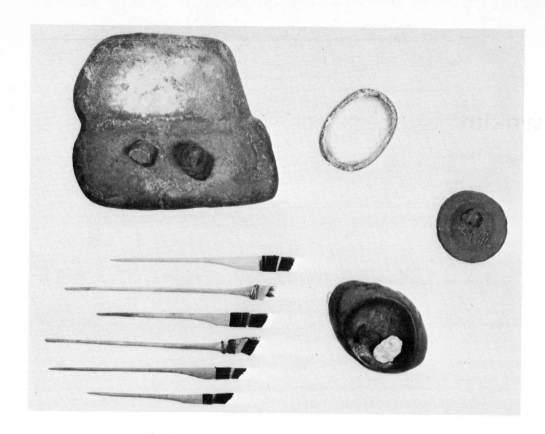

Fig. 8. (*Top and right*) Earth ochers, blue clay, and clamshell paints, A6070; (*left*) set of brushes, A3644

Fig. 9. Leather templates used as patterns for design forms, made and used by Charles Gladstone, Skidegate. A4354

Kwakiutl Religion and Mythology

In the early days of the ancestral people of the myths, birds, men, animals, and fish lived in their own worlds, occasionally entering those of the others. Differing from each other only in covering, they could, and did, doff at will their cloaks of skin, feathers, or fur.

The earth with its familiar mountains, forests, local villages, and landmarks was inhabited by the myth people: Raven, Bear, Tsonokwa, Sisiutl, and many others. In the sky another area was inhabited by beings who lived in great houses and occasionally descended to earth on stairways. In this world lived Thunderbird and his younger brothers.

Under the sea lived another set of supernatural beings— not only fish and sea mammals, but a range of animals and birds who were the counterparts of the earth people: Sea Raven, Tsonokwa of the Sea, Sea Bear, and others. All of these were ruled over by Komokwa, chief of the undersea people, who lived in a great and wealthy house guarded by sea monsters. And there were others, some of them so huge that, when they rose up from the sea, the waters became shallow and swirled in tidal races.

There was also an underworld of ghost people living the same lives as those above earth, except that their night was day and their summer the winter above. These people were not tangible or substantial, but their lives were the same as those of humans.

Local groups and families traced descent to an ancestor among the myth people who in the early days had received special powers and privileges from a supernatural bird, animal, or other being. Such powers and privileges—including songs, dances, and the right to wear certain crests— were perpetuated from generation to generation. These crest forms are the main subject of carving, painting, and decoration, and much of Kwakiutl ceremony is based on these legendary inheritances.

Inheritance

The Northwest Coast concept of property was basic to every action and purpose of life.

The chief of the lineage and those in his house shared the inherited material wealth of the family line, such as fishing grounds, berry fields, and hunting sites. These were well-defined places and rights. In addition, they amassed and created other material wealth: the large lineage house in which they lived, the totem poles that proclaimed their crests, and the boxes of preserved foodstuffs. The related intangible properties were fully as important. A series of rank names and positions were inherited and held by an incumbent until he retired or died, at which time his successor was installed. Inherited also were the series of ancestral myths and the right to recount these; the right to use certain crests, masks, and utensils; the right to use certain lineage names and to sing certain songs; the right to wear particular costumes and to perform the dramas of the family myths.

A recounting of a family myth—the legend of how crests, names, songs, and ceremonial privileges were obtained—is given by Curtis (1915:137). In an isolated place the individual encounters some supernatural beings, who grant these boons, as in the following legend of the gens Walas of the Lekwiltok sept Wiweakam:

Yakayálitnuhl was walking near Tēkya, when he saw sitting on a rock a very large bird covered with soft down of dazzling whiteness. The tip of its hooked beak could just be seen in the midst of the thick down. He cried out, "Whatever you are, I *tlúgwala* (to find a treasure; specifically, to obtain special powers and privileges from a spirit. [Curtis' note]) you!" The bird threw back the feathers and skin from its head, revealing the head of a man, and spoke: "I am *kólus*, yet I am a man. My name is Toqátlasaqiáq ('born to be admired')." His face was steaming with heat, because of the thick covering of feathers. Soon the entire coat fell away and he stood forth with the full figure of a man.

The bird man accompanied Yakayálitnuh̄l to his home, and told him: "Give a winter dance, and you shall have these dances from me: *sŭnqŭnhulikiyŭ* (thunder-bird), *hóh̓luq* (a fabulous bird), *nŭ'nálalah̄l* ('embodiment of the personation of weather'), *há'maa* (a large, fabulous bird), *hámasi̇́lah̄l* ('wasp-embodiment'), and *kólus*." All these dances came from creatures of the sky.

Yakayálitnuh̄l founded the Walas gens, this word ("big") being another name of the bird *kólus.* It is believed that members of this gens are easily thrown into perspiration, as was the bird man by his feather garment.

Each person held a ranked position reckoned in relation to the lineage chief, who was also a household head. All clan prerogatives and privileges were personified in him.

Curtis (1915:139) lists various titles of address in use among the nobility:

Áte is a title of respect and reverence, and is best translated "sir" or "lord." *Tlŭwŭ́lkŭmi* ("eldest son of a chief") is equivalent to "prince," and the corresponding feminine title is *ki̇ṭihl.* In many cases the chief of a gens refers to his eldest son by a special hereditary epithet, such as *tlúgwi* ("treasure"). *Ḱii* is a term of endearment applied to the eldest child by the parents and the other children, as well as by one lover to another. Any one of noble rank is *gýikŭmi* ("chief"), and the head chief of a tribe or a sept is *hámakŭmi gýikŭmi* ("leader chief"). . . . A person of humble birth, or one who wishes to humble himself for the time being, addresses a noble with the deprecatory word *ḱáqiti* ("slave owner," that is, "I am your slave"), or *wátsiti* ("dog owner").

Title and privilege in one's family were strengthened and increased by marriage alliances with families that possessed other privileges; the children of such marriages would become doubly rich. Among the northern tribes—Tlingit, Tsimshian, and Haida—the maternal line was the important one for the transmission of family privileges.

Kwakiutl social organization was characterized by a paternal reckoning of lineage, except in the transfer of family prerogatives and privileges via marriage agreements. Figure 306 shows a *gisukstola,* an old form of display board used during the special ceremony by which the inherited privileges of the wife's ancestors were transmitted to her husband by gift from her father. The transfer consisted of the legend, myth, dance, song, and crest form, represented by a special box containing masks, crest, and whistles. These were given to the husband in potlatch, not for his own use but to be transmitted through him to his children or other heirs. The blowing of the whistle was the sign of transfer to take place during the initiation ceremonies in the Tsetseka season.

This double inheritance of family privilege with its associated crests, recitation, songs, dances, and apparel is the endless theme of Northwest Coast iconography.

Several other ways of acquiring family crest privileges were open to the people of the Northwest Coast. One was the acquisition of privilege by murder: killing the original owner allowed the victor to assume his privileges and material regalia. So important an institution as the whole Hamatsa dance complex, of primary rank among the dancing societies of the Kwakiutl everywhere, was obtained in 1835 by killing a group of Heiltsuk who were out in a canoe and seizing their regalia. A similar result could be achieved through taking a prisoner who became a slave, and thus lost his possessions and his position in the social group.

Another form of acquisition was by a gift, which could then be used by the new owner as one of his family privileges. According to a myth of the Kwakiutl, they were given the Kwekwe dance, mask, and rattles of the Comox by the latter after the Kwakiutl had gone over prepared for war to take it from them because "that's a very fine dance they have over there" (Boas 1905:236).

One other method was not formally acknowledged, but it is likely that there were a number of irregular borrowings in which the object was simply copied and a myth invented to justify it. If this myth was performed before the potlatch audience without public ridicule or challenge, then it could become an established part of the repertoire. This has been possible during the last eighty years because of the great loss of population that followed the invasions of new disease. There were many more family privileges available in many lineages than there were people to fill them (Codere 1950:

97). A new condition arose, in which a person with social aggression but limited family privileges would pay an owner to recount the details to him. He then used these authenticating features so that he could publicly claim the privilege (Olson 1950).

Finally, there must have been some individual initiative and invention of prerogative. Curtis (1915:158-59) says that such an invention could be justified by its audacity, by the interest and charm of the new design, and by the failure of the audience or of a specific rival to challenge the invented myth.

The Potlatch

The Kwakiutl individual of rank was concerned that others should recognize his claims and status. The same preoccupation was characteristic of the lineage group and of the villages in relation to each other. This concern was expressed in the institution of the potlatch, which provided a channel for claims to be made publicly, privileges to be displayed, and generous ceremonial hospitality to be offered. By accepting suitable gifts, guests in effect took payment as witnesses. The claims thus established by the host would be accepted at future potlatches.

The word "potlatch" comes from the Chinook jargon, meaning "to give." Elaborate feasting and hospitality, accompanied by the bestowal of gifts, were the core of this ceremony, without which no important social event could take place and no claim could be made. All of the names, ranks, privileges, and honors of the lineage inheritance were meaningless without this formal ritual of hospitality and the acceptance of gifts by the guests.

The social occasions calling for validation by a potlatch were numerous: the transfer of marriage privileges, the assumption of a new name by a youth or the giving of a new rank, the new use of a family crest, the initiation of a new dancer into the dancing societies. Each of these was the occasion for a full-blown social effort, often involving intertribal invitations. Among the northern coastal tribes, the most important occasions were a series of mourning cycles and the raising of mortuary poles to a deceased chief; among the Haida, they were the raising of a new house and the introduction of a new lineage chief.

The basic procedure of the potlatch was always the same. The lineage chief would consult with the older members of his household group, for the potlatch effort involved the entire household or kin group. When it was agreed that the potlatch should be held, and the date had been set, preparations began. Food sufficient to feed guests over a period of time must be gathered, prepared, and stored. Enough gifts to give to all must be produced, and the needed goods bearing the family crest carvings must be amassed. The carver of the chief often lived in the chief's house (as did the speaker of the chief, who acted as official orator on ceremonial occasions), and since he knew all of the inheritances he could carve any item with its appropriate designs.

In order to make ample gifts available, outstanding loans were called in as of a certain date. A system of loans and interest, indebtedness and reckoning, was an elaborate aspect of Kwakiutl life. Most public actions were financed by loans of white wool blankets, valued at one dollar each, which had been brought in by the Hudson's Bay Company early in the nineteenth century. These rapidly became a standard unit of value, and the other goods were appraised in terms of their value in blankets. The rate of repayment, which was agreed on at the time of the loan, varied according to the period involved; 100 per cent interest for a year's loan was standard.

New wealth was created by labor. Mats, baskets and boxes, furs, canoes, jewelry, and dishes were made for the gift-giving. After the arrival of trade goods, new items such as sewing machines, china dishes, and crates of oranges were purchased with the family's monetary earnings and given away. The essence of wealth was that it be distributed ceremonially.

Emissaries of the chief set off to invite the guests. When the time came for the event, these same emissaries, wearing formal costumes, went back to act as guides for the visitors.

The family of the host with the song leader and the speaker, in their finest robes and headdresses, stood upon the beach singing and dancing to greet the visitors as they approached by canoe. Sometimes large figures carved of wood were placed facing the sea to reinforce the welcome. Visitors were announced by the speaker and were seated according to their rank, in a traditional seating arrangement.

For the feasting, food dishes of varying sizes were brought in and passed around according to proper ritual as the herald explained the ancestral names of the food dishes and their history. The speaker also urged the different chiefs by name to eat and enjoy themselves, in the name of the host.

Since the potlatch was tied in with many social occasions great and small, it varied in length. Many family members offered minor episodes, such as the naming of a small child, as part of the major event.

One or more major events would be offered as a feature of each day. Family dances and dramas were enacted by dancers in masks and costumes to the accompaniment of songs and explanations by the speaker. Even more dramatic were the days when members of the family were introduced into the dancing societies. Each occasion was followed by feasting, oratory, and some gift distribution. Usually there was a climax of one form or another —a dance, a drama, or a copper-selling ceremony—then the final feast and speeches, during which the finest gifts were given away.

Potlatch gifts were bestowed as free donations by the host and his household. They were distributed in order according to the rank and position of the tribal lineage heads. Correct precedence was maintained by an official who called out the names as the gifts were given out. This was in itself a public recognition of the ranking positions of the lineage. The most important chiefs received the important and generous gifts, while people of little rank received token gifts. Extratribal visitors were also presented with gifts. Gifts, as payment, were made to the carvers and others who had served in preparing the potlatch.

If the potlatch was successful, all of the family group shared in the glory and pleasure of the social effort. Such an event might be spoken of up and down the coast with approbation and appreciation.

The immediate effect of the coming of the white man was to increase the variety of goods available to the Indians, who proceeded to trade with him for copper sheeting, muskets, brass and copper wire, and blankets. With the founding of Hudson's Bay Company trading posts at Fort Langley in 1827, Fort Simpson in 1831, Bella Bella in 1833, Fort Victoria in 1843, and Fort Rupert in 1849, these materials became even more generally available, and the cultures reached a high point of activity in potlatching and carving (Codere 1950; Duff 1964:53 ff.).

Disease devastated the tribes, beginning in 1838 and reaching a peak in 1862, leaving 20,000 people dead, villages decimated and sometimes deserted, and much of the social system changed (Codere 1950:97; Duff 1964:42). In spite of disease, the reserve system, and the pressures on the Indians to become converted and assimilated into the white culture, lineage inheritance and the potlatch continued, and the southern Kwakiutl continued to borrow and adapt the ceremonial patterns of other tribes, particularly the dancing complex of the northern Kwakiutl.

In 1921, as a result of the disapproval of missionaries and government officials, the potlatch was made illegal. In spite of the prohibition, however, the potlatch was so interwoven with the purpose and meaning of Kwakiutl life that it continued, although away from the main centers. In the same year, acting on secret information given by an Indian, the police sent a contingent to interrupt the potlatch of Daniel Cranmer of Alert Bay. He and several of his family were imprisoned, and his masks and coppers were taken to the National Museum where they still remain.

Since potlatching was an inherent sanction of so many important transfers and relationships, its discontinuance made any coherent tribal life impossible. In 1951 the ban on potlatching was repealed, and the institution, which had operated under cover but in a diminished way, took on new vigor. For an account of a potlatch held in 1966 at Alert Bay, see Appendix II.

The potlatch made possible a wide distribution of vast amounts of goods and kept them moving as various forms of wealth, both material and nonmaterial, circulated among groups and individuals. It has been described as life insurance for the successor to a chief's position, for the new chief would receive all of the returns and interest for loans out in his predecessor's name, although against this he also owed to others the loans they had made. It was a socially integrating force for households, all of whose members benefited from the public recognition of their cooperative social effort. It was also integrative as a face-saving device for restoring the social equilibrium of an individual or group. If a mistake had been made publicly in ritual or etiquette, a potlatch could be given for the purpose of wiping out the incident, and those who received gifts would not refer to it again.

One type of potlatch that has received a great deal of attention is the rivalry potlatch. After the devastating effects of disease had decimated the

Kwakiutl tribes, there were a number of positions and names open in the various lineages. Originally there were 658 positions in the social ranking system of the Kwakiutl. By 1898, of 1,597 people surviving only 637 were men of 16 years or more—not even enough to fill these positions (Codere 1950:97). A number of *nouveau riche* individuals asserted their claims to vacant positions, and the possibility of giving away great wealth aroused other rivals to compete for the same places with more and more lavish ceremonies, characterized by conspicuous waste.

There had always been a formal rivalry between the heads of various lineages. This, of course, heightened the suspense of ritual demonstrations, as first one chief and then the other gained apparent precedence. Actual practice was usually characterized by mutual agreement and coexistence. With the intensified struggle of rivalry for places that became open because of the shrinking of the population, the destruction of property by flamboyant gestures became more frequent, and quantities of food and property were destroyed by the aggressive contenders for supremacy.

The Copper Complex

The copper was an item of essential importance in the potlatch economy of the Kwakiutl, as well as among the Haida, Tsimshian, and Tlingit. These decorated sheets of beaten copper, a symbol of prestige and of surplus wealth, appeared in the same form among all these people (see Figs. 152-57).

All known coppers were made of rolled sheet copper, which became an item much desired in trade soon after the first contact with the white man at the end of the eighteenth century. There is a tradition that earlier coppers were made of the naturally occurring metal traded down from the Coppermine River area, although there are apparently none of these now in existence.

Each copper had a name that boasted of its value: "all other coppers are ashamed to look at it," for which 7,500 blankets were paid; and "making the house empty of blankets," for which 5,000 blankets were paid. Each one represented the number of blankets paid in order to obtain it, and had no function except to serve as an index of wealth.

The copper among the Kwakiutl was valued at the actual price of its last purchase. New purchasers vied to invest more property in it than the previous owner had been able to do. Thus a copper that was bought at the climax of a potlatch represented the triumph of the wealth of the host and his kin group, since it made it clear that he retained a surplus even after the extensive feasting, gifts, and ceremonial payments. Such an "auction" was a focal point of drama and excitement, as rival chiefs bid higher and higher for the copper. To purchase it was to win ceremonial distinction.

The ritual involving the purchase of the copper is described in detail by Boas (1895:345):

The trade is discussed and arranged long beforehand. When the buyer is ready, he gives to the owner of the copper blankets about one-sixth of the total value of the copper. This is called "making a pillow" for the copper; or "making a feather bed" or "the harpoon line at which game is hanging," meaning that in the same manner the copper is attached to the long line of blankets; or "taken in hand, in order to lift the copper." The owner of the copper loans these blankets out, and when he has called them in again, he repays the total amount received, with 100 per cent interest, to the purchaser. On the following day the tribes assemble for the sale of the copper. The prescribed proceeding is as follows: the buyer offers first the lowest prices at which the copper was sold. The owner declares that he is satisfied, but his friends demand by degrees higher and higher prices, according to all the previous sales of the copper. . . . Finally, the amount offered is deemed satisfactory. Then the owner asks for boxes to carry away the blankets. These are counted five pairs a box, and are also paid in blankets or other objects. After these have been paid, the owner of the copper calls his friends—members of his own tribe—to rise, and asks for a belt, which he values at several hundred blankets. While these are being brought, he and his tribe generally repair to the house, where they paint their faces and dress in new blankets. When they have finished, drums are beaten in the house, they shout "hi!" and go out again, the speaker of the seller first. As soon as the latter has left the house, he turns and calls his chief to come down, who goes back to where the sale is going on, followed by his tribe. They all stand in a row and the buyer puts down the blankets which were demanded as a belt, "to adorn the owner of the copper." This whole purchase is called "putting the copper under the name of the buyer." . . . On the following day all the blankets which have been paid for the copper must be distributed by the owner among his own tribe, paying to them his old debts first, and, if the amount is sufficient, giving new presents. This is called "doing a great thing."

When rivalry was fierce, the aggressor might "break" his copper. In this case, the copper was literally cut up, and the pieces, representing deliberately shattered wealth, were handed to the rival chief. The latter then had to destroy wealth of equivalent value or suffer shame. After being cut up, the copper could be riveted together and reused, but its value had to be re-established. As an ultimate gesture of magnificent waste, the whole copper could be thrown into the water and "drowned."

The copper as a symbol of conspicuous and surplus wealth was an endless theme among the Kwakiutl. Names of high-ranking people often contained a "copper" word: "Born to be Copper Maker Woman" was the important name of the wife of Komokwa, "The Wealthy One," who also had the name of "Copper Maker," and so on. Copper was also conceived of as a material of magical properties affecting human health.

The Ceremonial Year

The active working months of a successful spring and summer led to the accumulation of vast preserves of smoked and sun-cured fish and oil stocks. Summertime was the Bakoos time, the nonceremonial, secular part of the year, a time for travel, family camping, and the gathering of food.

With the onset of the rainy winter months, the Kwakiutl retired to their home villages and into their large cedar plank houses. These wet, cold winter months were a time of elaborate theatrical performance and ceremonies. This was the climax of the year, the Tsetseka, the ceremonial or supernatural season.

The name Tsetseka was taken from the Heiltsuk word for "shaman," the magician of the northern peoples who dazzled his audience with his demonstration of tricks. Along with the word were borrowed the supernatural and even sacred overtones of secret and magical tricks. This was the time when the supernatural spirits came for the purpose of initiating the young into the dancing societies. Everything during this season was different from the rest of the year—names were changed, and there were penalties for those who forgot the new ones; songs were changed, and the ways of singing them were changed. Everything directed attention to the special nature of the Tsetseka season.

At this time a new social order came into force. Clan, rank, and Bakoos names were replaced by a system according to which individuals were related to the spirits. Those of high secular rank had claim to the highest ranking spirit dances, but each person had to be formally initiated into the society his inheritance entitled him to join.

The Klasila

The change-over from the Bakoos season to the Tsetseka season was marked by a four-day carnival interlude, the Klasila, devoted to celebration, joking, laughing, and feasting. Although this was essentially a time of pleasure and relaxation, it was introduced with a brief period of mourning songs commemorating those who had died since the last Tsetseka season. During the singing of each person's songs, members of his family lineage wore mourning masks (see Fig. 43).

After this memorial service, the masks were put away and the new order of merriment and revelry began. The costume of this period was a fine ceremonial blanket worn with a carved headdress. Masks worn were those of ancestral and family crest figures, different from those of the super-naturally inspired dancers of the days immediately to follow. They were Dluwalakha masks, representing local birds, animals, and forces of nature that illustrated family myths. These masks were also part of the winter dance series, but in minor roles, and were not a strongly integrated part of the winter dance complex.

If there were more family masks than there were members of the family, other dancers were hired to wear those left over. Boas and Curtis mention a special display of family masks that took place at the beginning of the Klasila time. This is described by Curtis (1915:171):

A peculiar pantomime in which none of the regular dancers appears . . . is conducted as follows: On the first night the giver of the ceremony announces . . .

34

Plate I. Front and back views of rattle from Alert Bay, with
bear design, almost certainly Haida. Wood; black, red, blue.
Height: 11½ in. MacMillan Purchase 1951. A6095

Plate II. A: Front and back views of Haida rattle from Queen Charlotte Islands, with hawk and whale design. Wood; black, red. Height: 9½ in. MacMillan Purchase 1959. A6983. *B*: Kwakiutl raven rattle from Sullivan Bay. Wood; black, red, blue. Height: 13 in. MacMillan Purchase 1952. A8333. *C*: Bella Coola raven rattle, collected about 1910. Wood; green, brown. Height: 17 in. Gift of Miss Fanta Tait 1965. A8532.

A

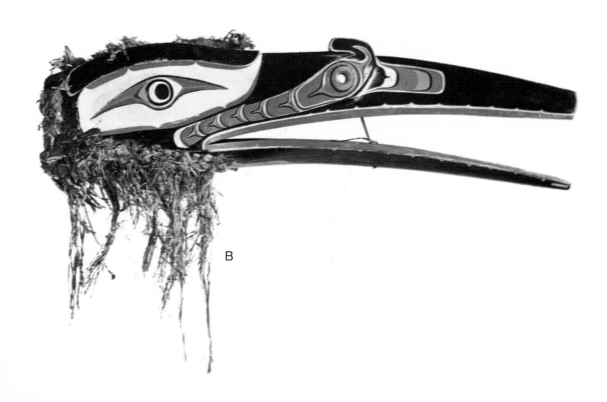

B

Plate III. A: Kwakiutl Hamatsa raven mask from Alert Bay, made by Mungo Martin. Wood and cedar bark; black, white, red. Length: 3 ft. 5 in. MacMillan Purchase 1952. A4243. *B*: Kwakiutl Hamatsa Hokhokw mask from Gilford Island, one of a set of four made by Jack James for Dick Hawkins. Wood and cedar bark; black, white, red, orange. Length: 3 ft. 8 in. MacMillan Purchase 1953. A6126

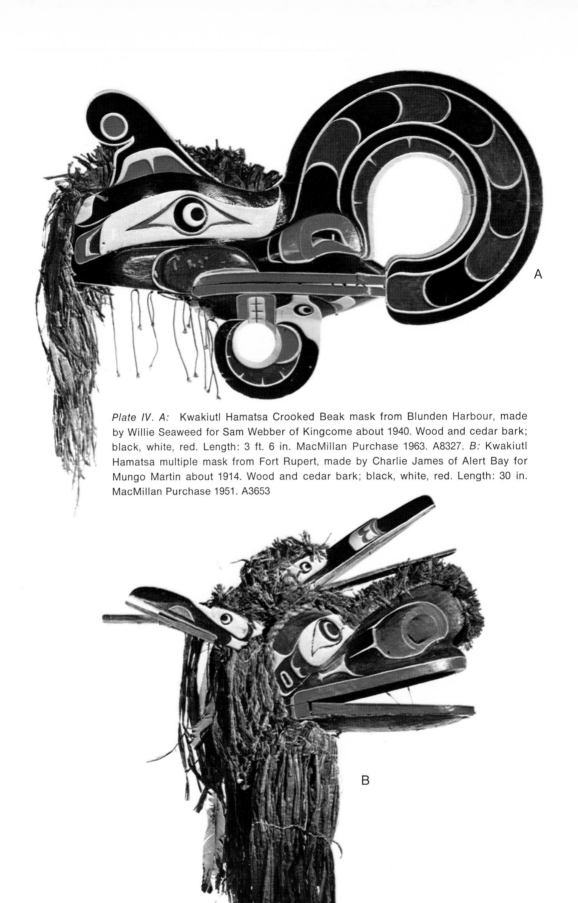

Plate IV. A: Kwakiutl Hamatsa Crooked Beak mask from Blunden Harbour, made by Willie Seaweed for Sam Webber of Kingcome about 1940. Wood and cedar bark; black, white, red. Length: 3 ft. 6 in. MacMillan Purchase 1963. A8327. *B:* Kwakiutl Hamatsa multiple mask from Fort Rupert, made by Charlie James of Alert Bay for Mungo Martin about 1914. Wood and cedar bark; black, white, red. Length: 30 in. MacMillan Purchase 1951. A3653

A

Plate V. *A*: Kwakiutl Hamatsa multiple mask from Blunden Harbour, attributed to Mungo Martin and Willie Seaweed. Wood and cedar bark; black, white, red. Length: 6 ft. 1 in. Dr. Walter C. Koerner Gift 1962. A7992. *B*: Kwakiutl Hamatsa multiple mask from Village Island, said to have come from Owikeno and to be very old, also attributed to Dick Price. Wood and cedar bark; black, white, red. Length: 23 in. MacMillan Purchase 1952. A4169

B

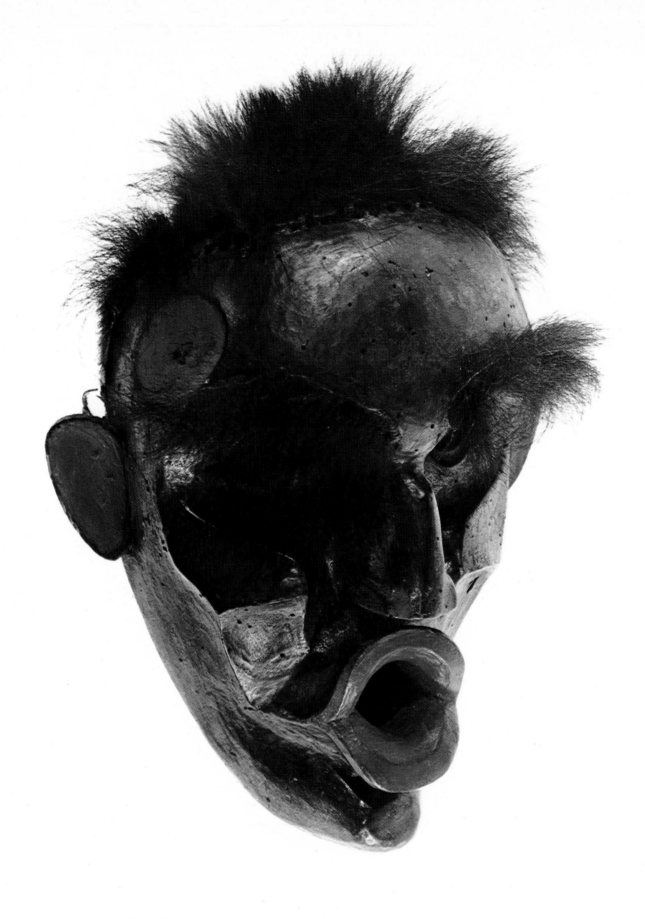

Plate VI. Kwakiutl Tsonokwa mask from Alert Bay. Wood painted with graphite and cinnabar, bearhide eyebrows and hair; black, red. Height: 13 in. MacMillan Purchase 1951. A3637

A

B

Plate VII. A: Kwakiutl button cloak from Sullivan Bay, with copper and T design in white buttons and red appliqué on green background. Width: 5 ft. 8 in. MacMillan Purchase 1952. A4171. *B:* Kwakiutl button cloak from Alert Bay, with tree design in white buttons and red appliqué on blue background. Width: 6 ft. 2 in. MacMillan Purchase 1951. A4251

A

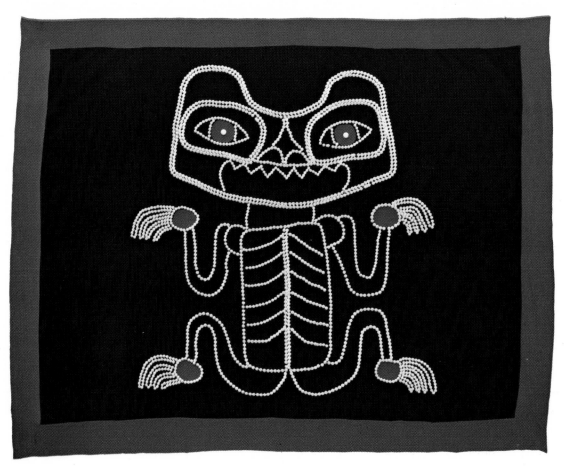

B

Plate VIII. A: Kwakiutl button cloak from New Vancouver, with design of sun and small broken coppers in buttons and red appliqué on dark blue background. Width: 6 ft. MacMillan Purchase 1961. A7490.
B: Haida button cloak from Prince Rupert, with bear design in pearl buttons and red appliqué on dark blue background. Width: 6 ft. MacMillan Purchase 1964. A8420

A

B

Plate IX. A: Kwakiutl Chilkat cloak from Fort Rupert. Commercial wool; black, red, green, yellow. Width: 5 ft. MacMillan Purchase 1962. A8041. *B*: Tlingit Chilkat cloak. Mountain goat wool woven on core of cedar bark fiber; black, yellow, blue, white. Width: 5 ft. 8 in. Gift of Mr. and Mrs. Sidney Garfield Smith 1956. A4454

A

B

C

← *Plate X. A*: Kwakiutl speaker's staff from Fort Rupert. Wood inlaid with abalone; black, red. Length: 5 ft. 5½ in. Illustrated in Curtis 1915: Vol. X, Pl. 333. MacMillan Purchase 1962. A8140. *B* and *C:* Front and back views of Tsimshian dance shirt from Prince Rupert. Muslin with eagle crest design painted on front, bullhead on back. Length: 34 in. MacMillan Purchase 1963. A6797

Plate XI. A: Kwakiutl chief's headdress from Sullivan Bay, with hawk design. Wood, abalone shell, sea lion whiskers, ermine, cloth mantle; black, green, blue, red. Height of carving: 8½ in. MacMillan Purchase 1952. A4173. *B*: Kwakiutl chief's headdress from Fort Rupert, with bear design. Wood, abalone shell, sea lion whiskers, ermine, cloth mantle; black, red, blue. Height of carving: 8 in. MacMillan Purchase 1962. A8226

A

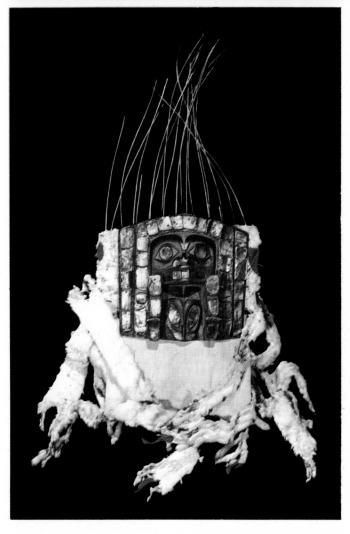

B

A

B

Plate XII. A: Kwakiutl chief's headdress from Alert Bay, with raven design. Wood and abalone shell; blue, red, black. Height of carving: 7½ in. MacMillan Purchase 1951. A3605. B: Tsimshian chief's headdress from Nass River, with bear design. Wood and abalone shell; red, black. Height of carving: 7½ in. Leon and Thea Koerner Foundation Grant 1959. A6810

Plate XIII. Kwakiutl heron and duck helmet headdress from Alert Bay. Wood and canvas; red, white, blue, black, green, yellow. Length of extended neck: 34 in. MacMillan Purchase 1951. A3633

Plate XIV. A: Haida frog bowl from Queen Charlotte Islands. Wood; green, black, red. Length: 8 in. MacMillan Purchase 1960, Rev. W. E. Collison Collection. A7053. *B:* Nootka duck from Kyuquot, used in the potlatch. Yew or hardwood, with brass plates along the sides; black, white, green, yellow. Length: 14 in. MacMillan Purchase 1961. A7861. *C:* Kwakiutl loon helmet headdress from Alert Bay. Wood; gray, yellow, green, black, red. Length: 19 in. MacMillan Purchase 1954. A6102

Plate XV. A: Kwakiutl eagle feast dish from Sullivan Bay. Wood; black, green, red, yellow. Length: 30 in. MacMillan Purchase 1953. A6433.
B: Kwakiutl eagle feast dish from Sullivan Bay. Wood; black, green, red, white. Length: 33 in. MacMillan Purchase 1953. A6432

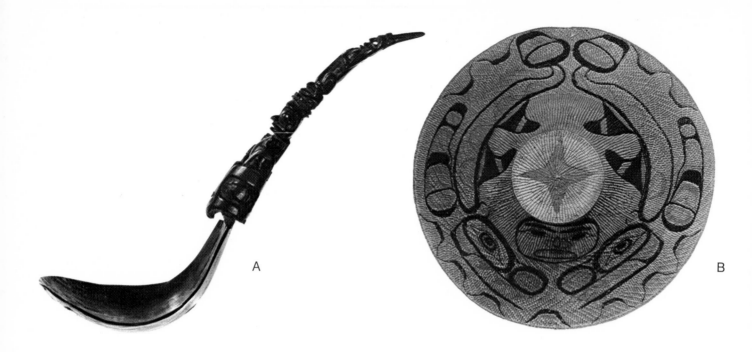

Plate XVI. A: Tsimshian spoon from Hartley Bay. Mountain goat horn. Length: 10½ in. Gift of Mr. Thomas Wallace. A6839. *B*: Haida hat from Skidegate, with killer whale design in black and red. Spruce root. Diameter of brim: 17 in. MacMillan Purchase 1948, Rev. G. H. Raley Collection. A1469. *C*: Haida drum from Queen Charlotte Islands, with killer whale design. Animal hide; red, black. Diameter: 19½ in. MacMillan Purchase 1948, Rev. G. H. Raley Collection. A4257. *D*: Tlingit killer whale crest basket. Spruce root; black, green, red, white, yellow. Diameter: 12 in. Gift of Mrs. W. C. Woodward 1951. A3763

Plate XVII. A: Kwakiutl killer whale mask from Sullivan Bay. Wood; black, white, red, green. Length: 5 ft. 5 in. MacMillan Purchase 1953. A6316. B: Kwakiutl killer whale mask from Alert Bay, with movable fins, tail, and jaw. Wood; black, white, red, blue, green. Length: 4 ft. 3 in. MacMillan Purchase 1960. A4506

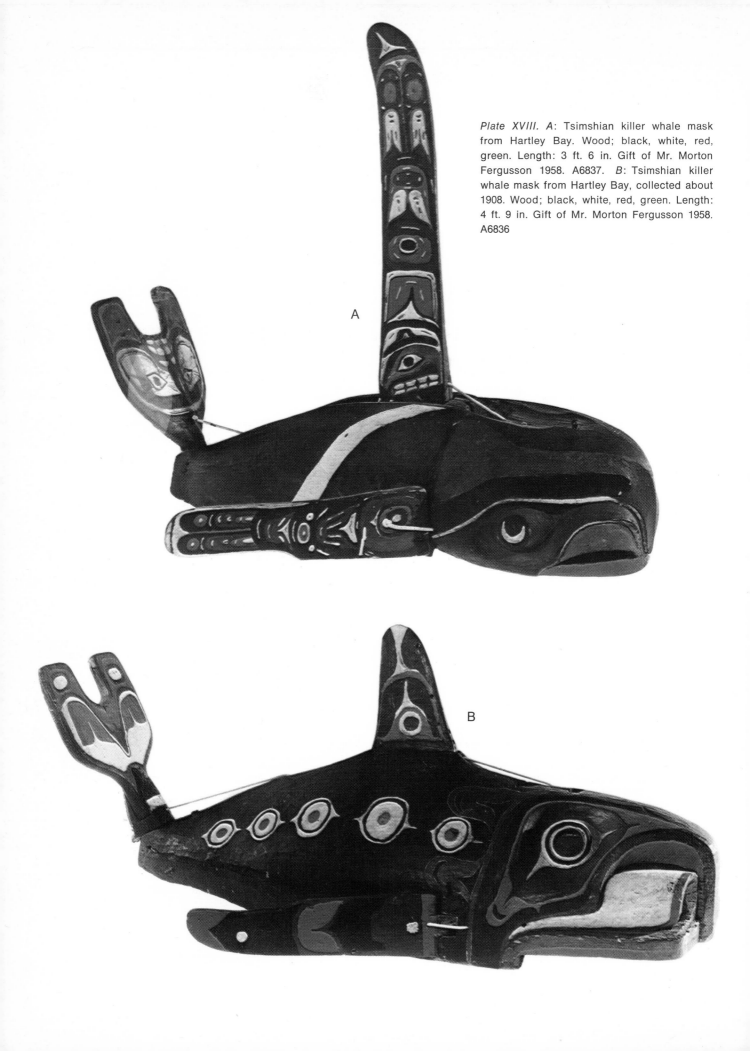

Plate XVIII. A: Tsimshian killer whale mask from Hartley Bay. Wood; black, white, red, green. Length: 3 ft. 6 in. Gift of Mr. Morton Fergusson 1958. A6837. *B*: Tsimshian killer whale mask from Hartley Bay, collected about 1908. Wood; black, white, red, green. Length: 4 ft. 9 in. Gift of Mr. Morton Fergusson 1958. A6836

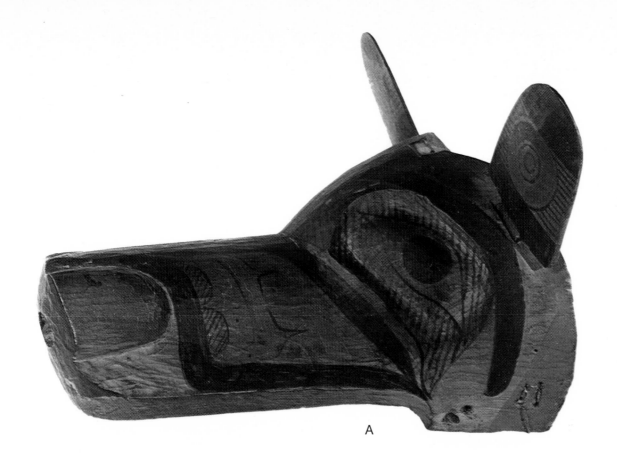

A

Plate XIX. A: Kwakiutl wolf mask from Kitlope. Wood; black, red. Length: 15½ in. MacMillan Purchase 1948, Rev. G. H. Raley Collection. A1744. B: Kwakiutl wolf mask from Sullivan Bay. Wood with mirror eyes; orange, yellow, green, black. Length: 15 in. MacMillan Purchase 1951. A6552

B

Plate XX. Kwakiutl Komokwa mask from Sullivan Bay. Wood; wings and neck of duck, canvas; green, red, black, blue. Height: 31 in.; wingspan of duck: 32 in. MacMillan Purchase 1950. A3588

Plate XXI. Kwakiutl moon mask from Kingcome Inlet, Bella Coola style. Wood; orange, red, black, blue, green. Diameter of rim: 21 in. MacMillan Purchase 1951. A3770

Plate XXII. Kwakiutl moon mask from Bella Bella, collected before 1945. Wood; black, red. Diameter: 12½ in. Museum Purchase 1949. A1797

Plate XXIII. Kwakiutl sun mask from Kingcome Inlet, carved by Arthur Shaughnessy and used at Gilford Island in 1918. Wood; black, white, red, green. Diameter with rays open: 22 in. The rays, attached to a flexible band, are shown open *(above)* and closed *(below)*. MacMillan Purchase 1951. A3553

A

Plate XXIV. A: Bella Coola moon mask, collected before 1910. Alderwood; blue, black, red. Diameter: 15 in. MacMillan Purchase 1963. A8367. *B*: Bella Coola cod mask. Alderwood; blue, black, red. Length 10½ in. MacMillan Purchase 1963. A8366

B

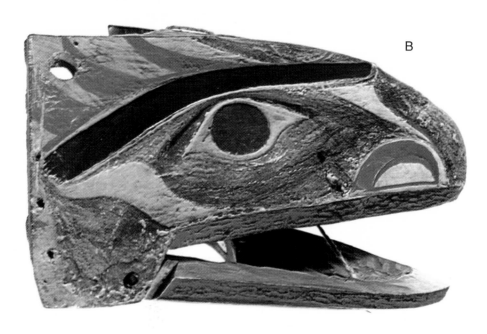

Plate XXV. Kwakiutl eagle mask from Kitamaat, said to have been used by the Sonahed people up to 1884. Wood and feathers; black, red. Height of carving: 11½ in. MacMillan Purchase 1948, Rev. G. H. Raley Collection. A1965

Plate XXVI. Kwakiutl echo mask from Sullivan Bay, a complex mask with interchangeable mouthpieces. Originally from Owikeno, the mask passed to Blunden Harbour and then to Gilford Island through marriage. The mouthpieces represent (*a*) Bookwus, (*b*) bear, (*c*) echo, (*d*) frog, (*e*) eagle, (*f*) echo, (*g*) Tsonokwa, (*h*) killer whale. Wood; black, orange, blue, green. Height: 12½ in. MacMillan Purchase 1950. A3587

A

B

Plate XXVII. A: Tsimshian mask of woman's face from Skeena River. Wood; black, red, blue. Height: 8 in. MacMillan Purchase 1961. A7367. *B*: Haida bird and human face mask from Queen Charlotte Islands. Wood and copper; black, red, blue, gray. Height: 8½ in. MacMillan Purchase 1960, Rev. W. E. Collison Collection. A7068. *C*: Bella Coola human face mask. Wood; blue, red. Height: 10½ in. MacMillan Purchase 1963. A8372. *D*: Haida mask of woman's face from Queen Charlotte Islands. Wood; black, red. Height: 9 in. MacMillan Purchase 1960, Rev. W. E. Collison Collection. A7064

C

D

Plate XXVIII. A: Kwakiutl mask of woman's face from Sullivan Bay, Bella Coola style. Wood; black, green, orange. Height: 12 in. MacMillan Purchase 1950. A3586. *B*: Kwakiutl fish mask from Gilford Island. Wood; black, red, white, green. Height: 13½ in. MacMillan Purchase 1952. A4094

A

B

A

B

Plate XXIX. A: Kwakiutl kerfed box with lid from Kitamaat, used by a shaman to store his gear. Wood and shells; black, red. Height: 13 in. Mac-Millan Purchase 1948, Rev. G. H. Raley Collection. A1764. *B*: Haida kerfed wooden box with lid from Queen Charlotte Islands, with bear carved on front. Wood; black, red, blue. Width: 3 ft. Mac-Millan Purchase 1960, Rev. W. E. Collison Collection. A7103

A

Plate XXX. A: Haida kerfed oil dish from Queen Charlotte Islands. Wood; unpainted. Width: 10 in. MacMillan Purchase 1960, Rev. W. E. Collison Collection. A7055. B: Tshimshian kerfed food dish from Port Simpson. Wood; unpainted. Width: 18 in. MacMillan Purchase 1953. A6189

B

A

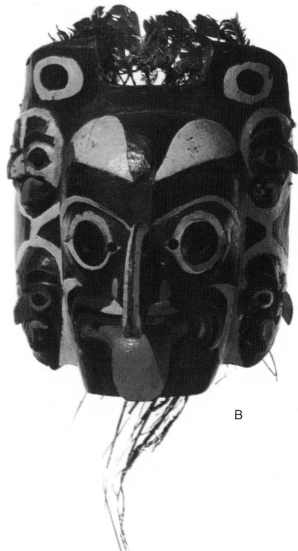

B

Plate XXXI. A and B: Nootka Kwekwe masks from Friendly Cove, Vancouver Island; two welcome masks made in 1905. Wood; black, red, white, green. Height: 22½ in. Gift Purchase of Dr. Walter C. Koerner 1965. A: A8547; B: 8546.

Plate XXXII. A: Kwakiutl model canoe from Bella Bella. Wood; black, red, blue. Length: 25 in. MacMillan Purchase 1948. A1545. *B*: Haida model canoe from Queen Charlotte Islands, with two men and sail, carved by Charles Edenshaw. Wood with cedar bark sail; black, red, blue, green. Length: 19½ in. MacMillan Purchase 1960, Rev. W. E. Collison Collection. A7095. *C*: Haida model canoe from Queen Charlotte Islands, with sea wolf design. Wood; black, red. Length: 3 ft. 5 in. MacMillan Purchase 1948, Rev. G. H. Raley Collection. A1531. *D*: Tsimshian canoe paddle from Nass River. Wood; black, red. Length: 5 ft. 6 in. MacMillan Purchase 1948, Rev. G. H. Raley Collection. A1538. *E*: Haida canoe paddle from Queen Charlotte Islands. Wood; black, red, blue. Length: 5 ft. 1 in. MacMillan Purchase 1960, Rev. W. E. Collison Collection. A7087 [that he will show] . . . all the masks owned by his family, which have been arranged in rows behind a curtain stretched across the rear of the room. While the people strike with their batons without singing, the curtain is raised with three ropes passing over a roof-beam, and every mask suddenly rises and moves about in its place. In a few minutes the curtain is lowered, and with brief intervals the spectacle is repeated three times more. The maskers are supposed to be carried away by the spirits which they represent, and hence they remain hidden during the next three days. On the second and the third night there is no dancing, but a feast is given, and on the fourth night the dancing with masks is repeated in order to recover the maskers from the spirits that have captured them.

Feasting, oratory, and the display of family privileges in drama and dancing were all part of the Klasila. The description which follows is a summary of the details of the ceremony practiced by the southern Kwakiutl, in particular those of Alert Bay and the adjacent islands. This account differs in its elaboration from that given for the northern Kwakiutl by Olson (1954 and 1955) and Drucker (1940). There the character of the "Masked Intruder" (Gakhula) does not appear in a recognizable form. Since, however, there is much illustrative material from Alert Bay, the sequence of ceremonial procedure as reported from that area is given here.

On the fourth day, during the height of the merriment, while the dancers were dancing about the dance floor, songs were being sung and batons were striking the beat against the boards, suddenly a masked intruder would enter through the doorway. This intruder, Gakhula (see Figs. 44, 45), with his forbidding and aggressive air, changed the emotional climate of the gathering. He made a speech to the effect that this was supposed to be a serious time, and by the time he had finished all the dancers had gone. Everything was quiet, until whistles were heard in the woods on the edge of the village, signaling the arrival of the spirits. Then the speakers announced that the next day would begin a new season; new names would be given, and new songs sung.

The people went home, bathed ritually, and completed the preparations for the days to come—the days in which the spirits would return and initiate the descendants into the secrets of their dancing orders. The next day whistles were heard again in the woods. This was the start of the true Tsetseka season.

The Tsetseka Season

The essential element of the Tsetseka season was the initiation of the novices. The day after the whistles of the spirits were blown, the novices disappeared, supposedly taken away by the appropriate spirit to be inspired. During the time of their absence they were prepared for their role. Each dancing society initiated its novices secretly, closing its house to all non-initiates, each night being devoted to feasting for the members of the dancing house.

On the fourth or final night of each novice's apprenticeship, the whole village, and even outsiders, were invited to see a dramatic performance showing how the novice had been seized by the spirits, how he had acted while under their power, and how he had once again become human. On cue, the novice made a dramatic entrance, gave his cries, danced, and showed by convincing behavior that he was in a state of spirit possession. In the course of his dancing he demonstrated his magical tricks.

In a series of ritualized acts the attendants and assistants to the novice helped to gentle him, to calm him. Eventually, when he had been tamed, he returned to human society and danced more quietly. The length of this performance varied, the more elaborate ceremonies taking several days.

At the end of each stage of initiation, gifts were distributed and payments were made to those who were to be indemnified and to those who had assisted the novice. With each day's performance a feast was held.

In each village there were two groups: the uninitiated, who acted as an audience for the novices, and the initiated. The initiated were divided into two orders: the Seals—the Hamatsa and the war spirit dancers who were the high-ranking dancers; and the Sparrows, who included all the others, from children to old men and women. Those who had been initiated into the Seals but who wished to retire went into the Sparrow group. They were still high-ranking elders, who continued to direct events but were no longer under the influence of the supernatural spirit. The Sparrows comprised a series of age-grade groups: the youngest boys, called Sea Parrots; boys from thirteen to fifteen, called Mallards; the strong young men, called Killer Whales; the oldest men, called Whales. Girls and women had equivalent names; the oldest group of women were called Cows (see Curtis 1915:164 for a complete list).

In some northern Kwakiutl tribes there was a separate dancing order, Mitla, whose novices were initiated by the spirits. In other dances Mitla was the name of a character who danced with supernatural tricks among those initiated by the war spirit. Another supernaturally inspired dancing order, Nootlem, or "Dog-Eaters," was common in the north, but among the southern Kwakiutl this word was used for dances not supernaturally inspired.

The Sparrows acted as jeering, mocking teasers of their high-ranking rivals, the Seals. This made for a comic interplay. Curtis (1915:205) reported this dialogue when the Tokwit, the female war spirit dancer, was looking for a box large enough to climb into so that she could (apparently) burn herself up:

At the end of the song she stood beside the fire, unwilling to leave. Now and then she cried ep ep, ep, ep ep! or, op op, op op!

The sparrows, who sat squatting about the room now began to call: "Well, ask her what she is going to do. If she is going to do anything, hurry and have it over! If she wants us to do something for her, say so and let us get about it!"

Some little distance from the singers sat . . . "Quick hearer," who holds his position by inheritance. The winter-dance speaker rose, saying, "I will ask what she wants." He went to the woman and appeared to whisper to her, but she made no reply. . . . "Quick hearer" in his place bent forward as if listening intently, and exclaimed: "I know what she wants! She says she wishes to be burned in the fire!"

The sparrows at once began to shout their willingness to perform whatever duties were necessary in carrying out the torture, but the woman turned and walked characteristically here and there in the space between the people and the fire, with gestures indicative of throwing magic power from her palms into the floor, and constantly crying op op, op op! Each utterance was accompanied by soft beating of the batons. Then she went to the fire and repeated her cry. Immediately the sparrows set up a babble of shouts: "She wants to go into the fire! Build up the fire! Push her into the fire, friends!" She moved round the fire, which was at the rear and somewhat to the left of the room, and the sparrows continued to make disparaging remarks about her: "Ha! Dancers of that kind are full of lies! They pretend to have been around the world!" The woman stood there for a while, then started again turning around and around and going over the entire floor, putting magic into it. Some of the sparrows followed her, imitating her motions and cried, and saying, "I can do the same thing!" Their leader . . . was particularly active. He now called to some of his companions, "Come, stand close to me and burn me up, instead of this liar!"

After the woman had encircled the fire the second time and stood at the rear of the room, the . . . [leader] went to her, broke off a few twigs from her kirtle, and put them on his head, saying to his men, "How do I look?" The sparrows gathered round him in the right rear corner of the house, while the *tokwit* went to the left rear and on round the fire for a third time. At once . . . [the leader] started after her, imitating her. After the third circuit, some of the sparrows cried to the speaker . . .: "Well, are we going to stay here all night watching this woman go round the fire? Ask her what she is going to do!"

The Sparrows tried to provoke the other group into violent behavior, especially to prevent the retirement of the Seals from active dancing.

Associated with each of the winter dancing societies in its own dance house was the order of seating, with a place for the song leader, the drum beater, and the heralds who directed the events, and specially ordered places where the singers sat. Each society followed its own order and ritual. All the societies used certain outward signs taught to them by their supernatural ancestors: red cedar bark to be worn on the head and neck; eagle-down to float on the people softly, as a sign of peace; red or black paint to adorn the face.

After all who claimed membership in the societies had been initiated, food supplies in the houses were low, and each host prepared a special farewell feast. When the final gifts and payments had been made, the speaker warned that soon the season would change again. Everyone sang the last Tsetseka songs, danced, and used the Tsetseka names. The red cedar bark was burned; the face paint was removed. Then a summer song was sung; the people turned and addressed each other by their secular, nonceremonial names; and the Tsetseka season was over for another year.

Staging the Tsetseka

In a sense, the whole of the Tsetseka season was staged. Each portion of it was under the guidance of the heads of the dancing societies and was carried out under their instructions by a group of officials—speakers, heralds, and hereditary officials with specialized duties. These controlled the time of beginning, agreed on the sponsor's dancing houses, and helped arrange for the spiriting away of the novices. Within the dancing society, the initiated ones participated in planning the proceedings, with the proper ways of appearing, dancing, uttering the special cries, and staging the dramatic tricks. The intention was always to convince the village of the real presence of spirits and the supernatural.

The house itself was a stage, with seating arranged so that the wall next to the curtain was shielded, and the dancers could come and go unseen. The central fireplace was the focus of attention. Dancing took place around the fireplace—the dancers moved four times around, counterclockwise, pivoting at the front and the back of the house, then disappeared. The performers entered suddenly through the front door, while others left unnoticed.

Illusion was managed in many ways. "Prop" men hidden above the beams of the house manipulated the strings that helped the dancers to control their magic tricks. Supernatural birds or other creatures, announced by thunderous noise on the roof, flew down through the air, appeared to pick up a person, and then flew up again. Underground passages increased the repertoire of magical tricks; such illusion gave credence to the presence of

39

spirits. Curtis noted that some people even stayed home in the deserted village during the summer berrying and fishing times in order to prepare the tunnels under the floor of the Ghost Dancers' House.

Staging was always deliberate. Even the apparently spontaneous destructive frenzy of the Hamatsa was subject to planning (Curtis 1915:179): "He advances on certain lines which have been secretly marked out on the floor, and those who have been previously warned by the initiator that hamatsa will bite them sit where these lines touch the edge of the open space, so that hamatsa can easily reach them."

During the winter dance season the whole village, not only within the houses but also outside, become the scene of the pageant. A novice was sought after and captured on the edge of the woods. Another novice—balanced on boards over a low-slung canoe—arrived apparently dancing on the water. The use of illusion was an important element: one novice was seen arriving by canoe with his sponsor when there was a sudden accident, the canoe overturned, and the novice was drowned. He was later revived and danced amid general rejoicing. Actually the drowning figure was a cedar carving which was weighted down and sunk. In another example of illusion the Hamatsa novice, fleeing to the woods, apparently disappeared in midflight. The Hamatsas, wearing red cedar bark head and neck rings, went into the woods to capture the novice. On the way they were handed hemlock boughs, which they donned. They advanced toward the Hamatsa novice, who, in order to mystify the village spectators, quickly substituted red cedar bark ornaments for his green hemlock rings. When the crowd opened, he had apparently disappeared, quickly to reappear at a considerable distance in the person of a second substitute dressed exactly like him. This one was then surrounded and "lost" in the same manner (Curtis 1915:174).

In one part of the drama, the Hamatsa novice rushed out from the house with everyone else in pursuit. The Killer Whales, who had been teasing him, ran to take refuge in the water, where they were cornered by the novice. He was afraid to go into salt water, and they were afraid to come close to him for fear of being bitten. Several novices of the sea-creature spirits appeared for initiation at the edge of the ocean as though they had just come up from its depths.

Terror, drama, and comedy were balanced to produce good theater:

During the feast the grizzly bear may become aroused, growl and roar, and try to get out of the room.

The people scramble back to their seats along the walls, while attendants rush over to restrain the beast. After a terrific struggle, despite their efforts, a board will be torn loose, and they will all be sent sprawling, but instead of a grizzly bear the figure of a decrepit old man will totter forth [Drucker 1940:207].

Some dancers acted as buffoons and created a disturbance. Some were clumsy; some were mimics who staggered around imitating the actions of others:

While the real dancers are making their secret preparations behind the screen, the jesters amuse the audience. They dodge behind the screen, parody the coming performance. Or one may accuse the other of lying, then peek behind the screen and come out to report "the real truth" to a convulsed audience [Olson 1940: A:5, 175].

Meticulous attention to the details of theatrical illusion and dramatic impact characterized the productions of the ceremonies.

Within the large plank house, the central fire cast lights and shadows. At the far end opposite the entrance door was a theatrical curtain made of wooden planks or muslin with the crest of the initiating spirit of the dancing house painted on it (see Figs. 10-14). Behind the curtain, awaiting their cues, were the dancers in costume. At one side was a small hidden cubicle to which the novice retreated. There were several such small rooms for the various dancers.

The dancing house in which the Tokwit dancers were going to perform was vacated and carefully guarded several days before the initiation. Underground passageways were dug, down which the dancer could disappear. A system of kelp speaking tubes was installed. Elaborate gear was brought to the house, such as false-bottomed chests in which the dancer would be concealed while apparently being consumed by fire.

Every opportunity to create drama was exploited. Here is an example cited by Drucker in a description of a Dluwalakha dance (1940:207):

The novice . . . flies away for four days, descends again, is caught and dances four nights like the rest. On the fourth night, the master of ceremonies . . . is bade to call the dancer's spirit down from the sky. He stands under the smoke hole, shouting his request that the "honored one from heaven" descend to show himself to the people. He tries very hard. Suddenly there is a tremendous thud on the roof, a blare of spirit horns, and a commotion at the door. The master of ceremonies sends the attendants to see if the spirit he has been calling has arrived. They report that there is something strange and terrifying without. They assemble at the door, holding their blankets out to form a screen, then back in. All at once they break away, revealing the spirit—a naked dancer, painted black, wearing a hominoid mask. The spirit dances, enters the cubicle, and is sent away when the novice is purified.

During the dances various tricks were employed to create convincing illusions. An apparent beheading used portrait carvings and bladders filled with seal blood. The fire thrower handled burning embers in leather gloves with wooden palms skillfully put on by his attendants. He walked on the fire over wooden boulders wearing protective footgear. The Tokwit dancer climbed into a wooden box, was consumed by fire, and in due course was reconstituted.

Curtis (1915:212-13) described two other examples of illusion, summarized as follows:

> Kinkalatlala walks about the house, making her cries. A noise is heard, and a wooden kingfisher appears. The bird descends to the dancer and follows him, darts at him and spears him with its long beak. It then flies up to the roof. The dancer has strings which raise and lower the bird, and there is a man above on the roof who also controls the strings.

> The female Mitla spirit produces salmonberries out of season. Four masked female attendants dance around her. Salmonberry shoots are let down from the roof. The berries are pebbles covered with resin gum dyed with iron oxide. The people eat them and pretend to fall dead, but are then revived.

A simple device was the use of the dancer's blanket to aid in concealment. A gesture of a blanket-covered arm would make a screen behind which one mask could be changed for another, or a whistle held under the blanket could be blown secretly.

Hereditary Officials and
Their Ceremonial Roles

Each functionary among the Kwakiutl had a specific job to perform during the winter ceremonials. Most of these jobs were hereditary, passed on from father to son. The speaker (Alk) was a hereditary official who acted as spokesman for the chief on all public and ceremonial occasions. He had a badge of office, the speaker's staff, which he held at all times while addressing the crowd. This official, who usually lived in the household of the lineage chief whose spokesman he was, also acted as "taster" for the chief, helping to divert the immense amounts of food that were served out at ceremonial feasts.

Each society had a song master who invented, and then memorized, every song belonging to every member of the society. This office was not hereditary; the song master was appointed because he was very quick at making up and learning songs. Most members had four songs for each of their names. When a novice was to be initiated, the song master was called in by the sponsor and paid to invent the songs. He and his assistants retired to the woods, while the novice hid nearby, and after some experimentation devised a song which they and the novice memorized. These songs were subsequently brought out whenever needed as the theme of the dancer. During the dance the song master and his assistants sang the song while the people beat time with sticks as they danced around the room.

The baton master split the batons or music sticks for all the guests present and passed them out to the visitors to the house. He also brought in the long planks on which the sticks were struck. Later the sticks of the visitors, which were temporary, were collected and disposed of. Those of the leaders were carved and were permanent.

The senior members of the dancing societies who had retired from active service comprised a body of elders who directed proceedings to see that ritual and protocol were observed. Some of these kept watch during each dance and announced publicly when a mistake had been made in the dancing or behavior of the members. Those who had erred were publicly rebuked and might have to give a potlatch or gifts in restitution.

Other officials connected with the ceremonial organization included the following:

Four messengers for each sponsor of a dancing series, who invited the villagers. These messengers carried staffs of office. Other messengers invited other tribes and conducted them back to their villages.

The "Quick Hearer," who listened at dances and interpreted the movements of the dancers, calling out their wishes to the crowd.

The eagle down gatherer and dispenser.

The cedar bark distributor of head rings for visitors and guests.

The Takiumi, or special distributor of gifts, also called "Holding the Upper Part," who was in charge of the distribution of gifts at the potlatch. He held up each gift as he called out the name of the recipient. This was a very responsible position, for the Takiumi had to remember the proper order of precedence since any violation of this might give rise to new struggles between rivals. His assistants handed out the gifts as he called them.

Four copper holders, including two to hold the copper, one to cut it, and one to hold the pieces.

The "Word Passer," whose position depended on musical talent and the ability to memorize. He assisted the song master and acted as a prompter, having memorized the songs made by the maker for each new dancer.

The distributor of tallow and paint for facial painting.

The drum beater.

"Hotluliti," or "Obeyed by All," a director of ceremonies for each dancing society.

Various attendants at each dance society who interpreted, ran errands, built up suspense, and so forth.

Various police officers or monitors who kept order. These helped the elders keep "score" of mistakes made by people during the ceremonies and called out errors at the end of the day.

In addition to these, as further examples of the detailed allotment of chores, for the final purifying ceremonies of the Hamatsa there were a stone picker, a wedge splitter, a tong splitter, a cedar bark shaper, a cutter, a dish carrier, and a water carrier. All of these were engaged in the tasks connected with the making of a cedar bark figure which was elaborately constructed at the end of the Hamatsa sequence and then purified by smoke and embers, thus releasing the Hamatsa novice from his involvement with the spirits.

Other societies had less complex, but similar, sets of chores and officials.

Kwakiutl Dancing Societies

In 1895, Boas listed fifty-three different characters who had roles in the dancing societies of the southern Kwakiutl. By 1913, when Curtis listed those he found at Fort Rupert, there were sixty-three such dancing roles (Curtis 1913:156-58). Of these it appears that some had proliferated, such as Mitla, and had been divided between a man and a woman. In general a role assigned to a man was danced by a man, but if there was no male descendant to inherit the dance, a woman could be eligible for it.

The investigations by Drucker, in 1938, of the dancing roles that had survived among the Kwakiutl showed that a number of both major and minor roles were still inherited and danced, at least until recent times, in a series of two or three dancing orders (Drucker 1940:228).

The dancing societies of the Kwakiutl consisted of four main groups. Of these the most important and the most complex was the Hamatsa society under the supernatural inspiration of Bakbakwalanooksiwae, a powerful man-eating spirit, represented in the dance by the cannibal dancer or Hamatsa, in human form. The second group was under the inspiration of Winalagilis, the war spirit initiator. The third group, the Atlakim dance series, could be used either for Klasila or for Tsetseka displays by changing the symbolic decorations. The fourth group was made up of the Dluwalakha dancers (meaning "Once more from Heaven")—those who had been given supernatural treasures or *dloogwi,* which were passed on to the novice, but who were not, as a group, involved in the convincing and terrifying displays of supernatural seizure.

Among the northern peoples, the Tsetseka society comprised all those who acted as shamans, with the shamans' hereditary rights to supernatural healing powers and secrets.

A dinner attended by all the members of the dancing societies and given on the evening after the Hamatsa novice was tamed was described by Curtis (1915:231 ff.). A summary of his account follows.

At dusk, they began to assemble at the Hamatsa dancing house. The Sparrows, in their varied costumes representing animals, fish, and birds, filed in and were seated in their traditional seating places in the house. The guests from other villages, also in their costumes, were shown to their seats. Rushing in and shouting, two Fool dancers, tattered and unkempt, came carrying baskets of stones. They clumsily ran to their places, one to the left of the house, one to the right.

Two Hamatsa grizzly bears lurched in, their faces painted black, with great teeth. They growled, and sauntered to their positions. Thunderbird came in, with a flying motion.

The Hokhokws picked their way, stiff-legged like herons, as though looking downward into the water.

The War Dancers, with painted faces, carried lengths of rope. They looked up at the beams as though ready to swing from the rafters. All called out, "Don't do it, don't do it!" for these fierce warriors like to do violence. Tsonoqwa, great and shaggy, stumbled in the wrong way round the fire, tripping over people as she went. Attendants guided her to her seat, where she subsided and fell asleep.

The Mitla, or "Thrower" dancer, appeared in the doorway, glowering and clapping his sharp clapper. He glowered fiercely, reaching for his magic weapon. Everyone cried out, "Don't throw it, don't throw it!"

Then silence descended on all. This was "the weight of the winter dance pressing on the people."

The baton keepers handed around the music sticks. The dance leader held his rattle high. A long pause: then it fell. The batons crashed! Vibrated louder! He raised his rattle again. Silence. Then he shook it; it fell. He raised it; four times it fell. The batons drummed a rapid crescendo. Then the singing began. The song leader led: all sang the songs of the Tsetseka season. Three songs were sung in succession by all.

Then the house attendants brought dishes and feast spoons, first to each of the four Hamatsas in whose honor this dinner was held. The Sparrows reached for the spoons and dishes, crying "Give it to me! Me first!" Their dishes were placed before each three Sparrows, and other dishes in turn were placed before the other guests.

Boas (1895:545) describes the conversation at a similar dinner. He is reporting the conversation of the age grades of the Sparrows:

While the people were eating, the different societies uttered their cries:
    "The hens are pecking"
    "The great seals keep on chewing"
    "The food of the great killer whales is sweet"
    "The great rock cods are trying to get food"
    "The great sea lions throw their heads downwards"
When uttering these cries the members of the societies lifted their spoons and seemed to enjoy the fun. . . . Then they ate as quickly as they could, and all the different (sparrow) societies vied with each other, singing all at the same time.

Dancing Societies of Other Northwest Coast Tribes

The Bella Coola had two dancing societies: the Koosioot, a winter dancing society, in which supernatural spirits initiated the novices with tricks and violence; and the Sisauk, in which family and clan crests representing natural elements, flowers, and birds were given in connection with major intergroup potlatches.

The focal point of Haida society was the building and validation of a new lineage house and the installation of a chief. The potlatches for this occasion were accompanied by the initiation of members into a shamans' society in which the members learned and presented various tricks, usually violent.

The Tsimshian had four societies and four kinds of dances. These centered about the commemorative mourning cycle after a chief died, and the installation of his successor. Of the four societies, there were three in which the novices who were initiated learned tricks simulating states of supernatural possession.

The main dance of the Nootka was the wolf dance, in which the novice was initiated by wolves. Family crest masks might be shown.

The Salish had a series of "spirit quest" dances during the winter months. They only had one masked dance, which was inherited and performed by Kwekwe healers.

Hamatsa Ritual

The most important dance of the winter was that of the Hamatsa society. The Hamatsa complex originated among the Haisla, the northern Kwakiutl group at Kitlope, which was apparently the center for the dissemination of this dramatic dance complex. In recent times it was borrowed by the Tsimshian and the Haida of Skidegate. The Nootka and Tlingit alone are not recorded as having adopted it.

The Hamatsa dance was acquired by the Kwakiutl in 1835 when they attacked a Heiltsuk canoe, several of whose occupants had Hamatsa whistles and masks in their possession. This acquisition was then distributed by marriage transfer.

To become a full-fledged Hamatsa one must have danced a cycle of twelve years, four years through each of three grades. When the novice was ready to begin the series, the Hamatsa senior of his family line would retire in his favor. Usually the novice had already completed several other seasons of dancing in lower ranking societies. All of these stages involved feasting, gifts, payments, and ceremonial costs, and only people of wealth could afford them.

The popularity of this performance resulted from its complex cast of characters and the dramatic ritual, which took at least four days to complete. It was based upon legends of the bird-monsters who inhabited the sky-world and were eaters of human flesh, terrifying apparitions that searched for human bodies to consume. The horror they inspired was

50

heightened by the drama unfolded before the audience. Their behavior could not be accounted for in human terms, and thus it proved to the un-initiated the validity of spirit possession. Most early missionaries were certainly convinced of the literalness of the flesh-eating cannibalistic monsters, but the two most thorough students of the subject, Drucker and Curtis, have concluded that the apparent cannibalism was a carefully planned stage effect, involving effigies, sleight-of-hand, and other well-known theatrical devices much used by the Kwakiutl (Drucker 1965:165; Curtis 1915:221).

The performance consisted of the dramatic seizure of the novice by the Hamatsa initiating spirit, his disappearance into the woods, his four-day frenzy, and his ritual taming to the point where he became human again and a full-fledged member of the dancing society.

The chief cannibal spirit was Bakbakwalanooksiwae, whose spirit dominated the Hamatsa novice and all his assistants. He was invisible, but his presence was made known through a weird whistling sound—the winds blowing through millions of mouths in his body. Bakbakwalanooksiwae controlled a large household in the sky, whose members were portrayed in the dances of the Hamatsa society. These included the Hamatsa, an obsessive cannibal in human form, the representative cannibal spirit of Bakbakwala-nooksiwae; the Noonsistalahl or fire thrower, a being obsessed with fire; the Hamatsa's two attendants, who always danced with him—Komunokas, the rich woman, and Kinkalatlala, a female slave, both danced by women; Kwakwakwalanooksiwae, the cannibal raven; the Hokhokw, a fabulous long-beaked bird-monster; Galokwudzuwis, the "crooked-beak" bird-monster; Nanes Bakbakwalanooksiwae, the cannibal grizzly bear; Hamshamtsus, a less violent cannibal; and Noohlmahl, the fool dancer.

When the Hamatsa whistles sounded in the woods, the novice disappeared and remained invisible for a period of time during which it was said he was being initiated into the ways of Bakbakwalanooksiwae. With him were his two invariable companions, Komunokas and Kinkalatlala, each with four attendants of her own. (For examples of Hamatsa whistles, see Figs. 26 [A3620] and 27 [A7973].)

When the formal initiation was to begin, the novice appeared wearing hemlock branches in his hair and around his waist, over his shoulders, and around his wrists and ankles. He was in a state of animal-like ferocity, uttering cries of "*haap*" (eat), trying to bite people, and frequently breaking away from his captors, members of the society who were trying to soothe him. In his frenzy he ran into the woods, was brought back, and jumped down from the roof back into the room. At first he danced with a crouching step, very low, hands and arms akimbo, trembling, eyes starting, his head turning sharply this way and that, agitated by his spirit. At times he was completely overcome by his madness. Key words such as "body" and "eat," uttered by the audience or helpers, and their actions, goaded him into frenzied fits, and from time to time he disappeared into the closet at the rear house behind the *mawihl* (curtain or screen). When he reappeared he was wearing cedar bark ornaments. While he was absent, senior members of the Hamatsa society representing the various bird-monsters performed their dances in turn, wearing masks with a red cedar bark fringe, and long cedar fringes partially concealing their bodies and legs; each uttered his characteristic cries. All those who had "gone into the House of Bakbakwala-nooksiwae" to be initiated directly by him or his spirits were thought to have "learned his secrets." Such people were *lakhsa*. All others were *wikhsa*, "those who have leaned against his walls."

Each character danced four times around the central fire while the audience beat time for his dance and song. At the back of the house, a great cannibal tethering pole (*hamspek*) was put up. This was loosely fastened, so that it seemed to give way when the novice was tied to it, and it swayed and teetered, moved by his supernatural strength. From outside, the pole could be seen swaying above the housetop.

After four days and four nights of frenzy, during which he was subjected to various soothing practices—being offered "human" flesh to eat and ducked in sea water, having fish oil poured on him and ritual fire and smoke directed at him—the novice finally became calmed. Wearing his cedar bark head ring and neck rings and a button blanket, he danced and sang as a full-fledged Hamatsa and received a new Hamatsa name. Last of all, four officials performed a series of purifying tasks. They constructed a red cedar bark figure through which the new Hamatsa walked, after which it was burned in a cloud of smoke to complete the purifying process. On the final night there was great feasting and recounting of the legend, and payment was made to all those who had taken part in the ceremonies and to the others for any damage incurred through the violence of the novice. All the initiates gave Hamatsa dances and songs. Once the novice had been initiated, he danced with others of the society while new novices were brought along. An eye-witness account of the Hamatsa ritual is given in Appendix III.

The bird-monsters and the Noohlmahl wore masks. The other characters wore black face paint, and they all wore distinctive red cedar bark neck rings, skirts, capes, wrist rings, and sometimes cedar bark headdresses. The Hamatsa himself had a different set of head and neck rings at each stage of his initiation.

Ritual of Winalagilis, the War Spirit

The second high-ranking dancing order was made up of those who were inspired by the war spirit, Winalagilis. Characterized as brutal, violent, and impervious to pain, they possessed very dramatic tricks. Boas pointed out that these dancers may have represented the warriors of an earlier day, and they retained many of the warrior attributes such as fierce appearance, unkempt hair, and an aggressive demeanor.

The mythological basis of their performance was the possession of various magical gifts and powers: a quartz crystal that could cause death when it was thrown; the ability to fly, to become invisible, to control fire, and to touch it without harm; the use of "the water of life" to revive the dead; and a supernatural healing ritual. All of these were represented in a repertoire of tricks and demonstrations by the dancers.

Most of these dancers wore no costume except ordinary cedar bark skirts or kilts. They used hemlock boughs rather than cedar bark for head and neck rings. Their faces and frequently their bodies were painted with black pigment. They wore no masks, except those in the ghost dance, who sometimes wore masks representing skulls (Figs. 123, 124). The warrior dancers often wore headdresses in the form of the Sisiutl, the double-headed serpent which was a recurring theme of this series of dances.

The chief dancers of the Winalagilis ritual were the following:

The Mamaka (thrower) entered fiercely, looking about alertly for his "secret," a small tube that could expand to become quite long. This was

54

his "disease," which he pretended to throw into the crowd while they ducked their heads and covered them with their blankets. By telescoping his tube, the Mamaka seemed to catch it again magically. Finally he appeared to drive it into himself and fell dead, after which he withdrew the disease, arose, and danced off. The Mamaka carried a Sisiutl staff and bow.

The Noonsistalahl (fire thrower) was obsessed by fire and could not be kept away from it by his attendants. Wearing shoes and gloves of wood and leather, made to be as inconspicuous as possible, he seemed to walk across the fire, pick up embers, and throw the fire about without being harmed by it.

The Hayleekilahl (healer dancer) had the power to heal any of the effects of violence done to themselves by the warrior characters, who skewered themselves, swung from hooks, and by using seal bladders filled with blood appeared to inflict grave harm upon themselves.

The Matum (flyer) wore the magic quartz crystal on his head and flew from the roof into the room. Mitla was another war dancer, who wore a belt and carried a bow bearing the Sisiutl crest.

The most dramatic dancer of this group was the Tokwit, a female war dancer, who performed many magical tricks, using false-bottomed boxes, carved portrait heads, and kelp speaking tubes. Some of her tricks were having herself put into a box and apparently burned to death, having her head cut off or a sword run through her, and speaking from the underworld through the kelp tubes. At the beginning of the dance, the Tokwit, with her hands held palms up, singing her song, conjured the Sisiutl spirit up from the ground. The undulating, swaying, glittering *duntsik* ("power board"; see Fig. 130) rose up. When she struck it, it separated into two Sisiutl forms.

The ghost dancer was another character associated with the war dancers. Ghosts had the treasure or secret of being able to return the dead to life, and this was the theme of their performance. Their tricks all pertained to the underworld. During their dance they used underground tunnels to drag other dancers to the underworld and back. Each dancer in turn gave his dance and his cry ("hamamamama") and disappeared. This cry caused the Hamatsa, the war dancers, and the Sparrows to become excited. As each of them went toward the back of the room to see what was happening, he fell down as though stricken dead. The ghost dancers brought up the chief dancers from below, and revived the others. All then danced and sang together.

Atlakim Dancing

All of the Kwakiutl dancing societies had a dance called Atlakim ("taken far away into the woods" or "taken back into the woods"). The Atlakim was an inspired dancer who received and displayed a forest treasure or gift.

The southern Kwakiutl made this into a large-scale dance, including twenty-six young men and fourteen young women. On the whole, they were considered to be amusing. Their special sacred room was decorated with hemlock boughs instead of cedar bark. They wore masks (Figs. 131-44), each clearly recognizable as the character portrayed, and their head and neck rings were woven of hemlock and balsam, intertwined with strips of red cedar, salal branches, fern fronds, and moss—unusual materials for a Tsetseka dance. They also wore aprons of these same materials, hanging down in draperylike fashion. During the Klasila they also wore feathers.

There was only one song among them, repeated over and over as each dancer was called forth in turn. Each performed his dance and showed his treasure—usually the mask. Then a female dancer came out, danced, retired, and returned wearing red and white cedar bark neck and head rings, and finally a small group returned and performed a magical restoration of one of the dancers, who had been struck dead by supernatural power.

Dluwalakha Dancing and Masks

The fourth group among the dancing societies of the Kwakiutl were the Dluwalakha, or Nootlem—words used by Boas (1895) to mean "non-sacred." Dluwalakha dancers wore masks representing the family crest myth and family *dloogwi,* which were supernatural in origin, but the dancers were not supernaturally possessed as were the Hamatsa, Winalagilis, and Atlakim dancers. The supernatural gift passed on to the novice was of a simpler sort, often being the dance or other mimetic action, and the novice did not have a lengthy disappearance or an elaborate seizure. A description of a Dluwalakha dance is given by Drucker (1940:215):

The second night of the potlatch is the time for the novice to dance. He dances, then returns to his room. Now the master of ceremonies (alkw) is requested to call down the spirit of the dancer. He asks what he is to say, and the chief tells him. So he shouts (for example), "Come down, come down, you great Moon of Heaven!" There is a roaring noise, and something lands with a crash on the roof. Spirit horns are blown in the house and from the novice's room. Then a mask representing the Moon appears above the screen. The chief says to the master of ceremonies, "Blow the sacred eagle down on it, and ask if this is really the Moon." So he blows down toward the mask, and asks, "Is this really you, great Moon of Heaven whom we called?" The mask replies, "hm, hm, hm, hm," and waggles from side to side. The master of ceremonies announces, "Yes, this is the one." Now the musicians shout "wai!" and the spirit vanishes. They strike up a song. The novice comes out of his room to dance. After the dance, he reenters the room. The chief follows him in, emerging to report, "He is not speaking very plainly as yet. You had better call down (for example) the great Swan of Heaven."

So the master of ceremonies calls on the great Swan in the same fashion as he did the Moon. The novice comes out to dance again. The chief requests one of the guest chiefs who is a Healer (hailikila) to "heal" the dancer. The guest chief rises, and puts on his dance headdress and other regalia. Then he dances around and around the novice. He has a clapper (carved split-stick rattle) in each hand for keeping time. At the proper time he hands his clappers to an attendant, and takes a spirit (a wooden figurine, apparently) from the child's mouth. (The "spirit" is really handed to him by the attendant.) The healer displays the spirit three times and on the fourth, throws it (or pretends to) out the smoke hole, as all the people shout "wo:!" The spirit horns blow as the spirit departs.

The Dluwalakha dancing masks represented such mythological ancestors as Komokwa, Thunderbird, Kolus, and others. They also illustrated legends involving such characters as the sun, the moon, echo, and other elements of nature. A great number of them referred to the animals, birds, and local features of the landscape that played a role in the recounting and re-enactment of family myth. They made a colorful display in the stage productions of the winter ceremony, and were also used in Klasila time.

In the darkened house against the fire's flickering, these masks were powerfully evocative manifestations of the spirit world, with a compelling fascination. The high point in the evening's performance was often marked by the use of a transformation mask. The dancer drew attention to an approaching change by the rhythm of his dance and by the centrally prominent place he chose to stand, as the beat of the song sticks intensified. Slowly the mask opened, revealing within it another being who also belonged in the myth of the dance.

Wigs of shredded cedar bark, fur, feathers, or even burlap were worn with the masks, and the costumes were very cleverly devised to give the illusion of furred, feathered, or other nonhuman beings. Many of these can be seen in the photographs taken by Edward S. Curtis between 1912 and 1915 (Curtis 1915: Vol. X and Supplement). In later years these elaborate costumes were often replaced by button cloaks (see Figs. 186-88).

The rich and intense emotional experience of these dances, shared by the whole village, provided the major purpose and reward for the craftsman of the Northwest Coast. His audience, sophisticated in a tradition of masks and carvings, appreciated his ingenuity and virtuosity. They were interested in new theatrical invention. For a skillful and inventive craftsman there must once have been a nearly inexhaustible market for all the new carvings he could produce. This demand and the high standards of the audience were responsible for the great volume and high quality of the work of these tribal craftsmen.

Most family crest masks were shells of wood, hollowed out to fit over the face of the wearer. To support those of ordinary dimensions, light harnesses of wood and wire around the head were sufficient. Larger ones were often supported by a stick extending downward from the back of the mask framework to the wearer's waist and there tied to a belt. Still others were held in place by the dancer's hands. Some, made and supported in the same manner, were worn on the head, resting on the forehead.

It will be noted that these masks are not by any means all of equal artistic or technological quality. Some were simply and quickly hacked out for one occasion only, while others that show great dramatic and inventive power were meant to be a permanent part of a man's wealth. Some masks are crudely shaped and unfinished in surface and in treatment of detail and are painted in the same way, with carelessness and indifference. Moreover, there is an apparent relationship between crudity of workmanship and the choice of nontraditional colors, as in the orange and green Thunderbird (Fig. 369), although this is not invariable. The Thunderbird mask in Figure 371, painted an unusual pale blue, is very well carved, but the color is probably the result of repainting by someone of a later generation than the carver.

Well-carved masks exhibit the following characteristics:

1. Treatment of the wood is not rigid but plastic; parallel curved lines follow each other with ease and then diminish to a gently tapered and clean-cut finishing point.

2. Details of features show a certain technological virtuosity, an obvious enjoyment by the artist of his ability to elaborate the flare of a nostril, the curve of an eye, or the ridge of a cheek within the distinctive features of the mask.

3. The different parts or features are developed in a balanced relation to one another, and as a total form give an appearance of unity and strength.

The serious artist also accepted the limitations of traditional colors as part of the challenge and felt no necessity to introduce others.

These differences in craftsmanship have been interestingly reflected in the comments of Kwakiutl visitors to the museum. Some have noted the crudity of carving and painting of certain masks and showed some indignation and contempt for poor craftsmen. They seemed to feel that it was a reflection on the seriousness of the occasion for which the masks had been made. They appreciated the better pieces and were frequently able to identify the carvers. Not all Kwakiutl have been artists, however, nor are they all art critics. Some were apparently indifferent to the esthetic qualities of the masks, being concerned only with the questions of who had owned them and when they had been worn.

It is not easy to ascertain the age of some of the older masks, and it is impossible to give a date for the beginning of their use in the general region. Ethnographers in the second half of the nineteenth century noted an abundance of masks and a variety of uses. Masks from the Nootka were collected by Cook in 1778, and we know that the complex organization of the dancing societies and potlatching and the technology and style of the masks must have taken a long period of time to develop. So far archeology has not been able to throw direct light on the topic, and the problem is complicated by the fact that wooden objects in this moist region do not easily survive over a long period of time if subjected to ordinary weathering.

If there is any substance in the conjecture of Lieutenant T. Dix Bolles (1893:221-22) that the mask he illustrates was two hundred years old in 1892, this is one dating point, for this mask is well within the typological framework of those with which we are concerned. The three Tanis society masks shown in Figure 121, collected by the Reverend G. R. Raley in Kitlope in 1897, were found in a burial cave, and Dr. Raley reported that they were considered "very old" at that time. However, since the possessions of one's grandparents can seem "very old," this cannot be taken as a reliable indication. The information that has been gathered about the museum collection offers little on this subject, although it is helpful in coming to some conclusions about the development of masks the past hundred years or so.

In respect to standards of workmanship, it cannot be assumed that a well-made mask is old, and a poorly made one is modern. Some fine pieces and some poor pieces date, as nearly as can be determined, over the whole range of time during which these masks were made. Nor are depth of carving and detail accurate criteria of the age of a carving: some artists, both recent and of older times, have worked with great success with bold, high planes and strong features, without any extraneous detail, while some of the crudest and most inept items, new and old, are characterized by much non-essential detail, which serves only to emphasize the clumsiness of the whole (compare the bumblebee in Fig. 393 and the eagle in Fig. 382 [A4306]).

The Hamatsa raven mask shown in Figure 71, and two masks of Galokwudzuwis (Figs. 107, 108) were identified by all informants as "older than the others." If this is correct—and none of the other data gathered contradict it—it is possible to make certain generalizations about them.

All three are rather simple and massive. The detail of the carving, while carefully and precisely executed, is less elaborate than is customary on the masks we know to be later ones. All are mainly black, with a few faint white details that were evidently sparse from the first. It is possible that there is a link between these masks and the carvings from the northern area where the Hamatsa series originated.

Three outstanding characteristics emerge from an examination of the following carvings of the northern region, around Kitamaat and Kitlope: house posts (Figs. 492-94, 495 [A1789]), Tanis masks (Fig. 121), speaker's staff (Fig. 246), ladles (Figs. 290 [A1663] and 291 [A3580]), soul catcher (Fig. 523), grave effigy (Fig. 502 [A1706]), and wolf mask (Pl. XIX A). They are mostly black, with little or no other color. They are rather massive and forceful in concept, if not in actual size. They are finished in an extremely fine and polished manner. If this northern boundary is extended to the Xaihais, we may add the totem pole (Fig. 487), more ladles, and twin masks (Fig. 448) which exhibit the same qualities. It would seem, then, that the masks that should be considered early ones are those with dark color and rather simple, massive, but well-finished forms.

By these criteria the death mask from Kimsquit (Fig. 444 [A1749]) is also early, and the "ridicule" mask collected by Dr. Raley at Kyuquot (Fig. 439) should have its origin in a more northern area, such as Kitlope, rather than Nootka.

Three other pieces that are known to be comparatively old should be noted. Plate XXV shows an eagle mask from Kitamaat, worn by the Eagle people (called "Sonahed" up to 1884, according to Dr. Raley's notes). It is an extremely fine, beautifully finished and polished piece, with symbolic facial painting in very delicate red and black lines for which old paint was used. A seat used by the chief (Fig. 307 [A6520]) belongs to the same area and period. The wolf mask from Kitlope (Pl. XIX A) has the same qualities.

It should be possible for museums in the future to establish central documentary centers of data on comparable items. This will make it possible to analyze the stylistic and other features of all collected Northwest Coast masks in developmental sequences. With the help of such an index, many other items could be identified as to period, region, and function. Conclusions could then be more confidently drawn as to those traits that are diagnostic of style and period and the details that are the elements of creative invention.

PART II
Ceremonial Art

Ceremonial Curtains

The dancing house was a large plank house with a central fire whose flickering light accentuated the dramatic effects of the performance. At the rear of the dancing house there was a dressing room, to which the dancers retired in order to don their masks and change their costumes, and into which they could disappear. Here, too, there was a space where the novice could hide. To look into this territory was strictly forbidden to those who had not been initiated.

In the old days this room was a closet constructed of cedar plank walls which were painted with the design of the tutelary spirit of the house. Later large cotton sheets were painted with the Tsetseka spirit of the dancing house and used as curtains. Each dancing house had its own spirit-painted curtain, called a *mawihl.*

By tradition the *mawihl* was ceremonially burned at the end of each winter dance season. Several informants reported, however, that because of the expense of commissioning a new curtain every year, the *mawihl* was often saved and used in the following season.

Examples of these curtains are shown in Figures 10-14. They are painted in black—either water pigment, mud and charcoal, or (in one example) oil paint. The design in Figures 4 and 12 uses the motif of the Thunderbird, the enormous mythical bird who seized killer whales in his talons as if they were small fish. He is usually represented with supernatural horns curving from his head. Figure 13 has a raven design, and Figures 10 and 14 include in their designs the figure of the Sisiutl, the two-headed snake whose body is a human face (see also Figs. 126-30 and 251-54). Combined with the Sisiutl in Figure 14 is the T-shaped form of the copper (see also Figs. 152-57).

Fig. 10. Kwakiutl ceremonial curtain from Kingcome Inlet, attributed to Arthur Shaughnessy. Muslin with black painted design of Sisiutl and human figure. Width: 10 ft. MacMillan Purchase 1953. A4363

Fig. 11. Kwakiutl ceremonial curtain from Campbell River. Cotton with black Thunderbird motif. Width: 13 ft. 6 in. MacMillan Purchase 1951. A4024

Fig. 12. Kwakiutl ceremonial curtain from Alert Bay. Cotton with black Thunderbird motif, attributed to Arthur Shaughnessy. Width: 18 ft. 7 in. MacMillan Purchase 1952. A3773

Fig. 13. Kwakiutl ceremonial curtain from Kingcome Inlet. Cotton with black raven motif. Height: 7 ft. 2 in. MacMillan Purchase 1953. A4327

Fig. 14. Kwakiutl ceremonial curtain from Fort Rupert or Kingcome Inlet. Cotton with black painted design of Sisiutl, ravens, rainbow, and copper. Width: 13 ft. 1 in. MacMillan Purchase 1953. A6270

Supernatural Treasures

The *dloogwi,* or supernatural treasures, often consisted of small puppets or animal figures, sometimes in special boxes or cradles, which had supernatural significance. One way in which they were used is described by Drucker (1940:215):

On the appointed day the guests arrive. As they draw up in line before the beach, the villagers clap hands and sing while the host chief dances in honor of his guests. Then the chief stops suddenly and produces a "spirit doll" (a wooden figurine representing a nawalukw) from beneath his robe. He whirls it about his head four times, then pretends to throw it to the head chief of the guests. The latter "catches" it (really displaying one of his own). If he intends to dance himself, he keeps the spirit; if not, he returns it. If several tribes are invited, the spirit is "thrown" to the head chief of each. This transforms the guests from the secular to the ritual state, so they may enter the dance house.

The puppet shown in Figure 17, from Bella Bella, is of this type. It is very light, with a body made of cloth stuffed with grass. The others are made of wood. The puppet in Figure 15, representing Nootlemgeela, was conjured up out of the floor by the Tokwit dancer.

Figure 16 shows two puppets that were lowered by strings from the beams of the dancing house. Although they appear to be Christian angels, this is not necessarily their only inspiration, for the concept of magical flying with or without wings was a supernatural gift theme of several winter dances embodied in myth. All the wooden puppet figures have mica flakes or silver paint on some portion of them to enhance the glittering effect of their arrival.

Figure 18 shows a Tokwit box with a figure that was conjured up by the Tokwit dancer. The box was buried in a trench nearby, and when an assistant pulled the strings, which were attached to spools, the small puppet rose above the ground, its arms outspread. The Tokwit cradle in Figure 19 was recognized by Alert Bay people as a copy of an original one brought two generations earlier as a marriage transfer from the Heiltsuk. The original one is still in Alert Bay. The puppet, covered with a crest-painted sheet (now in fragments), sat up as the strings were pulled and appeared to be watching a spinning ball (now missing) that whirled around on the shaft in the front of the cradle.

The "supernatural crabs" (Figs. 22, 23) were made on spool rollers, so that they scuttled along the floor sideways when pulled. Each leg was attached very lightly to a piece of cloth along the edge of the crab, and the effect of the wooden pieces striking each other produced the dry, rustling sound of a crab scuttling on a rock.

The raven in Figure 21 was attached to strings across the roof beams which allowed it to fly down. Some birds are said to have picked up bundles or figures representing humans which then were lifted up and flown out through a hole in the roof.

Fig. 15. Kwakiutl Tokwit puppets from Kingcome Inlet. Wood; black, white, red. Height: 33 in. MacMillan Purchase 1951. (*Left*) A4514; (*right*) A4515

Fig. 16. Kwakiutl Tokwit puppets from Kingcome Inlet, about 35 years old. Wood. Height: 26 in. MacMillan Purchase 1951. (*Left*) A4516; (*right*) A4517

Fig. 17. Kwakiutl Tokwit puppets from Bella Bella. Wood with cloth bodies. Height: 22 in. Dr. and Mrs. G. E. Darby Valedictory Gift 1931. A3411

Fig. 18. Kwakiutl Tokwit box from Kingcome Inlet. The box was buried in the dirt floor with only the head of the figure showing. Wood; red, white, black. Height with figure extended: 35 in. Leon and Thea Koerner Foundation Purchase 1958. A6891

Fig. 19. Kwakiutl Tokwit cradle from Alert Bay, said to be a copy of an original that came from Heiltsuk through marriage 2 generations ago. Wood; red, black, green. Length: 3 ft. 5 in. MacMillan Purchase 1961. A7877

Fig. 20. Kwakiutl Tokwit frog from Kingcome Inlet. Wood; green, black, red. Length: 11½ in. MacMillan Purchase 1953. A6200

Fig. 21. Kwakiutl Tokwit raven from the top of a ceremonial staff, from Bella Bella. Wood; blue, black, red. Length: 11 in. Dr. and Mrs. G. E. Darby Valedictory Gift 1931. A1145

Fig. 22. Kwakiutl Tokwit crab from Port Hardy. Wood and nails; red, orange, black, white. Width: 26½ in. MacMillan Purchase 1954. A6362

Fig. 23. Kwakiutl Tokwit crab from Gilford Island. Underneath the crab is a spool roller. Wood; brown, white, black. Width: 29 in. MacMillan Purchase 1952. A4104

Batons, Whistles, Clappers, and Rattles

Songs and dances were part of all ceremony and ritual, a fundamental element of the inherited privilege. Equally important were the many whistles and other musical instruments that were specifically designated for most dances.

The transfer of the whistles and the box holding the gear for the dance was an important part of the transfer of privileges from father to son-in-law. Members of the society witnessed the transfer, meanwhile giving the ceremonial cry belonging to the Tsetseka season, even though the actual ritual might take place in the Bakoos time.

All performances for public or dancing society gatherings involved the use of long planks, placed near the seats of the dance house, on which wooden batons were beaten in time for the singers and dancers. To obtain and to pass out these batons was the inherited job of an official. Drumming to accent the beat was also basic to all performances, the most widespread drum form being a rectangular box suspended from a rafter by a rope and beaten with a leather-covered stick.

A round drum of hide stretched over a wooden frame and grasped from behind was another form frequently used, especially in the south. The drum and drummer had a designated place in each dance house arrangement.

The whistles blown in the woods to introduce the ceremonial season—usually four times for each of four nights—caused commotion and excitement in the village as the people prepared for the new season. There were several types of whistles, each with its characteristic sound, and a vast number were made. Of the 150 in the collection at the museum, a selection has been made to illustrate the main types. Wooden whistles of one, two, or three shafts, each with several holes and reeds, produced a strong, clear, rather eerie note, whose effect increased with the number of shafts. These were made of thin, hollowed shells of wood, glued with pitch and bound together. Whistles with reeds, which were bound together and fastened inside, were especially associated with the Klasila, and their tone was easily recognized. Bellows whistles like the one in Figure 29 (A8399), bound under the arm by a strap and completely covered by the wearer's costume, produced their sound from concealment. Other magical whistles were so small that they could be held inside the mouth and blown without revealing the source of the sound, or blown secretly when a hand or the corner of a blanket momentarily concealed the mouth in the course of the dance. Figures 26 (A3620) and 27 (A7973) illustrate examples of Hamatsa whistles, which were of great importance as part of the spirit manifestations.

Clappers were fashioned of a piece of wood cut, squared or rounded, hollowed out, and wrapped together with cedar withes or other vegetable fibers. The clapper was hinged flexibly on one side and produced a percussive noise when shaken. The sudden and loud noise was part of the drama. Thus the war-spirit dancer, the male form of Mitla, came in balefully and sounded his clapper before he used his magical weapon. A clapper said to have been "carried by Mitla while he was disrupting the singers" is shown in Figure 42 (A6368). The sound of the clapper was accompanied by the heavy clapping of the great wooden beaks of the Hamatsa dancers, stressing the beat of the dancers, the drummers, and the singers. The cockleshell clapper shown in Figure 42 (A8050) was said to be the "*dloogwa* of a Bookwus."

Rattles, like whistles, were an essential part of all inheritances. Their forms varied with their purpose, and they ranged from simple rings of pecten shells (associated only with the Kwekwe dancer) and rattles of puffin beaks and deer hoofs (see Figs. 39, 40) to the complex bird rattle (Figs. 30, 31) which was one of the outstanding art forms of the region.

The chief's rattle or bird rattle was a hollowed shell of wood, usually carefully carved and fitted, extremely light and finely finished in the form of a bird. Some adaptation of this form extended from the northern Tlingit down to the southern Kwakiutl and Nootka. Undoubtedly first borrowed by the southern groups from the northern tribes, it was used everywhere by high-ranking officials as an accessory to complete their costumes. It was employed only during the Klasila, not in Tsetseka times, when the round rattle was used. The chief, while he was making a speech, shook the rattle to emphasize what he was saying.

Originally this was probably a healing rattle used by shamans, its use symbolized by the protruding tongue of a recumbent figure identified as an otter, an animal associated with the shaman. The general form of the rattle was that of a bird, the handle being the tail, the back of the bird a platform on which assorted small figures were carved, and the belly emphasized by a bird's face and beak. In nearly every case the animal and human figures were exquisitely carved, detailed, and painted. Colors, usually limited to touches of red and black, were employed sparingly and softly.

The rough shape was cut from yellow cedar or alder and split in two. With a curved knife, the block was then hollowed to a shell with walls as thin as one-sixteenth of an inch. The shell was then carved carefully with a knife blade and finished smooth by the use of an abrasive such as shark-skin. Small stones or shot were put in, and the rattle was sewn together by a withe through small holes bored in the side—one, two, or three stitches at each side. The two halves of the handle were then bound by withes.

Shamans' rattles were generally round, hollowed shells made with the same care and finished but unadorned. The rattles associated with the Tsetseka season were of this hollowed form, and many of them, particularly those used by the Hamatsa, were carved to imitate a skull. The Solatlala, attendants of the Hamatsa, carried rattles, sometimes in the form of human heads, which were used to pacify the cannibal dancer and help to calm him down as he became tamed (Figs. 32 [A6296, A8046], 33 [A6100], 38). Rattles made of copper, or of wood in the shape of a copper, were used in the copper ceremonials (Figs. 35, 36 [A4031, A6099]).

Fig. 24. (*Left to right*) Kwakiutl baton from Alert Bay. Wood. Length: 13 in. MacMillan Purchase 1952. A4377. Kwakiutl baton from Alert Bay, with Thunderbird design. Wood. Length: 13½ in. MacMillan Purchase 1953. A6439. Kwakiutl baton from Alert Bay. Wood; blue, red, orange. Length: 13½ in. MacMillan Purchase 1957. A4291. Kwakiutl baton from Kingcome Inlet. Wood. Length: 13 in. MacMillan Purchase 1954. A3412

Fig. 25. (*Left to right*) Kwakiutl "seagull" whistle from Kingcome Inlet. Wood. Length: 17½ in. MacMillan Purchase 1953. A6203. Kwakiutl whistle from Turnour Island. 2 pieces of wood bound with string, with carved crescent slot; 1 tone. Length: 18 in. MacMillan Purchase 1954. A6364. Whistle, probably Kwakiutl. Wood. Length: 19½ in. Gift of Walter C. Koerner 1962. A8325. Kwakiutl whistle from Kingcome Inlet, with killer whale design. Wood; white, black, red, blue. Length: 15 in. MacMillan Purchase 1951. A3660

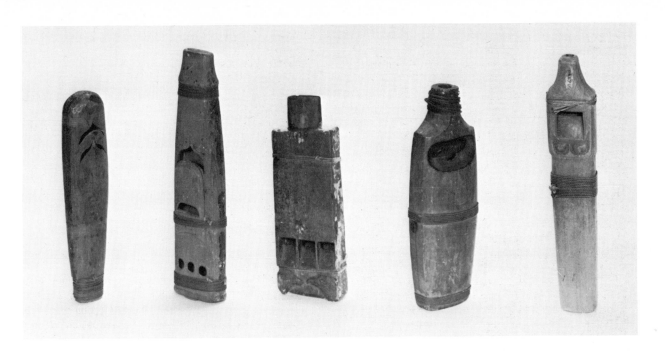

Fig. 26. (*Left to right*) Kwakiutl whistle from Alert Bay. 2 pieces of wood bound with cord, with 2 carved slits, some red paint; 1 tone. Length: 9½ in. MacMillan Purchase 1953. A4222. Kwakiutl whistle from Alert Bay. 2 pieces of wood bound with string, with 3 holes and 2 carved slits; 2 tones. Length: 11¼ in. MacMillan Purchase 1953. A4207. Kwakiutl Hamatsa whistle from Alert Bay. 2 pieces of wood bound with string, with 2 carved bird figures; 3 tones. Length: 9 in. MacMillan Purchase 1951. A3620. Kwakiutl "owl whistle" from Fort Rupert. 2 pieces of wood bound with cord; 1 tone. Length: 9¾ in. MacMillan Purchase 1953. A6263. Kwakiutl whistle from Blunden Harbour. 3 pieces of wood bound with string; 2 tones. Length: 11 in. MacMillan Purchase 1951. A6330

Fig. 27. (*Left to right*) Kwakiutl whistle from Sullivan Bay, with killer whale design; ½ missing. Wood; blue, green, black, red, white. Length: 16 in. MacMillan Purchase 1953. A4339. Kwakiutl Hamatsa whistle from Alert Bay. Wood and bone bound with cord and sealed with resin gum; 4 tones. Height: 4¾ in. MacMillan Purchase 1962. A7973. Kwakiutl "invisible" whistles from Fort Rupert, collected in 1885. Wood. Length: 2 in. MacMillan Purchase 1963, Cadwallader Coll. A8401, A8403, A8404. Kwakiutl "raven whistle" from Alert Bay. 2 pieces of wood bound with string and carved with a crude human face; 2 tones. Length: 11¾ in. MacMillan Purchase 1953. A4188

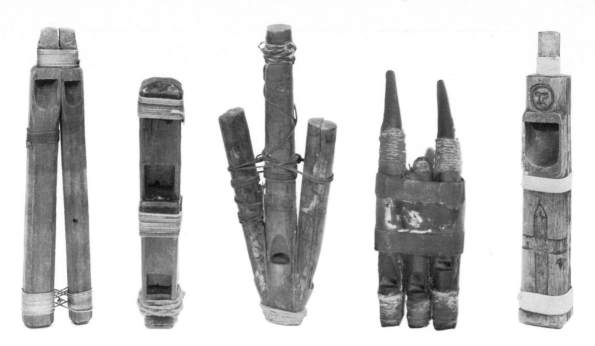

Fig. 28. (*Left to right*) Nootka whistle from Head Point. 2 wooden pipes, made up of 4 pieces lashed with string, bound together; 2 tones. Length: 13⅝ in. MacMillan Purchase 1961. A1497. Kwakiutl "eagle whistle" from Alert Bay. 5 pieces of wood bound with string; 4 tones. Length: 6½ in. MacMillan Purchase 1953. A4225. Kwakiutl whistle from Gilford Island. 3 wooden pipes bound with string and tied together; 4 tones. Length of middle pipe: 10½ in. MacMillan Purchase 1954. A6372. Kwakiutl whistle from Kitlope. 3 horn tubes bound together with paper, tape, and cord; 3 tones. Length: 5¾ in. MacMillan Purchase 1948, Rev. G. H. Raley Coll. A1758. Kwakiutl whistle from Simoom Sound. 2 pieces of wood bound with twine, carved with a Tsonokwa head; 1 tone. Length: 13⅝ in. MacMillan Purchase 1952. A3828

Fig. 29. (*Left to right, top*) Tsimshian whistle from Port Simpson, with killer whale design. Wood; black. Length: 15½ in. MacMillan Purchase 1948, Rev. G. H. Raley Coll. A1971. Kwakiutl bellows whistle from Kitsalas. Wood and leather; 4 tones. Length: 13½ in. MacMillan Purchase 1948, Rev. G. H. Raley Coll. A6516. (*Bottom*) Nootka whistle from Kyuquot. 2 pieces of yew wood bound with string; killer whale form with red paint in slots; 1 tone. Length: 16 in. MacMillan Purchase 1961. A7860. Kwakiutl bellows whistle from Fort Rupert, collected in 1885. Wood and deerhide. Length: 9 in. MacMillan Purchase 1963, Cadwallader Coll. A8399. Kwakiutl bellows whistle from New Vancouver Village. Wood and leather with nails; 2 tones. Length: 6¾ in. MacMillan Purchase 1961. A7486

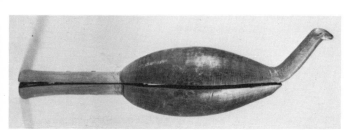

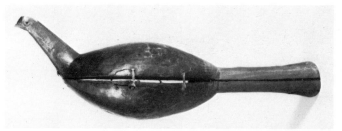

Fig. 30. (*Top to bottom, left*) Salish rattle from Cowichan. Wooden eagle with abalone shell eyes and face carved on underside. Length: 13 in. MacMillan Purchase 1962. A8047. Kwakiutl duck rattle from Quatsino, collected in 1900. Wood. Length: 13½ in. MacMillan Purchase 1964. A8417. Kwakiutl rattle from Bella Bella, with raven, frog, and sea otter design. Wood; black, red. Length: 13 in. MacMillan Purchase 1948, Rev. G. H. Raley Coll. A1760. Salish bird rattle from Nanaimo. Wood. Length: 17 in. Leon and Thea Koerner Foundation Purchase 1958. A6890a. (*Right*) Nootka duck-shaped rattle from Nuchatlitz, used in wolf dance. Wood. Length: 10½ in. MacMillan Purchase 1961. A7856. Nootka bird rattle from Nuchatlitz, said to be about 200 years old and to be associated with a harpoon used in the whale ritual. Wood. Length: 17½ in. MacMillan Purchase 1961. A7855. Nootka duck-shaped rattle from Ahousat, with dog and bird face on its back. Wood; black, white, red, brown. Length: 19¾ in. MacMillan Purchase 1962. A7969. Nootka bird rattle from Vancouver Island. Wood. Length: 15 in. MacMillan Purchase 1962. A8049

Fig. 31. (*Top to bottom, left*) Kwakiutl rattle from Minstrel Island, with raven and loon design. Wood; black, red. Length: 12 in. MacMillan Purchase 1954. A6366. Tsimshian raven rattle from Prince Rupert, over 100 years old. Unpainted wood. Length: 13½ in. MacMillan Purchase 1963. A6795. Haida raven rattle from Queen Charlotte Islands. Wood; red, black, blue. Length: 13½ in. MacMillan Purchase 1960, Rev. W. E. Collison Coll. A7058. Kwakiutl raven rattle from Simoom Sound. Wood; red, black, green, white. Length: 12½ in. MacMillan Purchase 1953. A6308. (*Right*) Bella Coola bird rattle with human face and bird's head on back and hawk's face on bottom. Wood; blue, red, black, green. Length: 18 in. MacMillan Purchase 1962. A8048. Kwakiutl rattle from Campbell River, with bird and bear design. Wood; black, red, green. Length: 16 in. MacMillan Purchase 1962. A8284. Kwakiutl raven rattle from Alert Bay. Wood; black, green, red. Length: 12 in. Leon and Thea Koerner Foundation Gift 1957. A6634. Tsimshian raven rattle from Prince Rupert, over 100 years old. Unpainted wood. Length: 15 in. MacMillan Purchase 1963. A6796

Fig. 32. (*Left to right, top*) Kwakiutl rattle from Campbell River, with hawk design. Wood and cedar bark; red, black. Length: 11 in. MacMillan Purchase 1951. A4027. Kwakiutl rattle from Blunden Harbour, with killer whale design. Wood, cedar bark, and abalone shell; white, black, green, red. Length: 11½ in. MacMillan Purchase 1951. A3656 *(Bottom)* Kwakiutl Solatlala rattle from Gilford Island. Wood and cedar bark; red, black. Length: 11 in. Mac-Millan Purchase 1962. A8046. Kwakiutl Solatlala rattle from Simoom Sound. Wood and cedar bark; white, black, red. Length: 13 in. MacMillan Purchase 1953. A6296

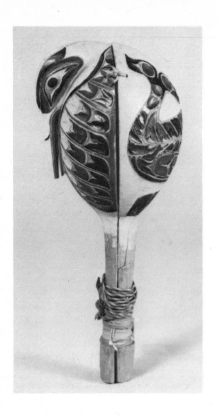

Fig. 33. (*Left to right, top*) Kwakiutl rattle from Kingcome Inlet, with crane and killer whale design. Wood; gray, black, red, green, yellow. Length: 11¼ in. MacMillan Purchase 1951. A3661. Kwakiutl Solatlala rattle from Alert Bay. Wood; red, black. Length: 9½ in. MacMillan Purchase 1951. A6100. Tsimshian rattle from Nass River. Wood; black, red. Length: 12 in. MacMillan Purchase 1948, Rev. G. H. Raley Coll. A1669. (*Bottom*) Tsimshian rattle from Kispiox, with eye designs, collected before 1890. Wood; black, red. Length: 8½ in. MacMillan Purchase 1961. A7539. Rattle, probably Tsimshian, collected between 1945 and 1948. Unpainted wood. Length: 9½ in. MacMillan Purchase 1961. A7296. Rattle, probably Tsimshian, collected between 1945 and 1948. Wood. Length: 10 in. MacMillan Purchase 1961. A7294

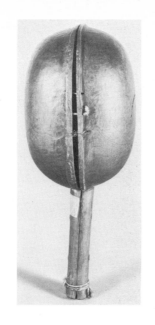

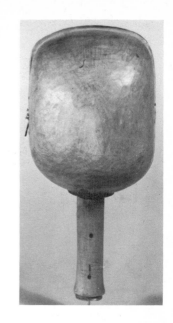

Fig. 34. (*Left to right*) Rattle, probably Tsimshian. Wood. Length: 9 in. MacMillan Purchase 1948, Rev. G. H. Raley Coll. A4457. Tsimshian rattle from Kispiox, collected before 1890. Wood and goat horn. Length: 11½ in. MacMillan Purchase 1961. A7541. Tsimshian rattle from Kispiox. Wood. Length: 10½ in. MacMillan Purchase 1962. A7967

Fig. 35. (*Left to right*) Tsimshian rattle from Nass River. Copper and wood, with whale design. Length: 9½ in. Gift of Bert Robson. A1756. Kwakiutl rattle from Alert Bay. Copper; green, red, black. Length: 7 in. MacMillan Purchase 1953. A4254. Kwakiutl rattle from Bella Bella. Copper. Length: 5¼ in. Dr. G. E. Darby, 1931 Valedictory Gift. A1111

Fig. 36. (*Left to right*) Haida bear-shaped rattle from Queen Charlotte Islands. Wood; blue, red, black. Length: 9¼ in. MacMillan Purchase 1960, Rev. W. E. Collison Coll. A7059. Kwakiutl modern ceremonial rattle from Alert Bay. Wood, shaped in the form of a copper; black, green, red. Length: 10½ in. MacMillan Purchase 1951. A6099. Kwakiutl rattle from Alert Bay. Wood, shaped in the form of a copper; green, red, blue. Length: 9½ in. MacMillan Purchase 1953. A4031

Fig. 37. (*Left*) Salish rattle from Cowichan, with bear and bird designs; 2 views. Wood with black paint outline. Length: 12 in. MacMillan Purchase 1962. A8054. (*Right*) Rattle with salmon head design, collected before 1890. Wood; red, black. Length: 9¼ in. MacMillan Purchase 1962. A7537

Fig. 38. 4 Kwakiutl Solatlala rattles from Fort Rupert, made by Dick Price in 1940 and depicting decapitated heads. Wood with woolen hair; white, green, black, orange. Height: 13 in. MacMillan Purchase 1952. A3793, A3794, A3795, A3796

Fig. 39. (*Left to right*) Rattle. Wood bound with fiber, with deer hoofs and skull. Diameter: 5 in. Gift of Mrs. J. Cuzen 1958. A6898. Tsimshian hand-shaped rattle from Kitsegukla. Wood; some red coloring. Length: 7¼ in. MacMillan Purchase 1962. A7959. Salish rattle from Cowichan. Wood, mountain goat wool, and nettles; red, white. Length: 15 in. MacMillan Purchase 1951. A3516

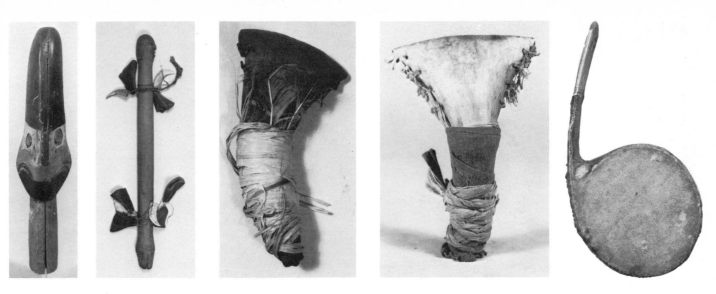

Fig. 40. (*Left to right*) Rattle with raven design, collected before 1890. Wood; black, green, red. Length: 9½ in. MacMillan Purchase 1961. A7538. Rattle wand, collected before 1890. Unpainted wood, deer hoofs, and claws. Length: 14 in. MacMillan Purchase 1961. A7536. Nootka rattle from Vancouver Island. Baleen and grass, steamed and bent, the handle bound with grass, with feathers fastened to the inner curve. Length: 4½ in. MacMillan Purchase 1962. A7970. Nootka rattle from Vancouver Island. Baleen and cloth, steamed, bent, and sewn at the edges; plain handle bound with strips of cloth. Length: 7½ in. MacMillan Purchase 1962. A8053. Haida drum-shaped rattle from Queen Charlotte Islands. Wood and leather. Length: 7 in. MacMillan Purchase 1960, Rev. W. E. Collison Coll. A7062

Fig. 41. (*Left*) Kwakiutl rattle from Kingcome Inlet, with killer whale design. Wood and cedar bark; yellow. Length: 16 in. MacMillan Purchase 1961. A7316. (*Right*) Kwakiutl rattle from Port Hardy, with killer whale design. Wood; black, white, red. Length: 9½ in. MacMillan Purchase 1954. A6363

Fig. 42. (*Left*) Kwakiutl clapper from Minstrel Island, with killer whale design. Wood; black, green, red. Length: 11¼ in. MacMillan Purchase 1954. A6368. (*Right*) Kwakiutl clapper from Alert Bay, in the shape of a cockleshell. Wood, with a black painted lining. Length: 5 in. MacMillan Purchase 1962. A8050

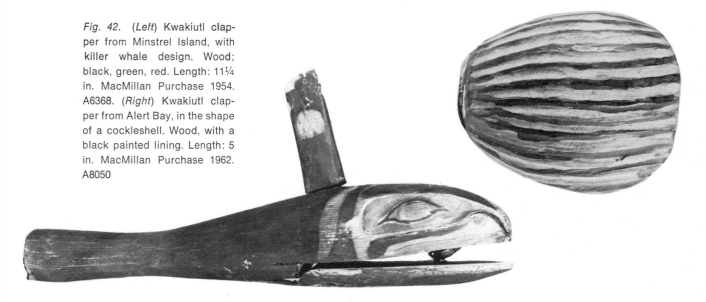

Mourning Masks

The brief mourning period that introduced the Klasila was marked by the singing of the songs of those who had died since the last Tsetseka season. Members of the family lineage of the deceased wore mourning masks like those shown in Figure 43. A6352 depicts a woman of the Koskimo, who practiced head-shaping, as shown by the sloping forehead. The lines painted on the mask represent furrows made by deliberate self-abrasion of the skin, a stylized form of grief demonstration. A6544 and A4176 have lines of copper, representing tears streaming down each cheek.

Fig. 43. (*Top*) Kwakiutl mourning mask from Sullivan Bay. Wood; orange, black. Height: 10¼ in. MacMillan Purchase 1952. A4176. (*Bottom, left to right*) Kwakiutl mourning mask from Smith Inlet. Wood; red, white, black. Height: 13 in. MacMillan Purchase 1953. A6352. Kwakiutl mourning mask from Sullivan Bay. Wood; black, orange, blue. Height: 10¾ in. MacMillan Purchase 1955. A6544

Masks of Gakhula, the Intruder

The masks shown in Figures 44 and 45 represent Gakhula, the Intruder, whose entrance interrupted the gaiety of the Klasila singing and dancing and marked the beginning of the Tsetseka season. This character is associated particularly with the southern Kwakiutl. A6300, which resembles a Tsonokwa mask, was identified as a *Gakhulagumhl* (mask of Gakhula) by an informant from Alert Bay.

Fig. 44. (*Top*) Kwakiutl Gakhula (Intruder) mask from Gilford Island. Wood; green, red, black, white. Height: 12 in. MacMillan Purchase 1952. A3816. (*Bottom, left to right*) Kwakiutl Gakhula (Intruder) mask from King-come Inlet. Wood; green, black, red, white. Height: 12¼ in. MacMillan Purchase 1953. A6274. Kwakiutl Gakhula (Intruder) mask from Kingcome Inlet. Wood; yellow, black, red. Height: 10 in. MacMillan Purchase 1953. A6211

Fig. 45. (*Top*) Kwakiutl Gakhula (Intruder) mask from Gilford Island. Wood; black, white, green. Height: 12 in. MacMillan Purchase 1962. A8101. (*Bottom, left to right*) Kwakiutl Gakhula (Intruder) mask from Kingcome Inlet. Wood; red, black. Height: 11 in. MacMillan Purchase 1953. A6184. Kwakiutl Gakhula (Intruder) mask from Kingcome Inlet. Wood; black. Height: 13½ in. Mac-Millan Purchase 1953. A6300

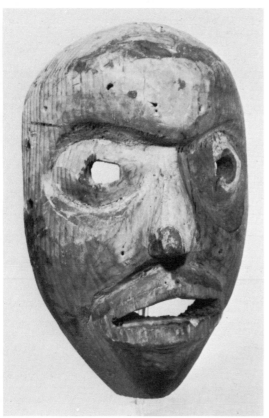

Hamatsa Bird-Monster Masks

Hamatsa bird-monster masks were worn with cedar bark fringes hanging from the back of the mask down over the shoulders, effectively concealing the dancer, who was further covered by a long cape of shredded cedar bark that fell to the ankles. The lower beak of the mask was jointed, so that when the proper string was pulled it shut with a clap. At one point in the dance a number of bird-monsters, dancing with a springy bird step in unison with the sharp beat of the batons, turned their heads in various directions and clapped their beaks to the beat. At high moments they clapped their beaks in fast vibration, while the beat of the batons and the dance steps increased rapidly.

The bird-monster masks were constructed to be worn on the forehead, with the cedar bark fringe concealing the face and shoulders. They varied in length from less than two feet to more than eight feet, and in weight from two to sixteen pounds. Considerable strength, not only of the neck and shoulder muscles, but especially of the legs, was required in order to wear these masks and dance with them in the difficult squatting position.

The masks were secured in two ways. In some, a strong stick fastened at the top and back of the mask went straight down the spine to mid-shoulders or waist. There it was fastened by a rope (originally of cedar bark, later of twine) around the waist or chest. The other method used was a rope harness going from the top back of the mask down around both armpits and tied around the chest or waist. Both methods held the mask securely and left the hands of the dancer free for manipulating the beak or for dancing gestures.

The traditional color of all these masks was black, with details of white paint and red added to the nostril or beak. Most of them were both carved and painted, and they were made with great care. A few had small wooden skulls added to the cedar bark fringe. These skulls were characteristic motifs of the whole Hamatsa drama (see Fig. 122).

Hamatsa masks represented the fabulous bird-monsters, Kwakwakwalanooksiwae, Hokhokw, and Galodwudzuwis, sometimes showing two of them in dual aspect. Kwakwakwalanooksiwae ("Raven-at-the-mouth-of-the-river") masks (Pl. III A; Figs. 46-72) can be identified by the heavy beak with flared nostrils, and are distinguished from non-Hamatsa raven masks (Figs. 384-89) by the cedar bark fringe covering the face and extending down to the shoulders. Hokhokw masks (Pl. III B; Figs. 73-79) are characterized by a long narrow beak, square at the end, with a high, flaring nostril. The Galokwudzuwis (Crooked-Beak) masks (Pl. IV A; Figs. 80-109) were worn by women. These masks have an elaborate prominence over the nostrils, often cut out to emphasize the strong curve. They provided the greatest range for individual variation by the artist because of the curved and frilled upper face.

Fig. 46. (*Top*) Kwakiutl Hamatsa raven mask from Alert Bay, attributed to Willie Seaweed. Wood and cedar bark; black, white, red. Length: 4 ft. 3 in. MacMillan Purchase 1954. A6121. (*Bottom*) Kwakiutl Hamatsa raven mask from Gilford Island, attributed to Dick Hawkins. Wood and cedar bark; black, white, red. Length: 4 ft. 5 in. MacMillan Purchase 1952. A3815

Fig. 47. Kwakiutl Hamatsa raven mask from Alert Bay, attributed to Chief George. Wood and cedar bark; red, white, black, orange. Length: 3 ft. 6 in. MacMillan Purchase 1954. A6361

Fig. 48. Kwakiutl Hamatsa raven mask from Sullivan Bay. Wood, cedar bark, and feathers; black, white, red. Length: 3 ft. MacMillan Purchase 1951. A3673

Fig. 49. Kwakiutl Hamatsa raven mask from Sullivan Bay, attributed to John Davis, repainted by Charlie George. This is an old-style mask, similar in form to some collected in the 1890's. Wood and cedar bark; red, green, black, white. Length: 15 in. MacMillan Purchase 1953. A4283

Fig. 50. Kwakiutl Hamatsa raven mask from Fort Rupert, attributed to Dick Price; 1 of a set of 4 including Figs. 73, 81, 85. Wood and cedar bark; black, white, red. Length: 3 ft. 9 in. MacMillan Purchase 1952. A3792

Fig. 51. Kwakiutl Hamatsa raven mask from Kingcome Inlet, attributed to Dick Hawkins, dated approximately 1935. Wood and cedar bark; black, white, red. Length: 25 in. MacMillan Purchase 1954. A6119

Fig. 52. Kwakiutl Hamatsa raven mask from Blunden Harbour, attributed to Willie Seaweed. Wood and cedar bark; black, white, red, orange. Length: 26 in. MacMillan Purchase 1953. A6334

Fig. 53. Kwakiutl Hamatsa raven mask from Sullivan Bay, attributed to Chief George. Wood and cedar bark; black, white, red. Length: 28 in. MacMillan Purchase 1953. A6169

Fig. 54. Kwakiutl Hamatsa raven mask from Alert Bay, attributed to Mungo Martin. Wood and cedar bark; black, white, red. Length: 4 ft. MacMillan Purchase 1952. A4248

Fig. 55. Kwakiutl Hamatsa raven mask from Kingcome Inlet, made in 1911. Wood and cedar bark; black, white, red. Length: 3 ft. 9 in. MacMillan Purchase 1951. A3538

Fig. 56. Kwakiutl Hamatsa raven mask from Gilford Island, attributed to Jack James. Wood and cedar bark; black, white, red. Length: 3 ft. 3 in. MacMillan Purchase 1953. A6320

Fig. 57. Kwakiutl Hamatsa Raven mask from Turnour Island, attributed to Mungo Martin. Wood and cedar bark; black, white, red. Length: 3 ft. 2 in. MacMillan Purchase 1961. A7476

Fig. 58. Kwakiutl Hamatsa raven mask from Blunden Harbour, attributed to Johnny Nolie. Wood and cedar bark; black, white, red. Length: 24 in. MacMillan Purchase 1953. A4321

Fig. 59. Kwakiutl Hamatsa raven mask from Kingcome Inlet, attributed to Willie Seaweed. Wood and cedar bark; black, red, orange, white. Length: 34 in. MacMillan Purchase 1953. A4249

Fig. 60. Kwakiutl Hamatsa raven mask from Kingcome Inlet, attributed to Willie Seaweed. Wood and cedar bark; black, white, red. Length: 4 ft. MacMillan Purchase 1953. A6317

Fig. 61. Kwakiutl Hamatsa raven mask from Gilford Island, attributed to Dick Hawkins; 1 of a set including Fig. 102 and Pl. IIIB. Wood and cedar bark; black, white, red, orange. Length: 3 ft. 6 in. MacMillan Purchase 1953. A6127

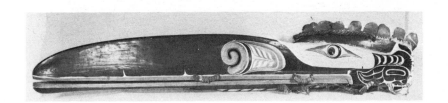

Fig. 62. Kwakiutl Hamatsa raven mask from Alert Bay, a 3-man mask carved by Mungo Martin in 1905. Wood, cedar bark, commercial rubber; black, white, red. Length: 8 ft. 3 in. Gift of Walter C. Koerner 1965. A8545

Fig. 63. Kwakiutl Hamatsa raven mask from Village Island. The cut-through beak is unusual for Raven, and possibly this should be identified as Hokhokw. Wood and cedar bark; red, green, white, black. Length: 4 ft. 9 in. MacMillan Purchase 1952. A4168

Fig. 64. Kwakiutl Hamatsa raven mask from Sullivan Bay. Wood and cedar bark; black, white, red. Length: 4 ft. 5 in. MacMillan Purchase 1951. A3674

Fig. 65. Kwakiutl Hamatsa raven mask from Kingcome Inlet, attributed to Tom Wamiss. Wood and cedar bark; black, white, red. Length: 4 ft. 4 in. MacMillan Purchase 1961. A7318

Fig. 66. Kwakiutl Hamatsa raven mask from Alert Bay. Wood and cedar bark; green, white, red, black. Length: 28 in. MacMillan Purchase 1951. A3627

Fig. 67. Kwakiutl Hamatsa raven mask from Sullivan Bay. Wood and cedar bark; black, white, red. Length: 5 ft. 8½ in. MacMillan Purchase 1951. A6551

Fig. 68. Kwakiutl Hamatsa raven mask from Alert Bay. Wood and cedar bark; black, white, red. Length: 25 in. MacMillan Purchase 1951. A3628

Fig. 69. Kwakiutl Hamatsa raven mask from Alert Bay, attributed to Charlie George, Sr. Wood and cedar bark; black, red, white, green. Length: 26 in. MacMillan Purchase 1953. A6307

Fig. 70. Kwakiutl Hamatsa raven mask from Kingcome Inlet, attributed to Charlie George, Sr. Wood and cedar bark; black, white, red, green. MacMillan Purchase 1952. A3807

Fig. 71. Kwakiutl Hamatsa raven mask from Kingcome Inlet, thought to be very old. Wood and cedar bark; black, white, red. Length: 3 ft. 3 in. MacMillan Purchase 1952. A3806

Fig. 72. Kwakiutl Hamatsa raven mask from Sullivan Bay. Wood; black, green, red. Length: 30 in. MacMillan Purchase 1952. A4512

Fig. 73. Kwakiutl Hokhokw mask from Fort Rupert, attributed to Dick Price; 1 of a set of 4 including Figs. 50, 81, 85. Wood and cedar bark; black, white, red. Length: 4 ft. 3 in. MacMillan Purchase 1952. A3789

Fig. 74. Kwakiutl Hokhokw mask from Sullivan Bay, attributed to Mungo Martin. Wood and cedar bark; black, white, red, brown. Length: 5 ft. 7 in. MacMillan Purchase 1951. A6554

Fig. 75. Kwakiutl Hokhokw mask from Fort Rupert, attributed to Dick Price. Wood and cedar bark; black, white, red. Length: 5 ft. 4 in. MacMillan Purchase 1953. A6269

Fig. 76. Kwakiutl Hokhokw mask from Blunden Harbour, attributed to Willie Seaweed. Wood and cedar bark; black, white, red. Length: 5 ft. 5 in. MacMillan Purchase 1953. A6346

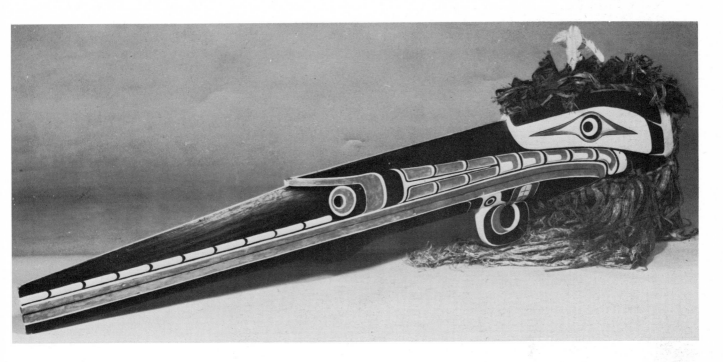

Fig. 77. Kwakiutl Hokhokw mask from Alert Bay, attributed to Willie Seaweed. Wood and cedar bark; black, white, red. Length: 5 ft. 10 in. MacMillan Purchase 1954. A6120

Fig. 78. Kwakiutl Hokhokw mask from Sullivan Bay. Wood and cedar bark; black, white, red. Length: 5 ft. 6 in. MacMillan Purchase 1951. A3672

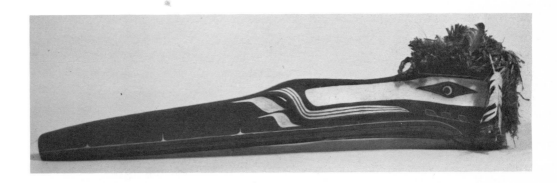

Fig. 79. Kwakiutl Hokhokw mask from Kingcome Inlet, made by Charlie George, Sr. Wood and cedar bark; black, white, red. Length: 5 ft. 5 in. MacMillan Purchase 1960. A4493

Fig. 80. Kwakiutl Crooked-Beak mask from Sullivan Bay. Wood and cedar bark; black, white, red. Length: 29 in. MacMillan Purchase 1951. A3675

Fig. 81. Kwakiutl Crooked-Beak mask from Fort Rupert, made by Dick Price; 1 of a set of 4 including Figs. 50, 73, 85. Wood and cedar bark; black, white, red. Length: 3 ft. 4 in. MacMillan Purchase 1952. A3813

Fig. 82. Kwakiutl Crooked-Beak mask from Kingcome Inlet, attributed to Tom Wamiss. Wood and cedar bark; black, white, red. Length: 33½ in. MacMillan Purchase 1960. A4496

Fig. 83. Kwakiutl Crooked-Beak mask from Kingcome Inlet, attributed to Willie Seaweed. Wood and cedar bark, with copper teeth; black, orange, red, white. Length: 28 in. MacMillan Purchase 1951. A3537

Fig. 84. Kwakiutl Crooked-Beak mask from Kingcome Inlet. Wood and cedar bark; black, white, red. Length: 30 in. MacMillan Purchase 1954. A6117

Fig. 85. Kwakiutl Crooked-Beak mask from Fort Rupert, made by Dick Price; 1 of a set of 4 including Figs. 50, 73, 81. Wood and cedar bark; black, green, white, red. Length: 26 in. MacMillan Purchase 1952. A3814

Fig. 86. Kwakiutl Crooked-Beak mask from Village Island. Wood and cedar bark; black, white, red. Length: 32 in. MacMillan Purchase 1952. A4158

Fig. 87. Kwakiutl Crooked-Beak mask from Blunden Harbour, attributed to Willie Seaweed. Wood, cedar bark, and feathers; red, orange, white, black. Length: 30 in. MacMillan Purchase 1953. A4250

Fig. 88. Kwakiutl Crooked-Beak mask from Smith Inlet, attributed to Charlie George, Sr. Wood and cedar bark; black, red, orange, white. Length: 26 in. MacMillan Purchase 1953. A6173

Fig. 89. Kwakiutl Crooked-Beak mask from Gilford Island. Wood and cedar bark; black, white, red, green, gray. Length: 32½ in. Mac-Millan Purchase 1952. A4510

Fig. 90. Kwakiutl Crooked-Beak mask from Alert Bay, attributed to Charlie George, Sr. Wood and cedar bark; black, white, red. Length: 20 in. MacMillan Purchase 1951. A4019

Fig. 91. Kwakiutl Crooked-Beak mask from Alert Bay, attributed to Charlie George, Sr. Wood and cedar bark; black, white, red. Length: 32 in. MacMillan Purchase 1954. A6360

Fig. 92. Kwakiutl Crooked-Beak mask from Gilford Island. Wood and cedar bark; black, white, red. Length: 20 in. MacMillan Purchase 1961. A7479

Fig. 93. Kwakiutl Crooked-Beak mask from Kingcome Inlet, attributed to Willie Seaweed. Wood and cedar bark; black, white, red. Length: 18 in. MacMillan Purchase 1951. A3536

Fig. 94. Kwakiutl Crooked-Beak mask from Blunden Harbour, attributed to Charlie George, Sr. Wood and cedar bark; orange, red, white, black. Length: 22½ in. MacMillan Purchase 1953. A6132

Fig. 95. Kwakiutl Crooked-Beak mask from Smith Inlet, attributed to Charlie George, Sr. Wood and cedar bark; orange, red, black, white. Length: 31 in. MacMillan Purchase 1953. A6174

Fig. 96. Kwakiutl Crooked-Beak mask from Allison Harbour, attributed to Charlie George, Sr. Wood and cedar bark; orange, red, black, white. Length: 17½ in. MacMillan Purchase 1953. A6131

Fig. 97. Kwakiutl Crooked-Beak mask from Kingcome Inlet, attributed to Chief George. Wood, cedar bark, and cloth; black, white, red. Length: 17½ in. MacMillan Purchase 1960. A4499

Fig. 98. Kwakiutl Crooked-Beak mask from Kingcome Inlet. Wood and cedar bark; black, white, red. Length: 30½ in. MacMillan Purchase 1953. A6151

Fig. 99. Kwakiutl Crooked-Beak mask from Sullivan Bay, attributed to Joe Johnny. Wood and cedar bark; black, white, red. Length: 19 in. MacMillan Purchase 1953. A6170

Fig. 100. Kwakiutl Crooked-Beak mask from Village Island, attributed to Charlie George, Sr. Wood and cedar bark; black, white, red. Length: 31½ in. MacMillan Purchase 1952. A4167

Fig. 101. Kwakiutl Crooked-Beak mask from Alert Bay, said to have been made at Blunden Harbour by Charlie George, Sr. Wood and cedar bark; black, white, red, orange. Length: 27 in. MacMillan Purchase 1951. A4018

Fig. 102. Kwakiutl Crooked-Beak mask from Gilford Island, attributed to Dick Hawkins; 1 of a set including Fig. 61 and Pl. IIIB. Wood, cedar bark, and feathers; red, orange, black, white. Length: 3 ft. 2 in. MacMillan Purchase 1953. A6125

Fig. 103. Kwakiutl Crooked-Beak mask from Fort Rupert, attributed to Charlie George, Sr. Wood, cedar bark, and feathers. Length: 32 in. MacMillan Purchase 1953. A6268

Fig. 104. Kwakiutl Crooked-Beak mask from Bella Bella. Wood and cedar bark; black, white, red. Length: 20½ in. Mac-Millan Purchase 1948, Rev. G. H. Raley Coll. A1745

Fig. 105. Kwakiutl Crooked-Beak mask from Sullivan Bay. Wood and cedar bark; black, white, red, pink. Length: 3 ft. 7 in. MacMillan Purchase 1951. A3680

Fig. 106. Kwakiutl Crooked-Beak mask from Village Island. Wood and cedar bark; black, white, red. Length: 3 ft. 8 in. MacMillan Purchase 1952. A4170

Fig. 107. Kwakiutl Crooked-Beak mask from Kingcome Inlet, said to be older than the other Crooked-Beak masks. Wood; black, blue, red. Length: 3 ft. MacMillan Purchase 1953. A6290

Fig. 108. Kwakiutl Crooked-Beak mask from Gilford Island, said to be older than the other Crooked-Beak masks. Wood and cedar bark; black, white, red. Length: 25 in. MacMillan Purchase 1952. A4096

Fig. 109. Bella Coola Crooked-Beak mask. Wood and cedar bark; black, white, red. Length: 3 ft. 5 in. Gift of Mrs. F. G. Sherbourg 1950. A1806

Fig. 110. Kwakiutl Hamatsa multiple mask from Sullivan Bay, attributed to Jim Howard of Blunden Harbour. Wood and cedar bark; black, white, red. Length: 25 in. MacMillan Purchase 1952. A4133

Hamatsa Cedar Bark Head and Neck Rings

Other headdresses representing bird forms were traditionally made of red-dyed cedar bark and were much lighter than the wooden ones. These were worn by the two women attendants in the dance, Kinkalatlala and Komunokas. Kinkalatlala wore a forehead mask called a *hetliwey* (Fig. 111 [A 3664]). Komunokas wore another shape of red cedar bark helmet headdress.

Red cedar bark was an integral symbol of the Tsetseka dance series. In the Bakoos, or nonsupernatural, season, white bleached cedar bark and often feathers were used. The use of both red and white cedar bark indicated that the object was used in both seasons.

The headdresses worn by the Hamatsa dancers were particularly elaborate and specialized. The Hamatsa novice wore a different set of head, neck, and wrist rings every night of his performance. Each of these was elaborately plaited, twisted, and stiffened, and to the initiates each was a specific badge of identification.

The head rings of the Hamatsa (Figs. 111, 112) were often square or had squared plaiting, symbolizing the Milky Way, which was the tethering pole of Bakbakwalanooksiwae, or other associated themes. The amount of energy expended by the women who dyed the cedar bark red by steeping it in alder bark juice, and then plaited, knotted, and decorated these items must have been considerable. When yarn, which is less fragile than cedar bark, became available, it was treated in the same fashion as cedar bark—dyed red, plaited, and knotted.

116

Figure 114 (A6584) shows a Haida neck ring collected in 1880 and reported by the collector to have been a shaman's neck ring. The fact that it is identical with the Hamatsa ones is an interesting further confirmation of the fact that the northern shaman group had a wide influence on southern dancing societies.

A7951 in Figure 114 shows the badge of a retired Hamatsa, one who had retired from the Seals but retained his role as a director of the dancing series.

Cedar bark ornaments similar to these, worn by other dancers, are illustrated in Figures 167-80.

Fig. 111. (*Top*) Kwakiutl Hamatsa head ring from Gilford Island, attributed to Jim Howard. Metal stovepipe with birds made of wood and cedar bark; black, white, red. Diameter of stovepipe: 8 in.; length of birds: 10 in. MacMillan Purchase 1954. A6377. (*Center, left to right*) Kwakiutl Hamatsa head ring from Alert Bay, said to have been 1 of a pair. Red cedar bark with 2 abalone shells attached. Length: 3 ft. MacMillan Purchase 1951. A4021. Kwakiutl Crooked-Beak headpiece from Gilford Island, attributed to Jim Howard, about 1935. Cedar bark. Length: 17 in. MacMillan Purchase 1951. A3664. (*Bottom*) Kwakiutl Hamatsa head ring from Fort Rupert. Red cedar bark mounted on cloth. Diameter: 7½ in. MacMillan Purchase 1948, Rev. G. H. Raley Coll. A1467

Fig. 112. (*Top to bottom, left*) Kwakiutl Hamatsa head ring from Alert Bay. Plaited natural cedar bark, Diameter: 10 in. MacMillan Purchase 1962. A7952. Kwakiutl Hamatsa head ring from Allison Harbour. Red cedar bark. Diameter: 6½ in. MacMillan Purchase 1953. A6136. Kwakiutl Hamatsa head ring from Kingcome Inlet. Red cedar bark and red cotton knitting. Diameter: 7 in. MacMillan Purchase 1951. A6083. (*Right*) Kwakiutl Hamatsa head ring from Kitamaat. Red cedar bark. Diameter: 9 in. MacMillan Purchase 1948, Rev. G. H. Raley Coll. A1747. Kwakiutl Hamatsa head ring from Kingcome Inlet. Red cedar bark. Diameter: 8½ in. MacMillan Purchase 1952. A3842. Kwakiutl Hamatsa head ring from Alert Bay. Natural cedar bark and cotton coiling. Diameter: 8 in. MacMillan Purchase 1960. A4522. Kwakiutl Hamatsa headpiece from Alert Bay. Diameter: 17 in. Deep red cedar bark. MacMillan Purchase. A8331

119

Fig. 113. (*Left to right, top*) Kwakiutl Hamatsa neck ring from Alert Bay. Red cedar bark. Diameter: 26 in. MacMillan Purchase 1951. A4518. Kwakiutl Hamatsa neck ring from Alert Bay. Red cedar bark. Diameter: 17 in. MacMillan Purchase 1951. A3602. Kwakiutl Hamatsa neck ring from Alert Bay. Red cedar bark and red yarn. Diameter: 16½ in. MacMillan Purchase 1953. A3729. (*Bottom*) Kwakiutl Hamatsa neck ring from Sullivan Bay. Red cedar bark and red yarn tassels. Diameter: 17 in. MacMillan Purchase 1952. A4122. Kwakiutl Hamatsa neck ring from Fort Rupert, said to be originally from the Heiltsuk and made about 1848. Red cedar bark and Hudson's Bay blanket. Diameter: 22 in. MacMillan Purchase 1953. A6272

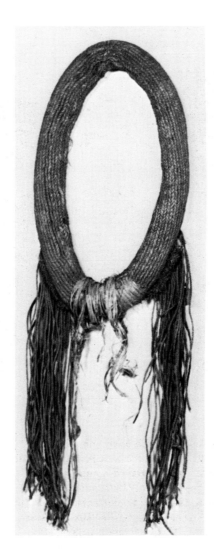

Fig. 114. (*Left to right, top*) Kwakiutl Hamatsa neck ring from Fort Rupert. Red cedar bark, red Hudson's Bay blanket, and red yarn. Diameter: 16 in. MacMillan Purchase 1953. A6262. Kwakiutl Hamatsa neck ring from Allison Harbour. Red twine. Diameter: 12 in. MacMillan Purchase 1953. A6137. Kwakiutl Hamatsa neck ring from Alert Bay. Plaited red cedar bark. Diameter: 31 in. MacMillan Purchase 1962. A7951. (*Bottom*) Haida "Hamatsa" neck ring from Queen Charlotte Islands, collected in 1880. Red cedar bark. Diameter: 15 in. Museum Purchase 1952. A6584. Kwakiutl Hamatsa neck ring from Alert Bay. Red cotton knitting. Diameter: 17 in. MacMillan Purchase 1953. A6254

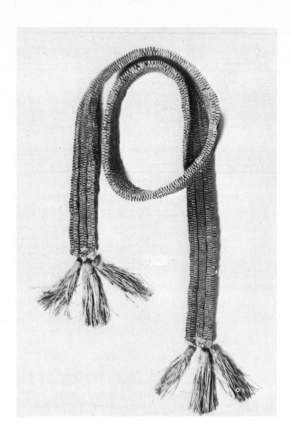

Fig. 115. (*Left*) Kwakiutl Hamatsa neck ring from Alert Bay. Plaited red cedar bark. Length: 8 ft. MacMillan Purchase 1962. A7950. (*Right*) Kwakiutl Hamatsa neck ring from Alert Bay. Red yarn. Diameter: 15 in. MacMillan Purchase 1953. A4302

Fig. 116. (*Left*) Kwakiutl Hamatsa neck ring from Alert Bay. Red yarn. Diameter: 16 in. MacMillan Purchase 1953. A4301. (*Right*) Kwakiutl Hamatsa neck ring from Alert Bay. Knitted red yarn. Diameter: 17 in. MacMillan Purchase 1953. A6306

Noohlmahl Masks

The Noohlmahl or "fool" dancers were messengers for the Hamatsa, ran errands for them, and acted as a sort of police during the Hamatsa series. They were violent, foolish, and nonhuman. They kept a kind of order by loudly threatening people, pushing back crowds, glaring at anyone who laughed, and throwing rocks and clubs. They were said to be under the control of the Ahlasimk spirits, who lived on a remote inland lake and hated everything calm, clean, or attractive.

Boisterous and unruly, the Noohlmahl buffoons were also filthy. Their garments were in dirty tatters, their hair unkempt and matted, and their repulsive, twisted masks matched the rest of their horrid appearance (Figs. 117-20). The chief feature of the Noohlmahl mask was an exaggerated, huge nose, and this aspect was emphasized in the pageant. Words referring to nose, smell, or mucus sent these creatures into a towering rage.

Their furious reaction caused them to strike out with their clubs and demolish any property in the way. For this reason no property of value was left in the dancing house, since the possessor would have to be indemnified by the sponsor of the dance for any damage done. Sometimes, however, the destruction was deliberately arranged, in order that the owner would receive a gift in payment afterward.

The Noohlmahl dancers were assisted in their enforcement of the ritual by the Hamatsa grizzly bears (Nanes Bakbakwalanooksiwae). These dancers, clad in bearskins and with long wooden claws, had faces painted red to rep-

123

resent an immense bear's mouth. Angry and menacing, they threatened anyone in the audience who moved or laughed, rattled the walls of houses, and smashed any property placed in their way. The owner of such property, or anyone scratched by one of these bears, was later compensated by a potlatch gift.

Fig. 117. Kwakiutl Noohlmahl mask from Gilford Island, attributed to Willie Seaweed. Wood; black, red. Height: 11 in. MacMillan Purchase 1953. A4305

 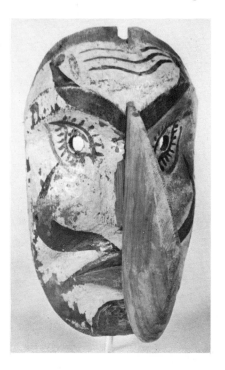

Fig. 118. (*Left*) Kwakiutl Noohlmahl mask from Allison Harbour. Wood, cedar bark, and feathers; orange, red, black, white. Height: 12 in. MacMillan Purchase 1953. A6217. (*Right*) Kwakiutl Noohlmahl mask from Turnour Island, said to be very old and to have been often copied. Wood; yellow, black, red. Height: 12 in. MacMillan Purchase 1961. A7483

Fig. 119. (*Left*) Kwakiutl Noohlmahl mask from Blunden Harbour. Wood; brown, black, white. Height: 11 in. MacMillan Purchase 1953. A4322. (*Right*) Kwakiutl Noohlmahl mask from Gilford Island. Wood and hair; black, red. Height: 10¾ in. MacMillan Purchase 1952. A3821

Fig. 120. (*Left*) Kwakiutl Noohlmahl mask from Alert Bay. Wood, cedar bark, and animal hair; red, orange, white, green, gray-green. Height: 8¾ in. MacMillan Purchase 1951. A6093. (*Right*) Kwakiutl Noohlmahl mask from Alert Bay. Wood and cedar bark; white, black. Height: 9¼ in. MacMillan Purchase 1951. A6094

Tanis Masks

The masks shown in Figure 121 are from Kitlope, at the center of origin of the Hamatsa dance complex. In this northern Kwakiutl area, the "house name" or "initiated" term for Hamatsa was "Tanis" (cf. Olson 1940:176; Olson 1954: 243; Drucker 1940:208, 211, 216).

According to the accounts, there were four chiefs eligible to wear these masks. One may be missing from this set collected by Dr. Raley from the burial cave of a former Kitamaat chief. These were said by Dr. Raley to have been considered "very old" in 1897, when he collected them.

Since these masks are so different in representation from the bird-monster complex, they pose an interesting problem in the transmutation of form and perhaps of meaning when the ritual was adopted by the southern Kwakiutl. The masks are powerfully carved and very solid; although the blocks of wood are hollowed out behind, the walls are thicker than is usual with masks. All three are painted with black graphite. A1782 has a touch of red ocher on the lips, and a sheet of mica used for the eyes. The masks are flat on the bottom jaw, as though made to sit upright on a flat surface.

Fig. 121. Kwakiutl Tanis masks from Kitlope, collected 1897. Wood; black, red. (*Top*) Height: 17½ in. (*Bottom, left to right*) Height: 16 in., 17 in. MacMillan Purchase 1948, Rev. G. H. Raley Coll. A1784, A1782, A1783

Ceremonial Skulls

Figure 125 (A6080) is an example of a blanket worn by an initiated Hamatsa as the ritual covering of his dance costume. The small wooden skulls affixed to it are indicative of the number of times he had danced as Hamatsa. Skulls were a symbol of the Hamatsa's grisly concern. Wooden skulls were often used to adorn headdresses, masks, and head rings, and rattles (Fig. 122 [A6183]) were often carved in this form. Those illustrated in Figures 122 and 123 were small ones sewn to clothing at one time. A3823 was probably carried on a board by the Kinkalatlala attendant in her dance placating the Hamatsa.

The ghost dancers associated with the Winalagalis war spirit ritual also wore head and neck rings adorned with wooden skulls (Fig. 124), and sometimes a mask representing a skull (Figs. 123, 124).

Fig. 122. (Top) 3 Kwakiutl ceremonial skulls from Village Island. Wood painted white with cedar bark decoration. Height: 7½ in. Mac-Millan Purchase 1953. A4166. (Center) Kwakiutl Hamatsa rattle from Kingcome Inlet in the form of a ceremonial skull. Wood and bearskin. Height: 13 in. MacMillan Purchase 1953. A6183. (Bottom, left to right) Kwakiutl ceremonial skull from Alert Bay. Unpainted wood. Height: 4½ in. MacMillan Purchase 1953. A6344. Kwakiutl ceremonial skull from Kingcome Inlet, attributed to Dick Hawkins. Wood; green, purple, red, white. Height: 6 in. MacMillan Purchase 1953. A6160. Kwakiutl ceremonial skull from Gilford Island. Unpainted wood. Height: 8½ in. MacMillan Purchase 1952. A3823

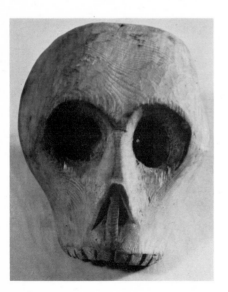

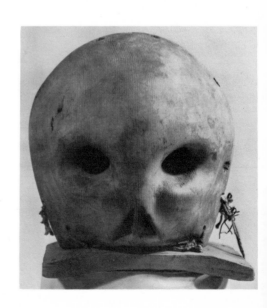

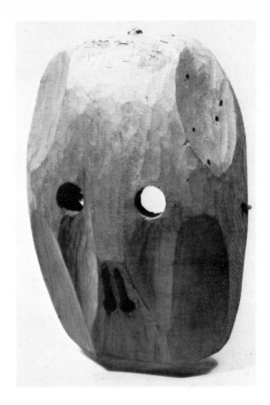

Fig. 123. (*Left*) Kwakiutl ceremonial skull from Alert Bay. Wood with green stain. Height: 5½ in. MacMillan Purchase 1953. A6309. (*Right*) Kwakiutl ghost dancer's mask from Alert Bay. Wood; green. Height: 11 in. MacMillan Purchase 1953. A6310

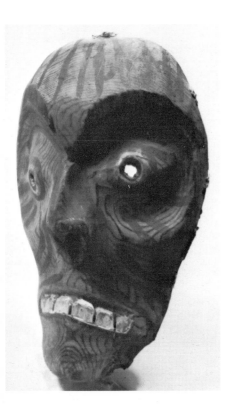

Fig. 124. (*Left to right*) Kwakiutl ghost dancer's mask from Alert Bay, also said to be the Wild Man of the Woods. Wood; black, white, red. Height: 12½ in. MacMillan Purchase 1951. A3613. Kwakiutl ghost dancer's mask from New Vancouver Village. Wood and horsehair; white, black, red. Height: 9 in. MacMillan Purchase 1961. A7488. Kwakiutl ghost dancer's headdress from Fort Rupert, said to be over 100 years old. Natural cedar bark with 4 wooden skulls painted white. Diameter: 15 in. MacMillan Purchase 1953. A6267

Fig. 125. (Top) Kwakiutl Hamatsa head ring from Kingcome Inlet. Deep red cedar bark with 2 unpainted wooden skulls. Diameter: 14 in. MacMillan Purchase 1951. A6082. (Bottom) Kwakiutl Hamatsa robe from Kingcome Inlet. Black velvet robe decorated with 9 wooden skulls and woven fringe of red and brown cedar bark. Length: 4 ft. 2 in. MacMillan Purchase 1951. A6080

Sisiutl Headdresses and Ceremonial Objects

The Sisiutl, the double-headed serpent whose body was a face, played an important part in the ritual of Winalagilis, the war spirit. This mythological creature was the warrior's assistant. It could be ridden and rowed like a canoe; its flesh was impervious to any spear; it could inflict instant death by its glance; and it could cause any enemy who looked upon it to be turned to stone, with all his joints turned backward. The Sisiutl was a frequently used design on the headdresses of the warrior dancers (Fig. 126), on ceremonial belts (Figs. 128, 129), on cloaks and aprons (Figs. 190, 191), on batons (Figs. 128, 129), bows (Fig. 163), feast dishes (Figs. 251-53), power boards (*duntsiks,* Fig. 130), and other ceremonial objects.

Fig. 126. *(Left to right, top)* Kwakiutl Sisiutl and loon headdress from Alert Bay. Wood; green, red, black, yellow. Height: 16 in. MacMillan Purchase 1953. A4036. Kwakiutl Sisiutl headdress from Alert Bay. Wood on leather base; black, red, green. Height: 10 in. MacMillan Purchase 1951. A3639. *(Bottom)* Kwakiutl Sisiutl headdress from Fort Rupert, made by Dick Price in 1940 and worn with small replicas around the wrists and ankles. Wood and cedar bark; white, black, red, green. Length: 15 in. MacMillan Purchase 1952. A3790. Kwakiutl Sisiutl headdress from Alert Bay, attributed to Dick Hawkins. Wood and leather; black, green, red. Length: 12 in. MacMillan Purchase 1951. A3604

Fig. 127. Kwakiutl Sisiutl ceremonial board from Alert Bay. Wood; red, green, black, white. Length: 11 ft. 6 in. MacMillan Purchase 1951. A3636

Fig. 128. (Top to bottom) Kwakiutl ceremonial belt with Sisiutl design from Village Island. Wood; red, black, green, blue. Length: 3 ft. 3 in. MacMillan Purchase 1961. A7472. Kwakiutl ceremonial belt with Sisiutl design from Alert Bay. Wood and cotton; white, green, black, red. Length: 4 ft. MacMillan Purchase 1952. A4263. Kwakiutl ceremonial belt with Sisiutl design from Fort Rupert. Wood and cord; white, black, orange, green. Length: 4 ft. 2 in. MacMillan Purchase 1952. A3791. Kwakiutl Sisiutl baton from Kingcome Inlet. Wood; black, red, green, white. Length: 3 ft. 7 in. MacMillan Purchase 1953. A6147

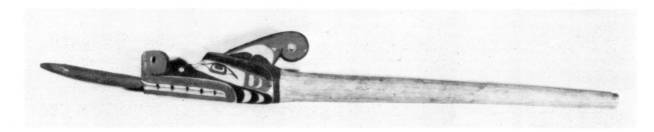

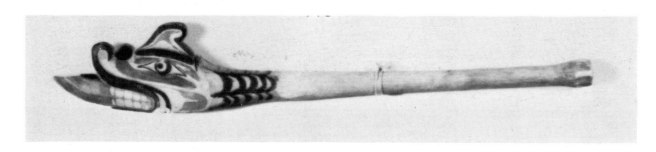

Fig. 129. (*Top to bottom*) Kwakiutl Sisiutl baton from Kingcome Inlet. Wood; black, white, green, red. Length: 27 in. MacMillan Purchase 1952. A3804. Kwakiutl Sisiutl baton from Kingcome Inlet. Wood; red, black. Length: 3 ft. 1 in. MacMillan Purchase 1952. A3800. Kwakiutl Sisiutl baton from Alert Bay. Wood; red, black. Length: 3 ft. 3 in. MacMillan Purchase 1951. A3632. Kwakiutl Sisiutl baton from Kingcome Inlet. Wood; black, green, red. Length: 28 in. MacMillan Purchase 1952. A3799. Kwakiutl ceremonial belt with Sisiutl design from Simoom Sound. Wood, rope, and cedar bark; red, black, green. Length: 22 in. MacMillan Purchase 1952. A3836

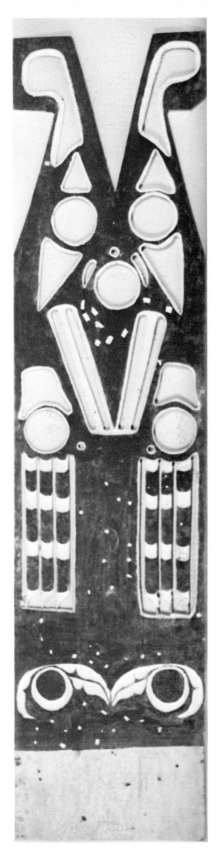

Fig. 130. (*Left*) Kwakiutl power board, with Sisiutl design, from Margaret Bay. Wood; black. Length: 8 ft. 9 in. MacMillan Purchase 1954. A6470. (*Right*) Pair of Kwakiutl power boards, with Sisiutl design, from Fort Rupert, attributed to Frank Walker. Wood; black, white. Length: 25 in., 24 in. MacMillan Purchase 1952. A3797, A3798

Atlakim Masks

Boas (1921:1193) gives the following list of dancers for the Atlakim dance:

1. "Calls Others into House" [Fig. 390 (A6088), "Grouse"]
2. "The Caller"
3. "Stump of the Woods" [Fig. 133 (A6348)]
4. "Laughing Woman of the Woods" [Fig. 131]
5. "Cannibal of the Woods"
6. "Dancer of the House"
7. "Raven of the Woods"
8. "Long Life Maker"
9. "Heat of House Woman"
10. "One Side Moss in Woods" [Fig. 140 (A4157)]
11. "One Side Rock in Woods" (one man and one woman)
12. "Frog Woman"
13. "Crooked Beak of the Sky"
14. "Hokhokw of the Sky" [Figs. 79, 392 (A4153)]
15. "Rich Woman"
16. "Woman giving Birth" (pretends to give birth, and her child gets up wearing a mask) [Fig. 140 (A4163c), "Woman"; Fig. 143 (A4163a and b), "Children"]
17. "Midwife" (comes out and shakes hands, dancing around. Another child is born and gets up wearing a mask—one boy and one girl)
18. "Salmonberry Woman"
19. "Sparrow Woman"
20. "Salmon Spirit" [Fig. 323 (A4161)]
21. "Listener" [Figs. 133 (A6341), 134 (A6340)]
22. "Sprinkler"
23. "Mountain Goat Hunter"

138

24. "Tying Woman" (blue jay)
25. "Dust-in-House-Woman"
26. "Helper-in-the-House"
27. "Door Keeper of Woods" [Figs. 141, 142 (A3657)]
28. "Partridge Woman"
29. "Thrush"
30. "Owl"
31. "Raindrop Maker"
32. "Answering Woman"
33. "Walking behind the Mountain Woman"
34. "Sneezer" [Fig. 142 (A6214)]

There would be forty called out in a full dance. It will be noted that some of these characters duplicate those in other Tsetseka dances—Raven, Hok-hokw, Crooked Beak, and Rich Woman—but most Atlakim masks, unlike the Hamatsa masks, were made roughly and hastily. Some were constructed of two boards fastened in a V form at the front of the face, not carved but rather crudely painted in white, orange, and black. They were meant to be worn in a dancing series for four years only and then burned. Only a few of the masks shown have been identified by informants. This is not surprising since there was a considerable amount of local variation in the group of forty, and not all of the characters would necessarily be often used. Probably the human face masks in Figure 447 are Atlakim as well, but it has not been possible to confirm this.

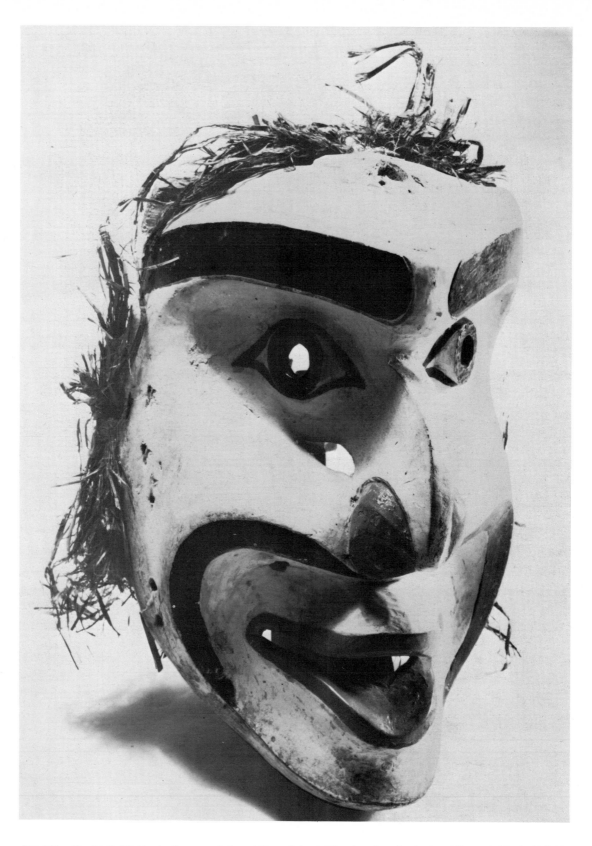

Fig. 131. Kwakiutl Atlakim buffoon mask from Village Island. Wood and cedar bark; white, red, black. Height: 12 in. MacMillan Purchase 1952. A4159

Fig. 132. Kwakiutl Atlakim mask from Blunden Harbour. Wood, cedar bark, and hide; white, red, blue. Height: 11 in. MacMillan Purchase 1953. A6347

Fig. 133. (Top) Kwakiutl Atlakim "tree stump" mask from Blunden Harbour, said to follow A6223. Wood, cedar bark, and feathers; white, red, black. Height: 10 in. MacMillan Purchase 1953. A6348. (Bottom, left to right) Kwakiutl Atlakim mask from Blunden Harbour, said to follow A6088 (Fig. 390). The hole in the forehead was where a small branch was inserted. Wood, cedar bark, and horsehair; white, black, red, orange. Height: 12 in. MacMillan Purchase 1953. A6223. Kwakiutl Atlakim buffoon mask from Alert Bay, attributed to Willie Seaweed. Wood and cedar bark; white, red, black. Height: 12 in. MacMillan Purchase 1953. A6341

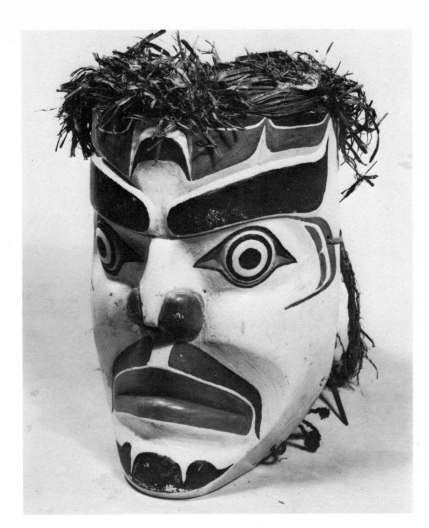

Fig. 134. (Top) Kwakiutl Atlakim buffoon mask from Alert Bay. Wood and cedar bark; white, red, black. Height: 12 in. MacMillan Purchase 1953. A6339. (Bottom, left to right) Kwakiutl Atlakim mask from Alert Bay. Wood and cedar bark; white, red, black. Height: 11½ in. MacMillan Purchase 1953. A6340. Kwakiutl Atlakim mask of a "spruce tree" clown, from Blunden Harbour. Wood and cedar bark; white, red, black. Height: 9½ in. Museum Purchase 1953. A6221

Fig. 135. Kwakiutl Atlakim mask from Smith Inlet, attributed to Joe and Willie Seaweed, 1940; 1 of a set of 5 including Figs. 135-39. Wood and feathers; white, black, blue, red. Height: 11½ in. MacMillan Purchase 1964. A8427

Fig. 136. Kwakiutl Atlakim mask from Smith Inlet, attributed to Joe and Willie Seaweed, 1940; 1 of a set of 5 including Figs. 135-39. Wood and feathers; white, black, blue, red. Height: 11½ in. MacMillan Purchase 1964. A8428

Fig. 137. Kwakiutl Atlakim mask from Smith Inlet, attributed to Joe and Willie Seaweed, 1940; 1 of a set of 5 including Figs. 135-39. Wood and feathers; white, black, blue, red. Height: 12½ in. MacMillan Purchase 1964. A8429

Fig. 138. Kwakiutl Atlakim mask from Smith Inlet, attributed to Joe and Willie Seaweed, 1940; 1 of a set of 5 including Figs. 135-39. Wood and feathers; white, black, blue, red. Height: 12 in. MacMillan Purchase 1964. A8430

Fig. 139. Kwakiutl Atlakim mask from Smith Inlet, attributed to Joe and Willie Seaweed, 1940; 1 of a set of 5 including Figs. 135-39. Wood and feathers; white, black, blue, red. Height: 12 in. MacMillan Purchase 1964. A8431

Fig. 140. (*Top*) Kwakiutl Atlakim mask of a mimic (Nenolu), from Village Island, last used in a potlatch at Alert Bay about 50 years ago. Wood and cedar bark; white, orange, black. Height: 15 in. MacMillan Purchase 1952. A4156. (*Bottom, left to right*) Kwakiutl Atlakim mask from Village Island, representing the mother of A4163a and A4163b (Fig. 143). Wood and cedar bark; red, black. Height: 9 in. MacMillan Purchase 1952. A4163c. Kwakiutl Atlakim "Moss Face" mask from Village Island. Wood and cedar bark; red, black, white. Height: 15 in. MacMillan Purchase 1952. A4157

Fig. 141. Kwakiutl Atlakim "door" mask from Alert Bay. Wood and cedar bark; white, green, red, black. Height: 16 in. MacMillan Purchase 1952. A4245

Fig. 142. (*Top*) Kwakiutl Atlakim "Sneezer" mask from Blunden Harbour, attributed to George Walkus. Wood and cedar bark; red, brown, white, black. Height: 13½ in. MacMillan Purchase 1953. A6214. (*Bottom, left to right*) Kwakiutl Atlakim mask from Blunden Harbour. Wood; white, red, black. Height: 11½ in. MacMillan Purchase 1951. A3657. Kwakiutl Atlakim mask from Alert Bay. Wood; red, white, black. Height: 11½ in. MacMillan Purchase 1951. A6107

Fig. 143. (*Top*) Kwakiutl Atlakim mask from Village Island, representing the daughter of A4163c (Fig. 140). Wood and cedar bark; red, white, black. Height: 7¼ in. MacMillan Purchase 1952. A4163a. (*Bottom, left to right*) Kwakiutl Atlakim mask from Village Island, representing the daughter of A4163c (Fig. 140). Wood; red, white, black. Height: 9 in. MacMillan Purchase 1952. A4163b. Kwakiutl Atlakim mask from Blunden Harbour. Wood; red, white, black. Height: 11½ in. MacMillan Purchase 1953. A6237

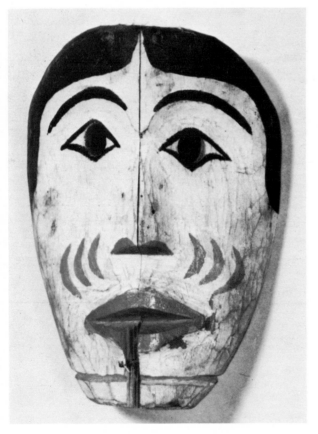

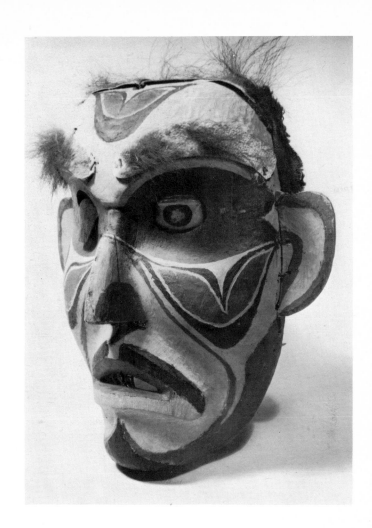

Fig. 144. (*Top*) Kwakiutl mask from Bliss Landing, possibly an Atlakim "Sleeper" mask. A system of stringing makes the eyes open and close. Wood and fur; green, red, black. Height: 14½ in. MacMillan Purchase 1948, Rev. G. H. Raley Coll. A1967. (*Bottom, left to right*) Kwakiutl Atlakim mask from Alert Bay. Wood and cedar bark; white, brown, black. Height: 13½ in. MacMillan Purchase 1951. A6092. Kwakiutl Atlakim mask from Village Island. Wood and cedar bark; black, red, white. Height: 10 in. MacMillan Purchase 1952. A4160

Tsonokwa Masks

A complex character in the dancing societies of the southern Kwakiutl was the giantess Tsonokwa, one of the large family of giants who lived in the faraway mountains and woods. Black in color, with bushy, unkempt hair and a pursed mouth through which she uttered the cry, *"Hu hu,"* she was a horrid and threatening figure. On her back she carried a basket in which she collected children, taking them home to eat. The children usually outwitted her, however, because she was vain, stupid, and clumsy. In another aspect, Tsonokwa controlled the magic "water of life," a gift she bestowed on a family that wrested her secrets from her. Her most important role was that of bringer of wealth and good fortune. In her house there were many boxes of treasure which were found by children who went to seek her, and there were also the magical Sisiutl house beams and posts, another indication of her treasure and her importance.

In the pageantry of the winter dances Tsonokwa appeared in two forms. As a dancer in the Tsetseka performance she was a shaggy, lumbering creature with half-closed eyes. She could not keep alert enough to dance the normal four circuits around the fire, but shambled in the wrong way and was guided to her seat, where she fell asleep. She kept falling asleep whenever anyone pointed a finger at her, and she did not participate in the events.

In her other role, as a figure of wealth-giving, she played an important part during the potlatch, especially among the southern Kwakiutl. She carried a basket in which were stored coppers, which she handed to the chief who was selling or giving them away. At a moment of climax in the copper dispersal, the chief put on a family crest mask of Tsonokwa, called a Geekumhl (Figs. 145-47). This mask, characterized not by the foolish face with half-closed eyes, but by a strong and vigorous face, usually had locks of human hair and was very carefully carved. As this creature, the chief "cut" the copper with a copper cutter, which often had the carved head of a Tsonokwa on its handle (Figs. 162, 164).

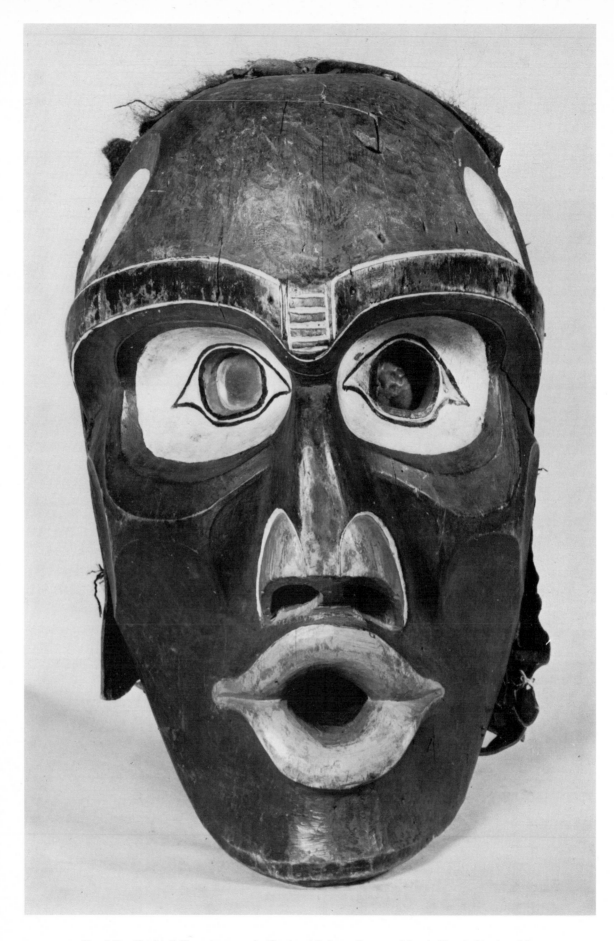

Fig. 145. Kwakiutl Tsonokwa mask (Geekumhl) from Turnour Island. Wood; black, white, red. Height: 17½ in. MacMillan Purchase 1961. A7491

Fig. 146. (Left) Kwakiutl Tsonokwa mask (Geekumhl) from Fort Rupert, made by Willie Seaweed. Wood and human hair; orange and black with red hair. Height: 10½ in. MacMillan Purchase 1953. A6271. (Right) Kwakiutl Tsonokwa mask (Geekumhl) from Gilford Island. Wood and horsehair; black, red, white. Height: 18 in. MacMillan Purchase 1952. A3774

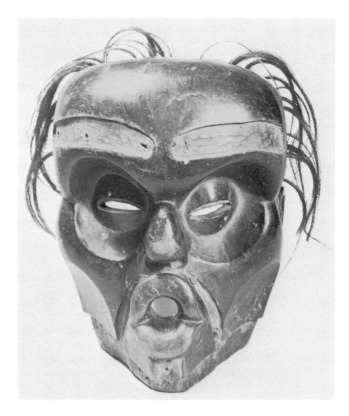

Fig. 147. (Left) Kwakiutl Tsonokwa mask (Geekumhl) from Alert Bay. Wood and human hair; red, green, black. Height: 11 in. MacMillan Purchase 1953. A4034. (Right) Kwakiutl Tsonokwa mask (Geekumhl) from Gilford Island. Wood and bear fur; black with reddish lips; eyebrows, chin, and area around mouth indented for inlay. Height: 11 in. MacMillan Purchase 1954. A6374

Fig. 148. (*Left*) Kwakiutl Tsonokwa mask from Alert Bay. Wood; black, white, red enamel paint. Height: 11½ in. MacMillan Purchase 1952. A4179. (*Right*) Kwakiutl Tsonokwa mask from Smith Inlet. Wood; red, black, white. Height: 15 in. MacMillan Purchase 1953. A4286

Fig. 149. (*Left*) Kwakiutl Tsonokwa mask from Kingcome Inlet. Wood; white, puce, black, with faint red line. Height: 14 in. MacMillan Purchase 1952. A3787. (*Right*) Kwakiutl Tsonokwa mask from Turnour Island. Wood and hair; black, red, gray, white. Height: 13 in. MacMillan Purchase 1954. A6369

Fig. 150. (*Left*) Kwakiutl Tsonokwa mask from Kingcome Inlet. Wood rubbed with charcoal; eyebrows of bear fur. Height: 22 in. MacMillan Purchase 1953. A6185. (*Right*) Kwakiutl Tsonokwa mask from Alert Bay. Wood with copper plate underneath and a mechanical device for opening and closing the eyes and jaw. Height: 30 in. Mac-Millan Purchase 1953. A6337

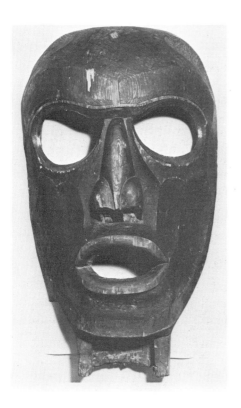
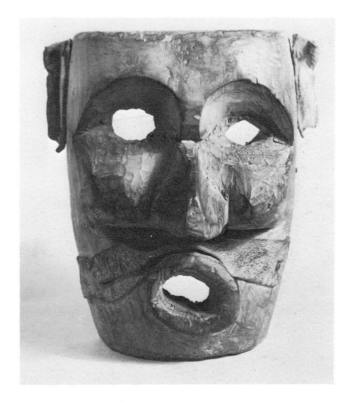

Fig. 151. (*Left*) Kwakiutl Tsonokwa head, part of a carved seated figure in a house at Kingcome Inlet; the rest of the carving had decayed. Unpainted wood. Height: 3 ft. 11 in. MacMillan Purchase 1953. A4342. (*Right*) Nootka Tsonokwa mask from the West Coast of Vancouver Island. Unpainted wood with leather strips. Height: 9½ in. MacMillan Purchase 1949, Rev. G. H. Raley Coll. A6817

Coppers

The copper was made of a large flat sheet of beaten copper cut in the shape of a shield with a T-shaped ridge imposed on it. It was painted with black lead, through which a crest design was incised. Coppers varied in height from six inches to two and a half feet. They were brought out as the climax of a potlatch, and were the preferred finish to the ceremony. They were particularly associated with the marriage transfer of privileges, with a wife's gift to her husband, and with naming ceremonies.

At naming ceremonies, a large ceremonial cradle *(yathla)* was constructed and hung from the beams at the front center of the house (Fig. 158). The copper was a "blanket" to keep the child warm. A herald or other official stood at each corner of the cradle and shook his rattle four times, pretending that there was a child in the cradle. A speech was then made naming the copper and the child. Rattles used in these ceremonies are among those shown in Figures 35 and 36. They were made either of copper or of wood in the shape of a copper.

Copper used as a decorative motif on garments (Pls. VII A, VIII A; Figs. 186, 190-92), staffs (Fig. 250), and crest carvings had the clear and unmistakable meaning of wealth.

Fig. 152. Kwakiutl copper from Fort Rupert. Height: 21 in. MacMillan Purchase 1962. A8059

Fig. 153. Kwakiutl copper from Kingcome Inlet. Height: 30 in.
Leon and Thea Koerner Foundation Grant 1957. A6834

Fig. 154. Haida copper from Queen Charlotte Islands. Beaten
copper, with an incised bear painted in black. Height: 29½ in.
MacMillan Purchase 1960, Rev. E. M. Collison Coll. A7102

Fig. 156. Kwakiutl copper from Sullivan Bay. Beaten copper roughly incised with a crude design. Height: 14 in. MacMillan Purchase 1952. A6113

Fig. 155. Kwakiutl copper from Kingcome Inlet. Beaten copper painted black. Height: 6½ in. MacMillan Purchase 1953. A6261

Fig. 157. (*Left*) Kwakiutl copper from Sullivan Bay. Beaten copper with bear face crudely incised. Height: 27½ in. Mac-Millan Purchase 1953. A6171. (*Right*) Kwakiutl copper from Allison Harbour. Beaten copper riveted together at the T ridge. Height: 31 in. MacMillan Purchase 1953. A4343

Fig. 158. One side of a Kwakiutl ceremonial cradle from Alert Bay, used in naming or copper ceremony; the other side is identical. Wood covered with painted cloth. Length: 5 ft. 2 in. MacMillan Purchase 1951. A3638

Ceremonial Weapons

Ceremonial weapons were associated particularly with the copper complex. The copper was sometimes "speared" with a harpoon (Figs. 159, 160) or spear (Fig. 161), in the ceremony associated with the transfer of privileges at the time of marriage. A wedge or "dagger" with a steel blade several inches wide was used to cut the copper. The copper shield was placed on a cutting platform (Fig. 166), and the wedge was hit so that the blade produced a rough, irregular cut in the copper. Often the wedges were symbolic daggers, carved of wood like the ones shown in Figures 161, 164, 165. In this case an additional cutting tool would be used. Daggers adorned with skulls (Fig. 164 [A3552]) were said to be used in the sense of "killing" the copper, that is, cutting it up with a wedge as a slave was killed with a stone dagger in the old days. The ceremonial dagger shown in Figure 165 (A8363) was said to have been used to "kill" the mask in Figure 442 (A8362) in a dance. Figure 163 shows a ceremonial bow decorated with a Sisiutl design.

Fig. 159. Kwakiutl ceremonial harpoon from Kingcome Inlet, used "to spear copper like a whale at marriage transfer ceremony." Wood with dagger point on end; black, red, white, with killer whale and eagle design at tip (*shown in detail above*), and face on other end (*left and below*). Length: 8 ft. 4 in. MacMillan Purchase 1951. A3630

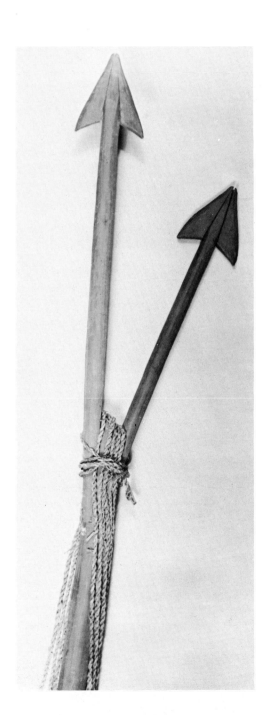

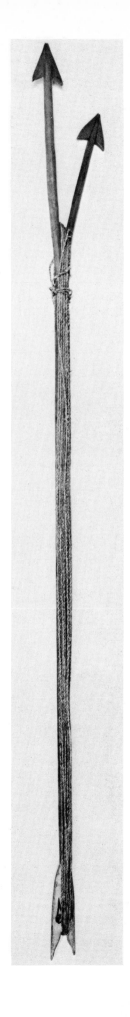

Fig. 160. Kwakiutl ceremonial harpoon from Kingcome Inlet. Wood with cedar bark rope line. Details show the 2 ends. Length: 10 ft. 9 in. MacMillan Purchase 1953. A6197

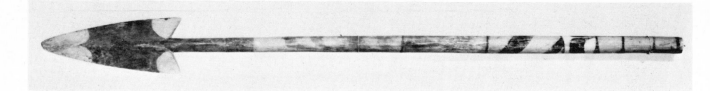

Fig. 161. Kwakiutl ceremonial spear from Alert Bay, used in copper ceremony. 2 pieces of wood with a carved point at the end; red, black. Length: 5 ft. 2 in. MacMillan Purchase 1951. A3631

Fig. 162. (Left and center) 2 views of Kwakiutl Tsonokwa wedge from Simoom Sound, with 2 carved Tsonokwa heads on the handle. Unpainted wood. Length: 15 in. MacMillan Purchase 1952. A3824. (Right) Kwakiutl Tsonokwa wedge from New Vancouver Village. Wood; black. Length: 18 in. MacMillan Purchase 1961. A7474

Fig. 163. Kwakiutl ceremonial bow with Sisiutl design from Alert Bay. Wood; red, black, green. Length: 5 ft. 8 in. MacMillan Purchase 1953. A6350

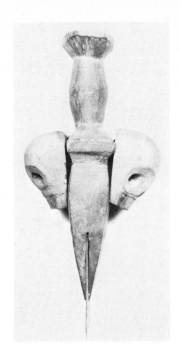

Fig. 164. (*Left to right*) Kwakiutl Tsonokwa wedge from New Vancouver Village. Wood; black, red, white. Length: 18 in. MacMillan Purchase 1961. A7487. Kwakiutl ceremonial dagger from Minstrel Island, with Tsonokwa head. Wood; black, red, white, yellow. Length: 17½ in. MacMillan Purchase 1954. A6367. Kwakiutl ceremonial Hamatsa dagger from Kingcome Inlet. Wood with steel blade; 2 skulls carved on handle. Length: 14 in. MacMillan Purchase 1951. A3552. Kwakiutl ceremonial dagger from Simoom Sound. Wood bound with cedar bark on handle. Length: 14 in. MacMillan Purchase 1952. A3837

Fig. 165. (*Left*) Bella Coola ceremonial dagger. Natural wood with cedar bark fringe. Length: 19 in. MacMillan Purchase 1963. A8363. (*Right*) Kwakiutl ceremonial dagger from Port Hardy. Unpainted wood. Length: 11 in. MacMillan Purchase 1962. A8075

Fig. 166. (*Right*) Kwakiutl copper-cutting stand from Alert Bay, carved in the form of a bear. Wood with an iron cutting platform on top of the head. Height: 3 ft. MacMillan Purchase 1961. A7878

Ceremonial Cedar Bark

The red-dyed cedar bark head and neck rings worn by the Hamatsa dancers have been shown in Figures 111-16. During the Tsetseka season similar ornaments were worn by other dancers, although some, as we have seen in the Atlakim dance, used hemlock, salal, and ferns instead. Some red cedar bark head rings were trimmed with ermine and abalone shell to make a ceremonial headband of a more permanent sort (Fig. 168).

White, bleached cedar bark had a different function, indicating that the Klasila season was in force and that the dance was not supernaturally inspired. In some cases a cape, skirt, or fringe was made of both red and white cedar bark, so that it could be used for any occasion.

Some Kwakiutl and non-Kwakiutl cedar bark head and neck rings are shown in Figures 167-78. The three with the cardboard fish, shown in Figure 167, were said to have been used by twins because of the mythical association between salmon and twins.

Fig. 167. 3 Kwakiutl head rings from Alert Bay. Red cedar bark with cardboard fish. Diameter: 8 in. MacMillan Purchase 1952. A4240

Fig. 168. (*Left*) Kwakiutl head ring from Alert Bay. Red Hudson's Bay blanket, ermine, and cedar bark. Diameter: 8 in. MacMillan Purchase 1960. A4523. (*Right*) Kwakiutl Klasila head ring from Simoon Sound. Cedar bark with abalone shell, ermine tails and skins. Diameter: 9 in. MacMillan Purchase 1953. A6298

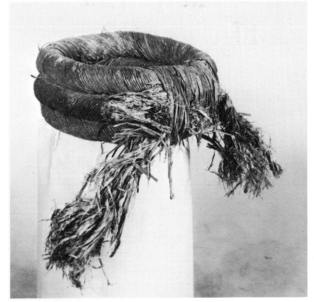

Fig. 169. (*Left*) 2 Kwakiutl head rings from Alert Bay. Red cedar bark. Diameter: 10 in. MacMillan Purchase 1952. A4228. (*Right*) Haida head ring from Queen Charlotte Islands. Red cedar bark. Diameter: 9 in. MacMillan Purchase 1952. A6583

Fig. 170. Coast Salish headdress from Patricia Bay, worn by a new dancer. Natural cedar bark and feathers. Width: 26 in. MacMillan Purchase 1962. A8184a

Fig. 171. (*Left*) Kwakiutl head ring from Alert Bay. Deep red and natural plaited cedar bark. Diameter: 9 in. MacMillan Purchase 1951. A3600. (*Right*) Haida head ring from Queen Charlotte Islands. Natural cedar bark with hide pompons. Diameter: 11 in. Mrs. F. L. Beecher Coll. 1950. A4143

Fig. 172. (*Left*) Coast Salish head ring from Patricia Bay. Deep red plaited shredded cedar bark. Length: 18 in. MacMillan Purchase 1962. A8188. (*Right*) Coast Salish head ring from Patricia Bay. Plaited red and natural cedar bark. Length: 18 in. MacMillan Purchase 1962. A8187

Fig. 173. Bella Coola head ring. Shredded deep red cedar bark. Diameter: 11 in. MacMillan Purchase 1963. A8375

Fig. 174. Kwakiutl Klasila neck ring from Kingcome Inlet. Red cedar bark with raven head, wing, and tail pieces of wood. Diameter: 35 in. MacMillan Purchase 1953. A6318

Fig. 175. Coast Salish headdress from Duncan. Shredded red cedar bark with feathers fastened at the center. Length: 24 in. MacMillan Purchase 1962. A8189

Fig. 176. Coast Salish headdress, probably from Duncan. Natural cedar bark. Length: 3 ft. 10 in. MacMillan Purchase 1962. A8134

Fig. 177. Coast Salish headdress. Natural cedar bark and hawk feathers. Length: 33 in. MacMillan Purchase 1962. A8135

Fig. 178. (*Left to right*) Tsimshian neck ring from Nass River. Red and natural cedar bark. Diameter: 18 in. MacMillan Purchase 1948, Rev. G. H. Raley Coll. A3736. Tsimshian neck ring from Nass River. Red and white cedar bark. Diameter: 21 in. MacMillan Purchase 1948, Rev. G. H. Raley Coll. A1742. Tsimshian neck ring from Aiyansh. Deep red cedar bark and deerhide. Diameter: 16 in. MacMillan Purchase 1962. A8231

Fig. 179. Coast Salish new dancer's harness from Patricia Bay. Natural cedar bark and feathers. Width: 26 in. MacMillan Purchase 1962. A8184b

Fig. 180. Kwakiutl cedar bark skirt from Kingcome Inlet. Natural shredded cedar bark. Length: 3 ft. 1 in. MacMillan Purchase 1960. A4520

Ceremonial Clothing

The dress for ceremonial occasions was as splendid and showy as human ingenuity could make it. Sea otter robes and fine furs were at first supplemented and later supplanted by the Chilkat blanket, a rectangular textile woven of mountain goats' wool and worn as a cloak. Such blankets, woven on a loom by Tsimshian and later Chilkat women, were composed of highly abstracted crest designs in blue, yellow, white, and black, with a long, heavy white fringe around the hem. (Pl. IX; Figs. 181-83). Each one took nearly a year to make and was highly valued up and down the coast among the other tribes, whose chiefs purchased one whenever possible. For all Chilkat weaving the pattern of the crest design was painted by a man on a "pattern board" (Figs. 184, 185) and then copied on the loom by a woman weaver.

A more common ceremonial costume was the "button blanket" or cloak (Pls. VII and VIII; Figs. 186-88). After trade blankets became available, a special kind of dark blue blanket was preferred for this special purpose. These were made into very brilliant cloaks decorated with red flannel appliqués of family crest motifs and with pearl shell buttons.

Another cloak, produced by the Salish women, was woven of white wool, in early times clipped from small domestic dogs kept for the purpose, and later from sheep and goats (Fig. 189). Some of these cloaks were decorated with colored geometric patterns, but for the most part they were plain, of coarse, rather heavy white wool, stiffened by the addition of white clay, milkweed down, and other substances to give body to the soft fibers.

Other clothing worn at ceremonies included a variety of dance aprons and leggings of flannel or of woven Chilkat cloth. Dance aprons were decorated with small items that created pleasant sounds, such as thimbles, cartridges, small coppers, puffin beaks, deer hoofs, and the like (Figs. 190-92). A shirt of Chilkat textile trimmed with fur was sometimes worn and was, like the cloak, a very costly item (Fig. 195). The black velvet Coast Salish costume shown in Figure 200 was worn with the staff illustrated in Figure 250 (A8141).

Among northern tribes a ceremonial robe of moosehide, decorated with painted designs, was sometimes worn (Fig. 198), as were painted or fringed deerhide aprons (Fig. 201).

Footgear was not worn in earlier times. Clothing for nonceremonial occasions was very simple—capes and skirts of woven or sewn cedar bark for the women (Fig. 180); cedar bark blankets or nothing for the men.

Fig. 181. Haida Chilkat cloak from Queen Charlotte Islands. Mountain goat wool; dark brown, yellow, blue. Length: 6 ft. MacMillan Purchase 1961. A7434

Fig. 182. Haida Chilkat cloak from Queen Charlotte Islands. Wool trimmed with otter fur; yellow, black, blue, white. Length: 5 ft. 1 in. MacMillan Purchase 1960, Rev. E. M. Collison Coll. A7079

Fig. 183. Tlingit Chilkat cloak from Sitka. Mountain goat wool; dark brown, light brown, yellow, white. Length: 5 ft. 6 in. Acquired 1960. A4504

Fig. 184. Tsimshian Chilkat pattern board. Wood with black painted design. Length: 34 in. Gift of Walter C. Koerner 1962. A8326

Fig. 185. Kwakiutl Chilkat pattern board, made by Mungo Martin for Mrs. Martin at U.B.C. Museum, 1951. Wood; white, green, yellow, black. Length: 4 ft. MacMillan Purchase 1951. A3658

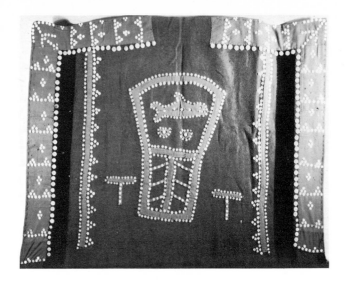

Fig. 186. (*Top to bottom, left*) Kwakiutl button cloak from Alert Bay. Blue textile with red appliqué and buttons; copper design with killer whale. Length: 4 ft. 8 in. MacMillan Purchase 1952. A4226. Kwakiutl button cloak from Alert Bay. Blue textile with copper design in red appliqué and sequins. Length: 6 ft. 1 in. MacMillan Purchase 1952. A4227. (*Right*) Kwakiutl button cloak from Allison Harbour. Green textile with copper design in red appliqué and buttons. Length: 4 ft. 3 in. MacMillan Purchase 1953. A6138. Kwakiutl button cloak from Kingcome Inlet. Blue textile with red appliqué and buttons; copper design with sun. Length: 6 ft. MacMillan Purchase 1953. A4326. Kwakiutl button cloak from Alert Bay. Blue wool with red flannel appliqué of Sisiutl, coppers, and Thunderbird. Length: 4 ft. 4 in. MacMillan Purchase 1953. A4325

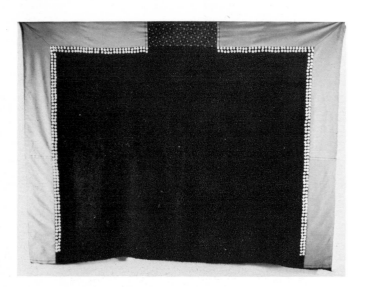

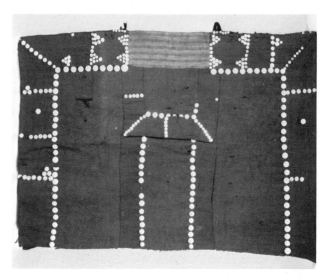

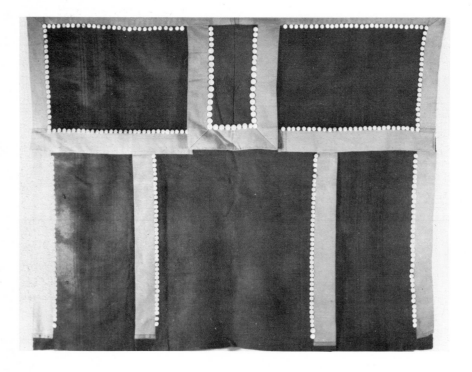

Fig. 187. (*Top to bottom, left*) Kwakiutl button cloak from Alert Bay. Tree design in red appliqué and buttons on blue background. Length: 6 ft. 2 in. MacMillan Purchase 1953. A3730. Tahltan button cloak from Telegraph Creek, possibly over 100 years old. Red flannel appliqué and pearl buttons on blue Hudson's Bay blanket. Length: 6 ft. MacMillan Purchase 1950. A3393. Tahltan button cloak from Telegraph Creek. Blue Hudson's Bay blanket with red appliqué and buttons. Length: 5 ft. 8 in. MacMillan Purchase 1951. A3554. (*Right*) Kwakiutl button cloak from Alert Bay. Blue textile with appliquéd red border, geometric button pattern, and abalone shell squares. Length: 4 ft. 10 in. MacMillan Purchase 1953. A6246. Kwakiutl button cloak from Kingcome Inlet. Blue Hudson's Bay blanket with button design. Length: 3 ft. 7 in. MacMillan Purchase 1952. A3840

Fig. 188. (Above) Tsimshian button cloak from Kispiox. Blue textile wtih Tahltan-style red flannel decoration and buttons. Length: 6 ft. MacMillan Purchase 1962. A7964

Fig. 189. (Right) Salish blanket. Natural color goat hair. Length: 9 ft. 2 in. MacMillan Purchase 1962. A8038

Fig. 190. Kwakiutl dance apron from Sullivan Bay. Black textile with bells attached; embroidered design showing a wolf on each side of a copper, and Sisiutl below; green, white, red, yellow, pink, blue. Length: 31 in. MacMillan Purchase 1952. A4172

Fig. 191. Kwakiutl dance apron from Sullivan Bay. Black wool with red cotton trim and chrome sleighbells on fringe; embroidered design of Sisiutl and copper. Length: 25½ in. MacMillan Purchase 1952. A4131

179

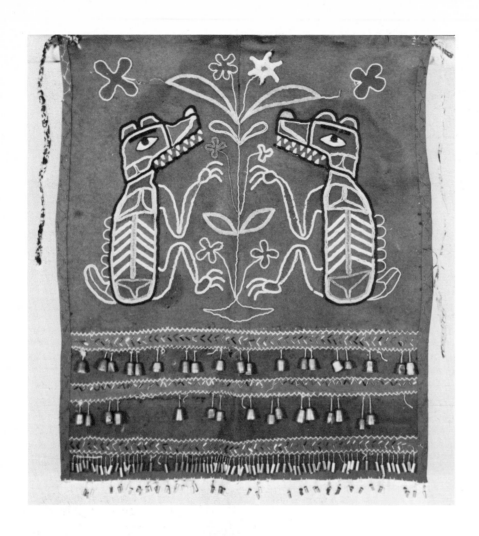

Fig. 192. (*Left*) Kwakiutl dance apron from New Vancouver Village. Red textile with beaded design of a flowering plant with a wolf on each side; fringe of thimbles and bullet shells. Length: 30 in. MacMillan Purchase 1961. A7489. (*Below, left to right*) Kwakiutl dance apron from Alert Bay, said to have been made before 1880. Black cloth with yellow and red beadwork design of a copper and 2 ravens, and small copper dangles. Length: 18½ in. MacMillan Purchase 1953. A6245. Kwakiutl Chilkat apron from Vancouver, woven by Mrs. Mungo Martin at U.B.C. Museum, 1951. Commercial wool; white, yellow, green, black. Length: 34 in. MacMillan Purchase 1952. A4184

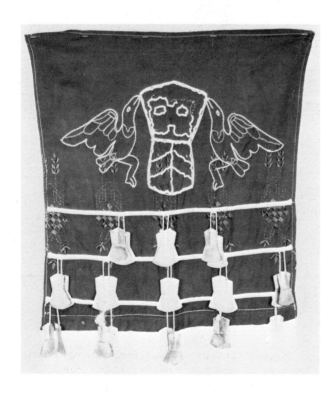

Fig. 193. Kwakiutl Chilkat apron from Vancouver, woven by Mrs. Mungo Martin at U.B.C. Museum, 1951. Commercial wool; black, white, yellow, blue, green, red. Length: 30½ in. MacMillan Purchase 1951. A3654

Fig. 194. Tlingit Chilkat apron from Sitka. Shredded cedar bark twine and mountain goat wool; yellow, blue, black, white. Length: 32 in. MacMillan Purchase 1960. A4505

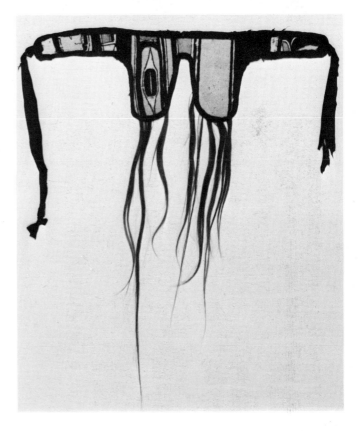

Fig. 195. Haida Chilkat shirt from Queen Charlotte Islands. Mountain goat wool; yellow, black, blue, trimmed with red feathers. Length: 3 ft. 2 in. MacMillan Purchase 1960, Rev. E. M. Collison Coll. A7080

Fig. 196. Tsimshian Chilkat headpiece from Kitwanga. Wool trimmed with tufts of hair; yellow, blue, black, white. Length: 24 in. MacMillan Purchase 1962. A8233

Fig. 197. Haida Chilkat leggings from Queen Charlotte Islands. Wool trimmed with deerhide fringe; yellow, blue, black, white. 13 in. square. MacMillan Purchase 1960, Rev. E. M. Collison Coll. A7078

Fig. 198. Tsimshian cloak from Skeena River. Moosehide with incised and painted design in black, red, green. Length: 4 ft. 8 in. MacMillan Purchase 1950. A1613

Fig. 199. Tsimshian dance apron from Nass River. Buckskin with deer hoof rattles. Length: 4 ft. 7 in. MacMillan Purchase 1962. A7955

Fig. 200. Coast Salish spirit dance costume from Vancouver Island. Black velvet jacket decorated with small wooden paddles, black velvet pants, wool socks. Length: 3 ft. 11 in. Leon and Thea Koerner Foundation Purchase 1958. A6887

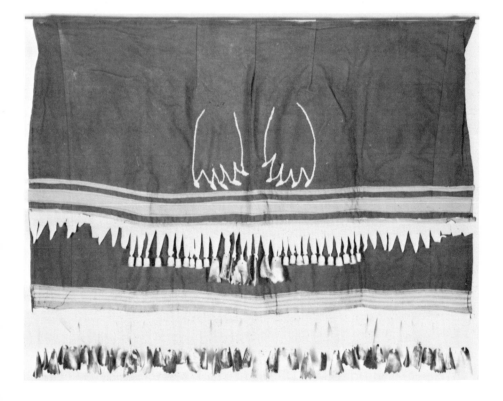

Fig. 201. Tsimshian dance apron from Kispiox. Embroidered hide with design of bear claws and deer hoof rattles attached to fringe. Length: 3 ft. 2 in. MacMillan Purchase 1962. A7962

Fig. 202. Coast Salish spirit dance headdress from West Saanich. Human hair. Length: 3 ft. 5 in. Leon and Thea Koerner Foundation Purchase 1958. A6886

Hats

Basketry hats were woven by the people of all tribes. Various shapes were associated with different areas. The Nootka and Salish had a dome-shaped hat (Fig. 213 [A3723, A1479]), which among the Nootka was elaborated for ceremonial occasions by the addition of a rounded spire or "sugar-loaf" form to this base.

The most popular form of hat was that worn by women of the northern regions. Curtis writes that the Kwakiutl women adopted this form about 1860, borrowing it from the Haida. The hat was woven of twisted spruce root fibers into a narrow cylindrical crown with a gently flaring brim (Pl. XVI B; Figs. 203-13). It was fitted firmly to the head by an inner rim around the forehead. Strong and well woven, it was a remarkably comfortable hat, light, airy, suitable both in sunshine and in rain. Women of upper rank who had successfully married and gone through the approved series of "redeeming" ceremonies were entitled to wear such a hat with their crest painted on it.

The crest designs on these hats were beautifully contrived. The "X-ray" technique, showing the whole animal body with both its inner and its outer features, and bisecting it so as to arrange it most gracefully around the rim, was a common way of filling the space. The bisected body of the crest bird or animal was so disposed that it joined in the center front at the face and the center rear at the tail. The designs were painted on with great skill, using some areas of solid color and many kinds of cross-hatching and other textural details. Colors were generally red and black, occasionally combined with green or blue paint.

A special kind of hat with interwoven rings was worn by chiefs to indicate the number of potlatches they had given (Fig. 213). Among the northern tribes, these basketry rings were often attached to a wooden crest rim with the same meaning.

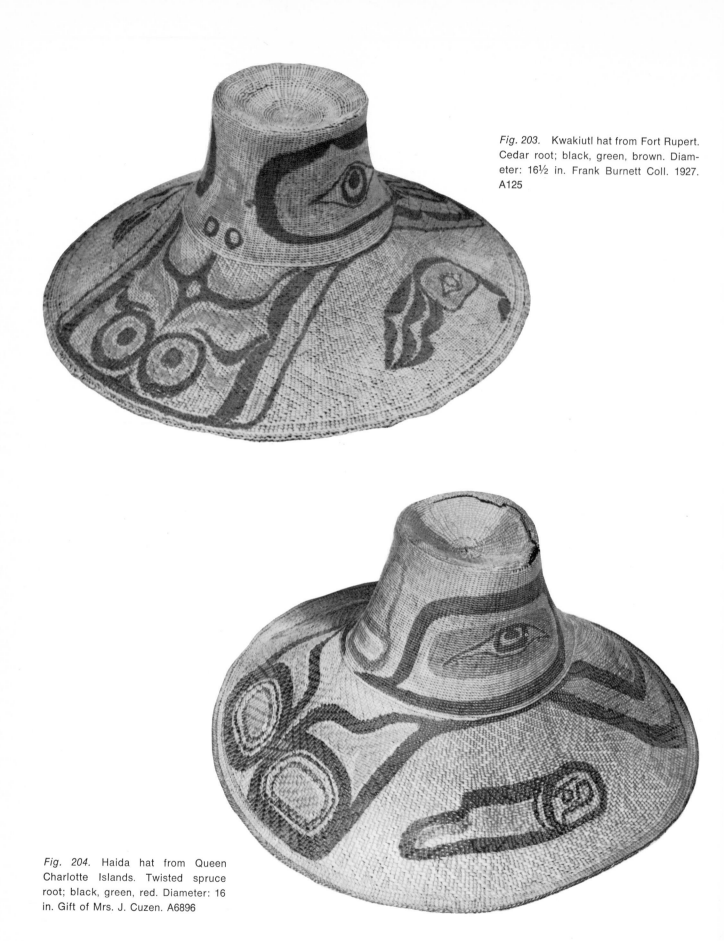

Fig. 203. Kwakiutl hat from Fort Rupert. Cedar root; black, green, brown. Diameter: 16½ in. Frank Burnett Coll. 1927. A125

Fig. 204. Haida hat from Queen Charlotte Islands. Twisted spruce root; black, green, red. Diameter: 16 in. Gift of Mrs. J. Cuzen. A6896

Fig. 205. Haida hat from Queen Charlotte Islands, with painted hawk design.
Twisted spruce root; black, red. Diameter: 18 in. Gift of Mrs. G. Galt 1954.
A6390

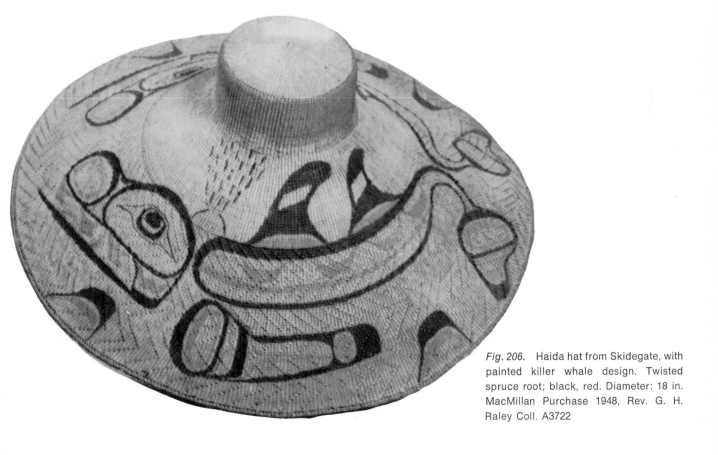

Fig. 206. Haida hat from Skidegate, with
painted killer whale design. Twisted
spruce root; black, red. Diameter: 18 in.
MacMillan Purchase 1948, Rev. G. H.
Raley Coll. A3722

Fig. 207. Haida hat from Queen Charlotte Islands, with painted design said to be shark's fin and kingfisher. Twisted spruce root; black, green, brown. Diameter: 16 in. Mrs. F. L. Beecher Coll. 1950. A4089

Fig. 208. Haida hat with painted killer whale design. Twisted spruce root; blue, black, brown. Diameter: 18 in. Museum Gift 1937, A. J. Buttimer Coll. A8343

Fig. 209. Kwakiutl hat from Bella Bella. Spruce root; black, red, green. Diameter: 16 in. Valedictory Gift 1931, Dr. G. E. Darby Coll. A1129

Fig. 210. Haida hat from Queen Charlotte Islands, with painted raven design. Twisted spruce root; black, red. Diameter: 16½ in. A. J. Buttimer Coll. 1937. A3238

Fig. 211. Haida hat from Queen Charlotte Islands, with painted design said to be a mountain goat. Twisted spruce root; black, green, red. Diameter: 17 in. Mrs. F. L. Beecher Coll. 1950. A4088

Fig. 212. Haida hat. Twisted spruce root; black, red, green. Diameter: 15 in. A. J. Buttimer Coll. 1937. A8341

189

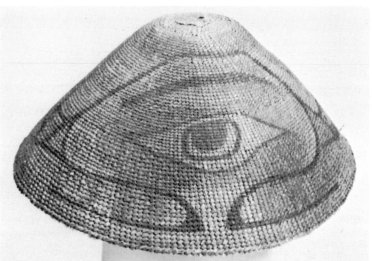

Fig. 213. (*Left, top to bottom*) Haida hat. Twisted spruce root; black, green. Diameter: 15 in. Museum Gift 1937, A. J. Buttimer Coll. A8344. Nootka hat from West Coast of Vancouver Island. Twisted spruce root; black, green, blue, red. Diameter: 17 in. MacMillan Purchase 1948. A3723. Salish rain hat from Fraser River. Twisted cedar rootlet; outside: brown, yellow; inside: blue, purple, black, white. Diameter: 14½ in. Donated by Mrs. Virginia Draper 1951. A1479. (*Above*) Kwakiutl hat from Kitamaat, collected about 1890; a potlatch hat with 4 rings, each representing a successful potlatch. Twisted cedar rootlet; black design. Diameter: 12½ in. MacMillan Purchase 1948, Rev. G. H. Raley Coll. A1465

Chiefs' Headdresses or Dancing Hats

Among the northern tribes, finely carved wooden crest badges attached to a head ring were traditional for all ceremonial Klasila wear. These *amhalayt,* as they were called by the Tsimshian, were copied by the Kwakiutl in the middle of the last century and constitute some of their finest crest carvings from then on. The Kwakiutl called them *yukweewae* (dancing forehead masks).

Fine carvers were employed for these headdresses (Pls. XI and XII; Figs. 214-27). A carved wooden frontal piece, inlaid with blue-green abalone shell glued with gum or pitch, was attached to a head ring of reinforced cedar bark and cloth. The top margin of the carved front was lined with a row of sea-lion whiskers that stood stiffly upright. Sometimes feathers were also used as decoration. The stiff sea-lion whiskers caught and held the eagle-down that was customarily strewn around at potlatches. A cloth or deerskin panel that covered the head and descended to the shoulders was sometimes attached to this elaborate headdress and then covered with white ermine skins, making an impressive and dignified chiefly adornment. Traditions of painting and the colors used varied.

Fig. 214. Kwakiutl chief's headdress from Alert Bay, with raven and Sisiutl design. Wood; green, blue, black, yellow. Height: 8½ in. MacMillan Purchase 1953. A3731

Fig. 215. Kwakiutl chief's headdress from King-come Inlet, with hawk design. Wood with abalone shell inlay missing; red, green, black. Height: 6¼ in. MacMillan Purchase 1953. A6149

Fig. 216. Kwakiutl chief's headdress from Sullivan Bay, with hawk design. Wood; green, black, red. Height: 5½ in. MacMillan Purchase 1952. A3839

Fig. 217. Kwakiutl chief's headdress from Fort Rupert, with raven design. Wood and abalone shell; black, blue, red. Height: 8 in. MacMillan Purchase 1953. A6273

Fig. 218. Kwakiutl chief's headdress from Allison Harbour, with hawk design. Wood and abalone shell, with glass eyes; black, green, blue, red. Height: 11 in. MacMillan Purchase 1953. A6322

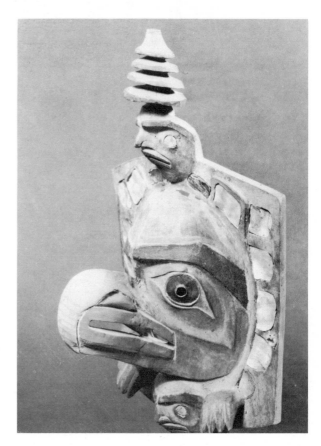

Fig. 219. (*Left to right, top*) Kwakiutl chief's headdress from King-come Inlet, with raven design. Wood and abalone shell; black, red, blue. Height: 9¼ in. MacMillan Purchase 1951. A6084. Kwakiutl chief's headdress from Kitamaat, with eagle design, used by Sonahed people up to 1888. Wood; brown, black, white. Length of plaque: 7½ in.: wingspread of eagle: 12 in. MacMillan Purchase 1948, Rev. G. H. Raley Coll. A4456. (*Bottom*) Kwakiutl chief's headdress from Sullivan Bay, with eagle design. Wood and abalone shell; green, red, black. MacMillan Purchase 1952. A4237. Bella Coola chief's head-dress. Wood and abalone shell; blue, red, black. Height: 11 in. Mac-Millan Purchase 1963. A8360

Fig. 220. Kwakiutl chief's headdress from Alert Bay, with sun and raven design. Wood, cloth, and sea lion whiskers; red, green, black. Height: 8½ in. MacMillan Purchase 1951. A6096

Fig. 221. Kwakiutl chief's headdress from Fort Rupert, with sun design, collected in 1885. Wood, abalone shell, and cedar bark; green, black. Height: 10½ in. MacMillan Purchase 1963. A8391

Fig. 222. Kwakiutl chief's headdress from Kitamaat, with double eagle design. Wood; black, red. Height: 6¼ in. MacMillan Purchase 1948, Rev. G. H. Raley Coll. A1736

Fig. 223. Kwakiutl chief's headdress from Blunden Harbour, with bear design. Wood with abalone shell inlay missing; red, yellow, black. Height: 8½ in. MacMillan Purchase 1953. A6333

Fig. 224. Tsimshian chief's headdress from Lakalzap. Wood and abalone shell; red, black. Height: 7¾ in. MacMillan Purchase 1948, Rev. G. H. Raley Coll. A1733

Fig. 225. Bella Coola chief's headdress, unfinished. Unpainted alderwood. Height: 11 in. MacMillan Purchase 1963. A8364

Fig. 226. Tsimshian chief's headdress from Hazelton. Unpainted wood. Height: 8½ in. MacMillan Purchase 1948. A4458

Fig. 227. Tsimshian chief's headdress from Aiyansh. Wood and abalone shell, with abalone shell teeth missing; red, blue, black. Height: 6 in. MacMillan Purchase 1948, Rev. G. H. Raley Coll. A1734

Helmet Headdresses

Headdresses of the "helmet" type, as distinguished from the chiefs' ceremonial dancing hats, were usually wood carvings representing family crest birds and worn on top of the head, with the button blanket completing the costume. The headdresses were held firmly in place by a ribbon or string tied under the chin, and were worn by both men and women.

Most of these were carved of solid wood, with a shell-like form hollowed out to fit over the head (Pl. XIII; Figs. 228-39). In some of them the carvings were attached to rings fitting around the head. Sometimes these headdresses were spectacular; the neck and wings of the heron illustrated in Plate XIII, for example, could be raised and lowered by strings.

Fig. 228. Kwakiutl loon or swan headdress, I of a set of 6, from Kingcome Inlet. Wood; black, white. Length: 19 in. MacMillan Purchase 1953. A6155

Fig. 229. Kwakiutl loon headdress from Village Island. Wood; black, red, green, yellow, purple. Length: 23 in. MacMillan Purchase 1952. A4162

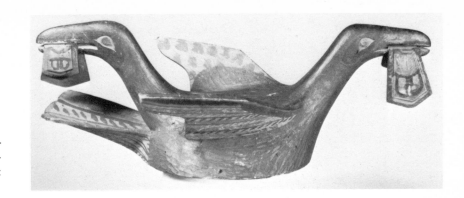

Fig. 230. Kwakiutl double loon head-dress with coppers, from Allison Harbour. Wood; black, green, red. Length: 19 in. MacMillan Purchase 1953. A6236

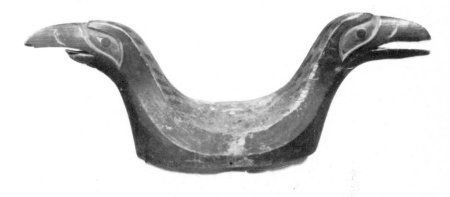

Fig. 231. Kwakiutl double raven head-dress from Fort Rupert. Wood; black, green, red. Length: 15½ in. MacMillan Purchase 1953. A6275

Fig. 232. Kwakiutl raven headdress from Alert Bay. Wood and plywood; black, red, white. Length: 20 in. Mac-Millan Purchase 1951. A6101

Fig. 233. Kwakiutl Thunderbird head-dress with movable wings, from Alert Bay, attributed to Willie Seaweed. Wood; red, orange, green, white, black. Length: 12 in. MacMillan Purchase 1951. A6090

Fig. 234. Kwakiutl Thunderbird head-dress from Blunden Harbour. Wood and cedar bark; red, orange, black, white. Length: 15 in. MacMillan Purchase 1953. A6219

Fig. 235. (*Above, left to right*) Kwakiutl hawk and killer whale headdress from Alert Bay. Wood decorated with plaid cotton and red feather; black, white, yellow. Length: 12½ in. MacMillan Purchase 1952. A4183. Kwakiutl killer whale headdress from Alert Bay. Wood, canvas, cloth, and fur; black, red, white, green. Length: 12 in. MacMillan Purchase 1951. A6103. (*Left*) Kwakiutl bear headdress from Alert Bay, made in 1900. Wood and sheep's wool with brass studs. Width: 15 in. MacMillan Purchase 1964. A8416

Fig. 236. Nootka hawk headdress from Kyuquot. Wood and baleen whiskers; green, white, orange, purple, black. Height: 12 in. MacMillan Purchase 1961. A7859

Fig. 237. Nootka hawk headdress from Nuchatlitz. Wood and sea lion whiskers; orange, green, maroon, silver. Height: 13 in. MacMillan Purchase 1961. A7858

Fig. 238. Nootka grouse headdress. Wood with tuft of twigs at top of head; yellow, green, red, white. Height: 11 in. MacMillan Purchase 1962. A8100

Fig. 239. Nootka grouse headdress. Wood, with tuft of twigs at top of head; yellow, green, red, white. Height: 11 in. MacMillan Purchase 1962. A8099

Jewelry and Cosmetics

Early jewelry consisted of dentalium shell necklaces; labrets of stone or ivory, which were inserted into the lower lips of women of rank in northern regions; pins of bone or ivory; and pendants and charms of carved ivory. With the advent of new trade goods new materials were adopted: brass and copper wire to be rolled into bracelet forms, and a variety of glass beads—red, dark blue, light blue, and brown, round or cylindrical, and in many sizes, which were bought from both Russian and European traders. These beads were combined with dentalium shells to make handsome necklaces. Figure 242 shows some of these ornaments which, although they were collected in different tribal regions, are typical of the Northwest Coast area generally.

Dark blue-green haliotis (abalone) shell, traded up from the Californian coast, was much favored. The contemporary generation of middle-aged people call the pieces about three inches square "the twenty-dollar" size, since they are said to have cost that amount of money. These squares of abalone shell were used to inlay masks, carvings, and headpieces. They were also sewn onto button blankets and cedar bark head rings.

Silver and gold coins were introduced by the Russians who settled in Alaska in 1798. Shortly afterward, the Indian craftsmen of the coast began to hammer the coins into flat bars which could be bent and incised with sharp lines in crest designs. Bracelets were worn by women of rank, usually several at a time. The practice of incising crest designs on silver and gold bracelets drew the attention of some very skilled craftsmen such as John

202

Cross of Skidegate. The finest bracelets have a slightly hollowed form, convex to the wrist (Figs. 240, 241). Among the Haida, silver and gold bracelets owned by the wife were pledged to her husband for his amassing of wealth for a potlatch or purchase. These were brought out on sticks, usually ten to a stick.

Hair was dressed with combs of wood, bone, or stone, but combs were not worn for decoration. Instead, hairpins and other ornaments called *tchenes,* made of iron and inlaid with shell, were popular with young girls, and women adorned their hair for festive occasions with pieces of red yarn and ribbon.

Some tattooing was done by most Northwest Coast groups, but the practice was common only among the Haida, whose high-ranking members wore black crest designs pricked into the chest, back, arms, and legs.

Face-painting for everyday wear was usually for cosmetic purposes, or as an over-all protection against sun, wind, and cold. For ritual occasions, elaborate designs colored red or black were applied and sometimes powdered over with a layer of bird's down.

Fig. 240. (Top to bottom, left) Kwakiutl bracelet from Sullivan Bay. Silver. Diameter: 2½ in. MacMillan Purchase 1955. A6172. Haida bracelet with bear head design, made by Charles Edenshaw. Silver. Diameter: 2½ in. MacMillan Purchase 1962. A8094. Haida bracelet with bear design, made by Bill Reid. Gold. Diameter: 2½ in. MacMillan Purchase 1961. A1501. *(Right)* Kwakiutl bracelet from Kingcome Inlet. Silver. Diameter: 2 in. MacMillan Purchase 1962. A3847. Haida bracelet with sea bear design, made by Bill Reid after a design by Charles Edenshaw. Silver. Diameter: 2½ in. Leon and Thea Koerner Foundation Purchase 1959. A1500

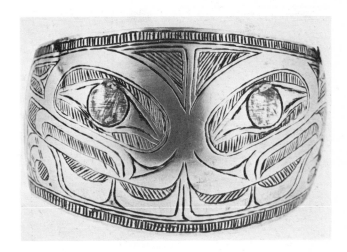

Fig. 241. (*Above*) Haida bracelet. Silver. Diameter: 2½ in. MacMillan Purchase 1963. A8411. (*Right, top to bottom*) Haida bracelet from Queen Charlotte Islands, made by Charles Edenshaw. Silver. Diameter: 2½ in. MacMillan Purchase 1962. A8093. Kwakiutl bracelet from Kingcome Inlet, with duck design. Silver. Diameter: 2¼ in. MacMillan Purchase 1952. A3848. Haida bracelet with eagle design, made by Bill Reid. Silver. Diameter: 2½ in. MacMillan Purchase 1963. A8412

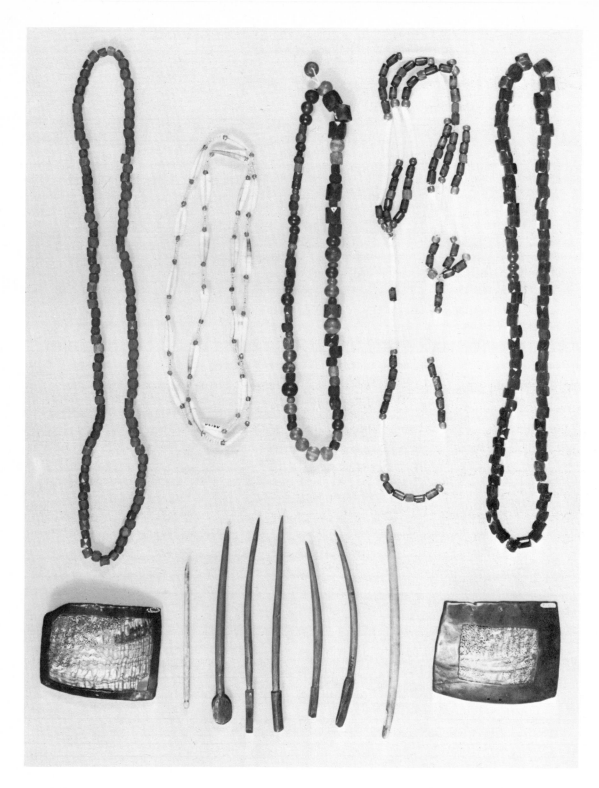

Fig. 242. Assorted jewelry. (*Top, left to right*) Glass trade beads, Russian type, origin unkown. A1726. Coast Salish dentalium shells interspersed with glass beads. A8130. Kwakiutl glass trade beads, English type. A6140. Tahltan dentalium shells and red glass Venetian beads. A3740. Nootka glass trade beads, English type. A8206. (*Bottom, left to right*) Kwakiutl "$20" size abalone shell backed by copper. A7881. Coast Salish bone blanket pin. A8178. 5 Kwakiutl vine maple hairpins. A3559. Haida bone nose skewer. A7176. Kwakiutl "$20" size abalone shell backed by copper. A7880

Ceremonial Staffs

The ceremonial staff, or "chief's talking stick" (Figs. 245, 246, 248, 249), carved and ornamented, was the badge of office of the speaker, who stood by the chief and relayed his sentiments to the gathered visitors. Other staffs, such as the *gwispeck,* were carried by the heralds who went from house to house to invite people to various events. These staffs were not always carved. The shaman also had a staff, an important part of his ritual gear, which was carved with the tokens and symbols of his vision and of supernatural spirits (Figs. 244, 247).

Fig. 243. Pair of Haida walking sticks from Queen Charlotte Islands, carved as wedding gifts by Charles Edenshaw for Rev. Collison's daughter and her groom. Wood with ivory handles, silver bands, and abalone shell inlay; serpents carved on each cane. Length: 3 ft. MacMillan Purchase 1960, Rev. W. E. Collison Coll. (*Left*) Frogs, A7090. (*Center*) Detail of A7090. (*Right*) Hawk, A7091

Fig. 244. Tsimshian shaman's staff from Kitsegukla. Unpainted wood. Length: 3 ft. 8 in. MacMillan Purchase 1962. A8230. (*Above*) 3 details

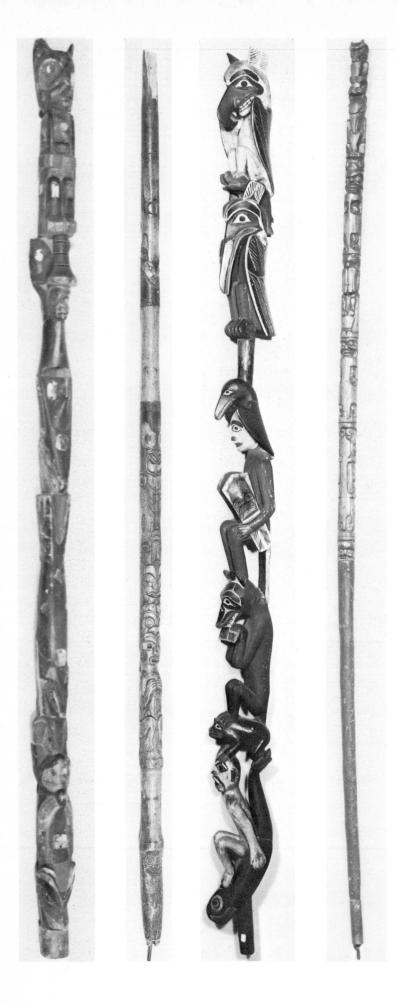

Fig. 245. (*Left to right*) Kwakiutl speaker's staff from Fort Rupert, illustrated in Curtis 1915: Vol. X, Pl. 333. Wood inlaid with abalone shell; black, red, green. Length: 5 ft. 5½ in. MacMillan Purchase 1962. A8140. Kwakiutl speaker's staff from New Vancouver Village. Varnished fir wood with some traces of red paint. Length: 6 ft. 4 in. MacMillan Purchase 1961. A7473. Kwakiutl speaker's staff from Bella Bella. Wood; green, brown, white, blue, red. Length: 6 ft. 3½ in. Dr. G. E. Darby Coll. 1949. A1927. Kwakiutl speaker's staff from Blunden Harbour. Varnished wood, the lower part painted green. Length: 4 ft. 9 in. Mac-Millan Purchase 1951. A3655. (*Above*) Detail of A3655

Fig. 246. Tsimshian speaker's staff from Kitkatlah, with carved eagle and heron design, shown with 2 details. Wood; black. Length: 35 in. MacMillan Purchase 1948, Rev. G. H. Raley Coll. A1762

Fig. 247. Haida shaman's staff from Queen Charlotte Islands, shown with 3 details. Unpainted wood inlaid with abalone shell. Length: 4 ft. 5 in. MacMillan Purchase 1960, Rev. W. E. Collison Coll. A7083

Fig. 248. Haida speaker's staff from Queen Charlotte Islands, shown with 2 details. Unpainted wood inlaid with abalone shell. Length: 4 ft. 6½ in. MacMillan Purchase 1960, Rev. W. E. Collison Coll. A7086

Fig. 249. Kwakiutl speaker's staff from Alert Bay. Wood; black, red. Length: 5 ft. 6 in. MacMillan Purchase 1951. A4035. (Above) Detail of A4035

213

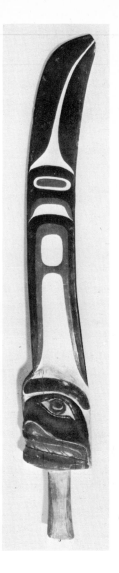

Fig. 250. (*Left to right*) Kwakiutl ceremonial staff from Alert Bay. Wood; black, white, red, with copper motif. Length: 5 ft. MacMillan Purchase 1953. A6029. Kwakiutl ceremonial staff from Turnour Island. Wood; black, red, with copper motif. Length: 4 ft. 2 in. MacMillan Purchase 1963. A8378. Salish spirit dance baton from Klemklemaletz, with bear design. Wood with deer hoof rattles; red, brown, black, white, orange. Length: 3 ft. 11 in. MacMillan Purchase 1962. A8141. Kwakiutl baton from Alert Bay, an imitation of a Tsimshian type. Wood; black, red, white, green. Length: 3 ft. 2 in. MacMillan Purchase 1953. A6165. Kwakiutl baton from Kingcome Inlet, with human head carved on handle. Wood; black, red. Length: 4 ft. MacMillan Purchase 1954. A3417

Feast Dishes

The feast was an invariable accompaniment to social gatherings, large or small. On ceremonial occasions when guests were being entertained, the food was served in crest dishes by the household members and passed out in the correct order of rank for that particular feast. The order varied, as we have seen, for Tsetseka, clan, or intertribal gatherings. The speaker spoke for the host, urging everyone to eat as much as he could. Food served depended upon the occasion, but consisted mainly of dried salmon, dried halibut, and smoked shellfish, with fish oil used as a condiment.

Feast dishes were part of the household crest belongings, and important ones were named. They varied in size. The first one used in a feast was a very large one which might be the size of a canoe, such as the twenty-foot Sisiutl feast dish shown in Figure 251 (see also Figs. 254, 257, 260-62). This contained generous portions of the food that was to be dispensed. Large ladles (Figs. 290-99) were used to serve food into smaller containers, which were placed before every four or six people.

Members of the household ladled food from these into individual serving dishes with smaller spoons. Small dishes of oil, in which the dried fish was dipped, were placed near at hand.

A Nootka whale display feast dish that was not used to serve food, but was carried through the village when the whale feast was announced, is shown in Figure 280 (A7851).

Most of the dishes were made of wood, either shaped from a hollowed-out log or formed of kerfed boards with convex sides. Kerfed wooden food dishes, illustrated in Figures 470-75, were made by grooving a cedar board and then steaming it so that it could be bent at right angles (see pp. 325-26).

Fig. 251. Kwakiutl Sisiutl feast dish from Turnour Island, attributed to Charlie James, 1907. Wood; green, black, red, white. Length: 20 ft. MacMillan Purchase 1950. A4147

Fig. 252. Kwakiutl Sisiutl feast dish from Kingcome Inlet, 1 of a pair with Fig. 253, and associated with the skull shown in Fig. 122 (A6160). Wood; green, blue, black. Width, including heads: 33 in. MacMillan Purchase 1954. A3413

Fig. 253. Kwakiutl Sisiutl feast dish from Kingcome Inlet, 1 of a pair with Fig. 252. Wood; green, blue, black. Width, including heads: 32¾ in. MacMillan Purchase 1954. A3414

Fig. 254. Kwakiutl feast dish from Campbell River in the shape of 2 Tsonokwa figures. Wood; some black and gray. Length: 7 ft. 5 in. MacMillan Purchase 1960. A4492

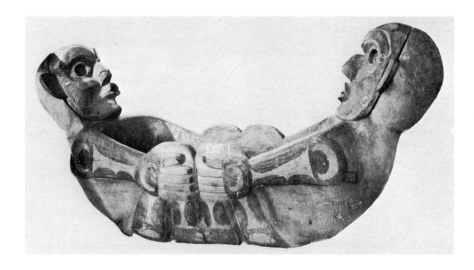

Fig. 255. Salish bear-shaped feast dish from Churchouse. Wood; black. Length: 24 in. MacMillan Purchase 1962. A8146

Fig. 256. Tsimshian bear-shaped oil dish from Skeena River. Shellacked wood and abalone shell. Length: 10½ in. MacMillan Purchase 1961. A7312

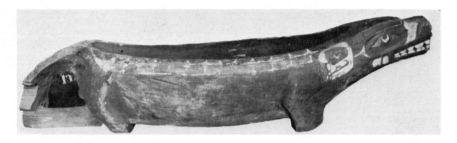

Fig. 257. Kwakiutl wolf-shaped feast dish from Kingcome Inlet. Wood; white, green, black, red. Length: 7 ft. 1 in. MacMillan Purchase 1951. A6937

Fig. 258. Kwakiutl wolf-shaped feast dish from Kingcome Inlet. Wood; traces of red paint on teeth. Length: 30 in. MacMillan Purchase 1951. A3669

Fig. 259. Kwakiutl wolf-shaped feast dish from Alert Bay, carved by Charlie James. Wood; black, green, red. Length: 12¼ in. Gift of the Lanning Family 1956. A6601

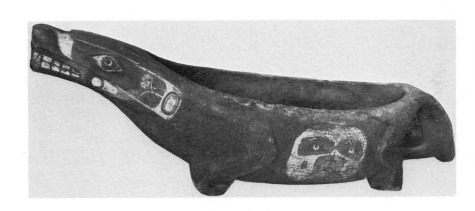

Fig. 260. Kwakiutl wolf-shaped feast dish from Kingcome Inlet. Wood; black, white, green, red. Length: 10 ft. 3 in. MacMillan Purchase 1952. A6557

Fig. 261. Kwakiutl wolf-shaped feast dish from Kingcome Inlet. Wood; white, green, black, red. Length: 7 ft. 1 in. MacMillan Purchase 1951. A6936

Fig. 262. Kwakiutl wolf-shaped feast dish from Kingcome Inlet, 1 of a pair. Wood, mostly unpainted, with touches of green and white. Length: 7 ft. 9 in. MacMillan Purchase 1950. A6938

Fig. 263. Kwakiutl feast dish from Kingcome Inlet, in the shape of 2 beavers. Unpainted wood. Length: 24 in. MacMillan Purchase 1951. A3668

Fig. 264. Pair of very old Kwakiutl feast dishes from Quatsino, made in the shape of 2 halves of a whale and commemorating the capture of the first whale by the culture hero Kula. Wood; black, red. Length (*left*): 26 in.; (*right*): 27 in. Mac-Millan Purchase 1948, Rev. G. H. Raley Coll. A1786, A1785

Fig. 265. Kwakiutl whale-shaped feast dish from Simoom Sound. Wood; brown, black, white, green. Length: 30½ in. MacMillan Purchase 1953. A6570

Fig. 266. Kwakiutl fish-shaped oil dish from Bella Bella. Wood with abalone shell eyes and operculum shell inlaid on back; black. Length: 10¾ in. Frank Burnett Coll. 1927. A1723

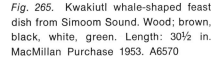

Fig. 267. Tlingit oil dish from Sitka, said to be in the shape of a flounder. Unpainted wood and turquoise glass trade beads. Length: 11 in. MacMillan Purchase 1962. A8061

Fig. 268. Kwakiutl seal-shaped oil dish. Wood, abalone and operculum shells; black. Length: 14 in. Gift of Mrs. Fyfe-Smith 1957. A6652

Fig. 269. Kwakiutl seal-shaped feast dish from Simoom Sound. Wood; white, black, red. Length: 29 in. Mac-Millan Purchase 1952. A3812

Fig. 270. Kwakiutl seal-shaped feast dish from Simoom Sound. Wood; white, black, red, green. Length: 29 in. MacMillan Purchase 1952. A3811

Fig. 271. Kwakiutl seal-shaped dish from Bella Bella. Wood; black, red. Length: 15 in. Gift of Frank Burnett 1927. A403

Fig. 272. Kwakiutl seal-shaped feast dish. Unpainted wood. Length: 7 ft. 2 in. Museum Purchase 1950. A7237

Fig. 273. (*Left*) Kwakiutl otter-shaped oil dish with carved eagle on lid, from Bella Bella. Wood; black, blue, pink. Length: 15 in. Frank Burnett Coll. 1927. A407. (*Right*) Kwakiutl beaver-shaped oil dish with lid, from Bella Bella. Wood; black, blue, red. Length: 15½ in. Frank Burnett Coll. 1927. A406

Fig. 274. (*Left*) Haida frog-shaped bowl from Queen Charlotte Islands, carved by Charles Edenshaw. Wood; black, red. Length: 9½ in. MacMillan Purchase 1960, Rev. W. E. Collison Coll. A7054. (*Right*) Haida frog-shaped oil dish from Queen Charlotte Islands. Wood inlaid with operculum shell; black. Length: 14 in. Gift of Mrs. J. Cuzen 1958. A6895

Fig. 275. (*Left*) Kwakiutl frog-shaped oil dish with lid, from Bella Bella. Wood; black, red. Length: 8½ in. Frank Burnett Coll. 1927. A405. (*Right*) Kwakiutl frog-shaped oil dish from Bella Bella. Wood; blue, black, red. Length: 7¾ in. Frank Burnett Coll. 1927. A404

Fig. 276. Tsimshian frog-shaped feast dish from Metlakatla. Wood with traces of green and black. Length: 7½ in. MacMillan Purchase 1948, Rev. G. H. Raley Coll. A1763

Fig. 277. (*Left*) Kwakiutl duck-shaped feast dish from Kingcome Inlet. Wood; gray, black, green, red, yellow. Length: 34 in. MacMillan Purchase 1951. A6566. (*Right*) Tlingit bird-shaped dish from Sitka. Wood; black, red. Length: 6½ in. MacMillan Purchase 1948, Rev. G. H. Raley Coll. A4260

Fig. 278. Haida food dish from Queen Charlotte Islands, with hawk design. Wood and abalone shell; black, red. Length: 20 in. MacMillan Purchase 1960, Rev. W. E. Collison Coll. A7082

Fig. 279. Kwakiutl feast dish in the shape of the bottom of a bird. Length: 30 in. Museum Purchase 1959. A3476

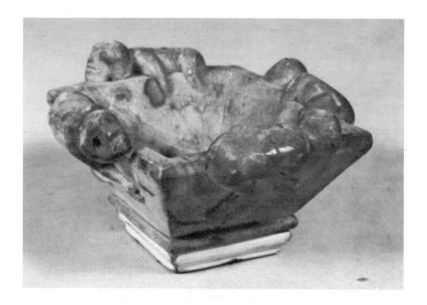

Fig. 280.   (Top) 2 views of Kwakiutl canoe-shaped oil dish from Kitamaat. Wood; black. Length: 9½ in. MacMillan Purchase 1948, Rev. G. H. Raley Coll. A1798 (Above) Nootka canoe-shaped festival dish from Nuchatlitz, with painted whale on the side, obtained by marriage from Rivers Inlet. This was used not for eating but for display in announcing the whale feast. Wood; black, green, red, white. Length: 5 ft. MacMillan Purchase 1961. A7851. (Left) Haida dish from Queen Charlotte Islands. Unpainted wood. Width: 7 in. MacMillan Purchase 1960, Rev. W. E. Collison Coll. A7057

Fig. 281. Kwakiutl canoe-shaped feast dish from Alert Bay. Wood. Length: 29¼ in. MacMillan Purchase 1962. A7953

Fig. 282. Tsimshian food dish from Kitkatlah. Wood. Length: 3 ft. 8½ in. MacMillan Purchase 1948, Rev. G. H. Raley Coll. A3388

Fig. 283. Salish food dish from Duncan. Wood. Length: 25 in. MacMillan Purchase 1962. A8133

Fig. 284. Kwakiutl canoe-shaped food dish. Adzed wood studded with brass nails. Length: 25½ in. MacMillan Purchase 1948, Rev. G. H. Raley Coll. A3389

Fig. 285. Kwakiutl canoe-shaped feast dish. Wood. Length: 27½ in. MacMillan Purchase 1948, Rev. G. H. Raley Coll. A6523

Fig. 286. Salish feast dish from Musqueam Reserve, made for a potlatch in 1895. Wood. Length: 3 ft. 11 in. Gift of Mr. Peter Hansen 1955. A6034

Fig. 287. Salish feast dish from Musqueam Reserve, made for a potlatch in 1895. Wood. Length: 3 ft. 9 in. Gift of Mr. Peter Hansen 1955. A6033

Feast Ladles and Spoons

Large feast ladles were generally made of wood, as were some plain eating spoons, although some smaller ladles were made of mountain sheep horn. The spoons most valued were the crest spoons of mountain goat horn (Pl. XVI A; Figs. 288, 289, 294, 296, 299). These delicate sculptured objects were manufactured mainly by the northern tribes, but they were eagerly sought by all other tribes and occasionally made by them as well. The horn was boiled to make it soft enough to carve, and was shaped in a two-piece wooden mold. Usually the bowl was made from another piece of horn and riveted onto the handle, sometimes with a small fragment of native copper. A bowl of different type of horn from that of the handle, such as mountain sheep, might be employed to provide variation in color and texture. The spoon handle was carved with a succession of small crest figures, following the tapering shape of the horn itself, and was sometimes inlaid with abalone shell. These small spoons were kept by the guests after the feast as one of the gifts of the occasion.

One further item of ceremonial eating was the slender spatula-shaped soapberry spoon, made of wood and used to whip soapberries *(Shepherdia canadensis)* into a froth for a dessert. The soapberry spoons shown in Figures 299 (A1566) and 300 are undecorated, but others were highly ornamented.

Fig. 288. (Left to right) Haida spoon from Queen Charlotte Islands. Mountain goat horn with sheep horn handle. Length: 11 in. MacMillan Purchase 1960. Rev. W. E. Collison Coll. A7141. Kwakiutl spoon from Douglas Channel. Horn. Length: 10¼ in. MacMillan Purchase 1948, Rev. G. H. Raley Coll. A1670. Haida spoon from Queen Charlotte Islands. Mountain goat horn. Length: 10¼ in. MacMillan Purchase 1960, Rev. W. E. Collison Coll. A7125

Fig. 289. (Left to right) Haida spoon from Queen Charlotte Islands. Mountain goat horn. Length: 10 in. MacMillan Purchase 1960, Rev. W. E. Collison Coll. A7131. Tsimshian spoon from Kispiox; very old. Mountain goat horn. Length: 10 in. MacMillan Purchase 1951. A3737. Kwakiutl spoon from Kitamaat, with carved eagle on handle. Horn. Length: 13 in. MacMillan Purchase 1948, Rev. G. H. Raley Coll. A1711

227

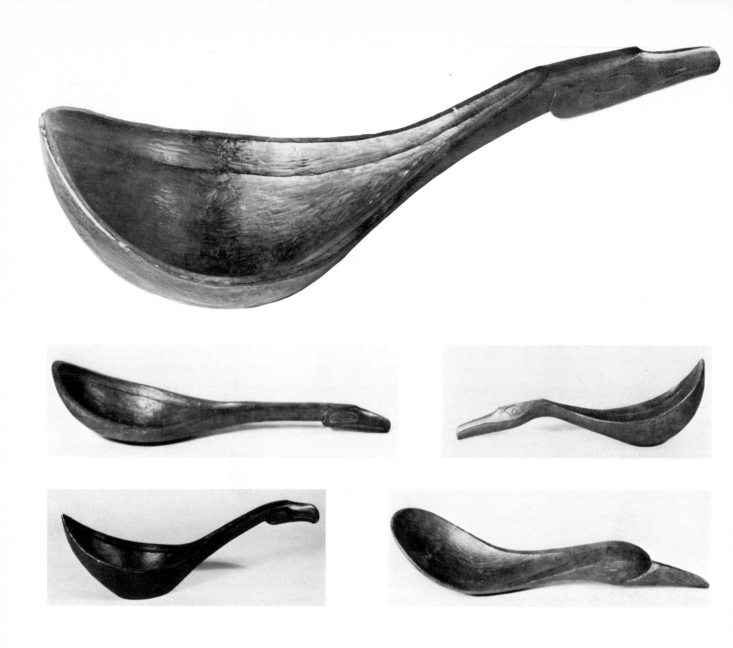

Fig. 290. (*Top*) Kwakiutl ladle from Kitamaat, with bird's head design. Wood; black. Length: 29 in. MacMillan Purchase 1948, Rev. G. H. Raley Coll. A6522. (*Top to bottom, left*) Tsimshian bird-shaped ladle from Kitsegukla. Natural wood with red paint in beak. Length: 3 ft. 2 in. MacMillan Purchase 1948, Rev. G. H. Raley Coll. A3391. Kwakiutl ladle from Kitlope. Cedar with eagle's head design. Length: 31 in. MacMillan Purchase 1948, Rev. G. H. Raley Coll. A1663. Kwakiutl bird-shaped ladle from Kitlope. Wood. Length: 18 in. MacMillan Purchase 1948, Rev. G. H. Raley Coll. A1565. (*Right*) Tsimshian bird-shaped ladle from Kispiox; very old. Cedar wood. Length: 3 ft. MacMillan Purchase 1948, Rev. G. H. Raley Coll. A3482. Kwakiutl ladle from Kitkatlah, with bird's head design. Wood. Length: 24 in. MacMillan Purchase 1948, Rev. G. H. Raley Coll. A1662

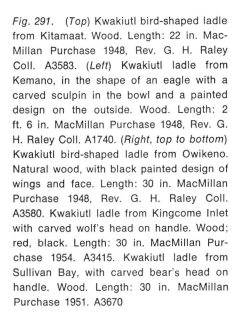

Fig. 291. (Top) Kwakiutl bird-shaped ladle from Kitamaat. Wood. Length: 22 in. Mac-Millan Purchase 1948, Rev. G. H. Raley Coll. A3583. (Left) Kwakiutl ladle from Kemano, in the shape of an eagle with a carved sculpin in the bowl and a painted design on the outside. Wood. Length: 2 ft. 6 in. MacMillan Purchase 1948, Rev. G. H. Raley Coll. A1740. (Right, top to bottom) Kwakiutl bird-shaped ladle from Owikeno. Natural wood, with black painted design of wings and face. Length: 30 in. MacMillan Purchase 1948, Rev. G. H. Raley Coll. A3580. Kwakiutl ladle from Kingcome Inlet with carved wolf's head on handle. Wood; red, black. Length: 30 in. MacMillan Purchase 1954. A3415. Kwakiutl ladle from Sullivan Bay, with carved bear's head on handle. Wood. Length: 30 in. MacMillan Purchase 1951. A3670

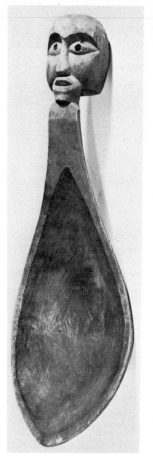

Fig. 292. (*Left to right*) Kwakiutl Tsonokwa feast ladle from Kingcome Inlet. Unpainted wood. Length: 3 ft. 2 in. MacMillan Purchase 1952. A3802. Kwakiutl ladle from Sullivan Bay, with carved human head on handle. Length: 3 ft. MacMillan Purchase 1953. A4284. Kwakiutl ladle from Sullivan Bay, with carved human head on handle. Wood. Length: 3 ft. MacMillan Purchase 1951. A3671

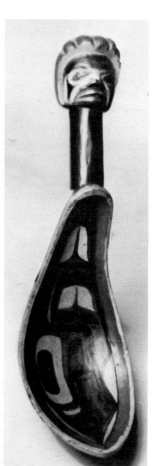

Fig. 293. (*Left to right*) Kwakiutl ladle from Bella Bella, with human head on handle. Wood; black, red, green, brown, blue. Length: 17 in. Valedictory Gift 1931, Dr. and Mrs. G. E. Darby. A1355. Kwakiutl ladle from Kingcome Inlet, with carved eagle on handle. Wood; red, green. Length: 4 ft. MacMillan Purchase 1954. A6428. Kwakiutl ladle from Kingcome Inlet, with carved eagle on handle. Wood; black, green. Length: 4 ft. MacMillan Purchase 1954. A6427

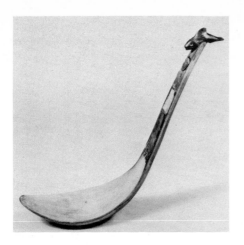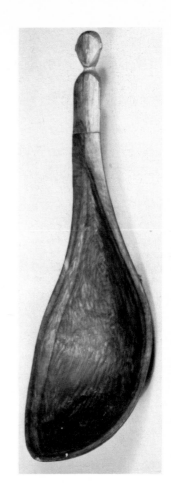

Fig. 294. (*Left to right*) Haida spoon from Queen Charlotte Islands, with killer whale design carved on handle. Horn inlaid with abalone shell. Length: 13 in. MacMillan Purchase 1960, Rev. W. E. Collison Coll. A7120. Kwakiutl spoon from Kitlope, with carved frog on handle. Wood. Length: 11 in. MacMillan Purchase 1948, Rev. G. H. Raley Coll. A1715. Kwakiutl ladle from Kitamaat, with human figure carved in outline on handle. Wild apple wood. Length: 3 ft. MacMillan Purchase 1948, Rev. G. H. Raley Coll. A3390

Fig. 295. Kwakiutl ladle from Turnour Island, with handle carved in the form of a sea lion. Wood. Length: 4 ft. 3 in. MacMillan Purchase 1963. A8377

Fig. 296. (*Left to right*) Feast ladle. Wood, with brass-rimmed lathe-turned knob. Length: 15 in. MacMillan Purchase 1961. A7285. Haida ladle from Queen Charlotte Islands. Horn. Length: 18½ in. MacMillan Purchase 1960, Rev. W. E. Collison Coll. A7100. Kwakiutl ladle. Horn inlaid with abalone shell. Length: 19 in. MacMillan Purchase 1961. A7534

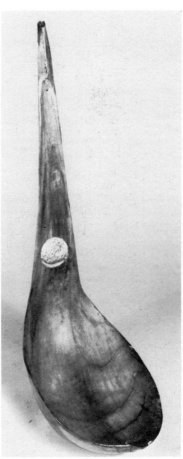

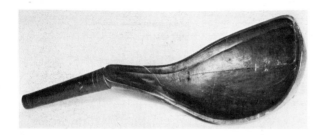

Fig. 297. (*Left to right, top*) Salish ladle from Koksilah. Unpainted wood. Length: 15 in. MacMillan Purchase 1948, Rev. G. H. Raley Coll. A4465. Tsimshian canoe-shaped ladle from Lakalzap. Wood; black. Length: 23 in. MacMillan Purchase 1948, Rev. G. H. Raley Coll. A8339. (*Bottom*) Kwakiutl ladle from Bella Bella. Wood. Length: 30 in. MacMillan Purchase 1948, Rev. G. H. Raley Coll. A6713. Salish ladle. Wood. Length: 15 in. MacMillan Purchase 1961. A8236

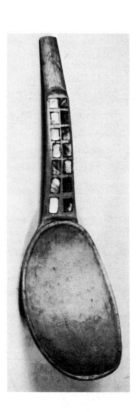

Fig. 298. (*Left to right*) Ladle, probably Tsimshian. Wood. Length: 26 in. MacMillan Purchase 1961. A7303. Kwakiutl ladle from Kingcome Inlet; very old. Wood. Length: 24 in. MacMillan Purchase 1952. A3801. Haida ladle from Queen Charlotte Islands. Unpainted wood inlaid with abalone shell. Length: 21½ in. MacMillan Purchase 1960, Rev. W. E. Collison Coll. A7101. Kwakiutl ladle from Gilford Island. Wood inlaid with abalone shell. Length: 12½ in. MacMillan Purchase 1953, Rev. G. H. Raley Coll. A4459

Fig. 299. (Left to right)
Kwakiutl spoon from Kitamaat.
Horn. Length: 14 in. MacMillan
Purchase 1948, Rev. G. H.
Raley Coll. A1714. Tsimshian
ladle from Nass River. Sheep's
horn. Length: 11 in. MacMillan
Purchase 1948, Rev. G. H.
Raley Coll. A1589. Kwakiutl
ladle. An old ladle of yellow
cedar, with a modern painting
in red, black, green, yellow,
white. Length: 28 in. MacMillan
Purchase 1961. A7304. Soapberry spoon, a very old form,
from Kitlope. Wood. Length:
11½ in. MacMillan Purchase
1948, Rev. G. H. Raley Coll.
A1566

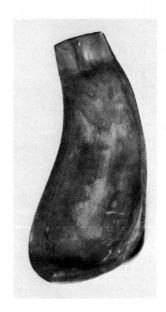
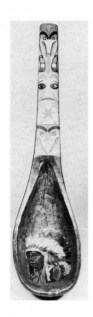

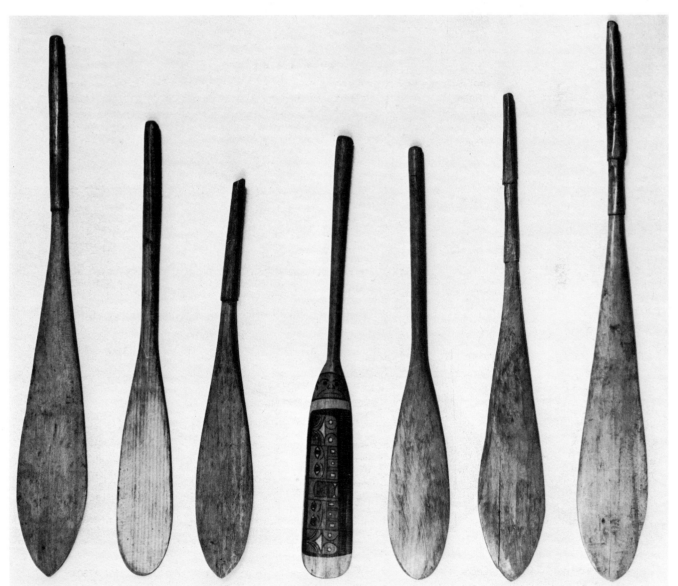

Fig. 300. Soapberry spoons. Wood. (*Left to right*) A1674 (Port Simpson), A1675 (Port Simpson), A6534 (Port Simpson),
A1567 (Kitlope), A1658 (Kitlope), A1611 (Port Simpson), A1659 (Kitamaat)

Baskets and Mats

The women of the Northwest Coast gathered natural fibers, prepared them, and wove them into baskets, mats, hats, and the clothing of everyday wear. In ordinary domestic life baskets were used to gather, store, and even cook foodstuffs. Made in a variety of forms and sizes, they were a substitute for pottery, which never developed in this region. Baskets were also used to store personal trinkets and jewelry.

Very fine baskets, embellished with crest decorations, were given as part of the valued gifts of the potlatch, and the workmanship was appreciated by all (Pl. XVI D; Figs. 301, 302). The crest design might be either woven in or painted on.

Mats were made generally for daily use, to be spread on the ground under the bowls of food at mealtime, to sit on, or as bed covers at night. Fine mats, often decorated with the family crest, were used for guests and were also given as part of the potlatch gifts (Fig. 303).

Fig. 301. 2 views of Haida basket from Queen Charlotte Islands, with painted frog design. Twined spruce root; black, red. Diameter of top: 7 in. MacMillan Purchase 1960, Rev. W. E. Collison Coll. A7178

Fig. 302. (*Right*) Haida basket from Queen Charlotte Islands, with painted killer whale design. Twined spruce root; brown. Diameter of top: 5½ in. MacMillan Purchase 1960, Rev. W. E. Collison Coll. A7190

Fig. 303. (*Below*) Kwakiutl mat from Alert Bay. Cedar bark with painted designs of killer whale and Thunderbird; black, red, brown. Length: 6 ft. 8 in. Gift of Mr. and Mrs. A. E. MacMillan 1960. A7278

Potlatch Properties

A number of objects associated with the potlatch are illustrated in Figures 305-7. Of special interest is a headdress worn by the official who directed the sequence of events in the potlatch by a series of whistle signals (Fig. 305). A duck with weighted strings which was whirled among the guests, who were "paid for their pains" if they were hit by it, is shown in Plate XIV B. The ceremonial display board shown in Figure 306, called *gisukstola*, was a box lid used in the transfer of marriage privileges.

Fig. 304. (*Above and right*) Kwakiutl potlatch bird from Quatsino, with a cannibal face on the bottom. Unpainted wood. Length: 28 in. MacMillan Purchase 1962. A8283

Fig. 305. (*Right*) Nootka headpiece from Kyuquot, said to have been carried by the man who gave the whistle signals to order the sequence of events in the potlatch. Wood with metal dome on each side of head; black, blue, white. Height: 9½ in. MacMillan Purchase 1962. A7982

Fig. 306. (*Below*) Kwakiutl ceremonial box lid from Campbell River, used as a display board in the marriage transfer of privileges. Wood set with otter teeth; the black painted design has mostly worn off. Length: 34 in. MacMillan Purchase 1960. A7281

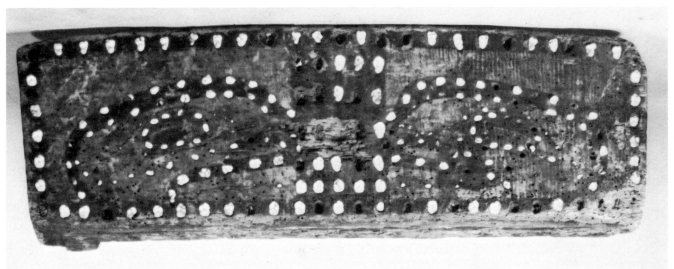

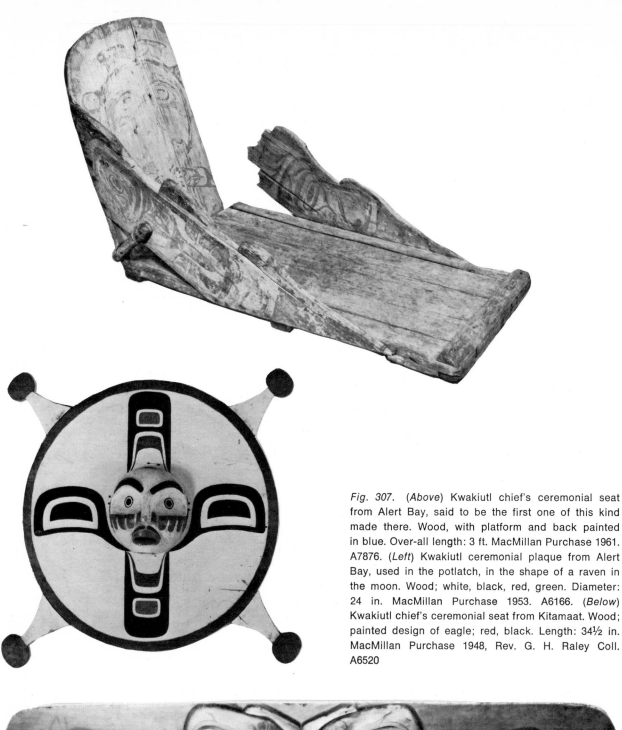

Fig. 307. (Above) Kwakiutl chief's ceremonial seat from Alert Bay, said to be the first one of this kind made there. Wood, with platform and back painted in blue. Over-all length: 3 ft. MacMillan Purchase 1961. A7876. (Left) Kwakiutl ceremonial plaque from Alert Bay, used in the potlatch, in the shape of a raven in the moon. Wood; white, black, red, green. Diameter: 24 in. MacMillan Purchase 1953. A6166. (Below) Kwakiutl chief's ceremonial seat from Kitamaat. Wood; painted design of eagle; red, black. Length: 34½ in. MacMillan Purchase 1948, Rev. G. H. Raley Coll. A6520

Komokwa Masks

Of major importance in Kwakiutl myth, Komokwa was King of the Undersea World, Master and Protector of the Seals, who were a symbol of wealth. His name means "Wealthy One," and he ruled from a great, rich house under the water. His house posts were live sea lions, who guarded the entrance. The house contained great wealth in blankets, coppers, and other treasures. Many human supplicants of legendary history tried to reach this kingdom, and those ancestral heroes who achieved their goal became wealthy and powerful, returning to their home village with magical boxes full of treasure.

One of Komokwa's other names was Copper Maker, and he married a high-ranking woman named Born To Be Copper Maker Woman—Tlakwa-kilayokwa—a very high-ranking name among Kwakiutl women. A myth of the Bella Bella claimed that it was her return home with various of Komokwa's gifts that was the occasion of the first Dluwalakha dance.

As ruler of the sea, Komokwa was associated with loons, seals, octopods, killer whales, and sculpins. This association was emphasized by the presence of several masked representatives of these, which accompanied him in the dance. Sometimes they were also represented by symbols on the masks of Komokwa.

Komokwa is also associated with rising tides and whirlpools. Among the Wikeno, when Komokwa was about to enter the dance house attendants rushed in to report that the ocean was rising far above high-tide line. Later, seemingly terrified, they reported that the water was nearly up to the door. Komokwa then entered (Drucker 1940:208).

One of the most beautifully carved masks in the museum collection, the mask of Komokwa illustrated in Plate XX, was associated with a woman's face mask when purchased from its owner (Pl. XXVIII A). This probably represents Komokwa's wife, for the two were undoubtedly made by the same carver, probably as a pair.

An interesting point of identification associated with the Komokwa masks concerns the round protuberances on the masks seen in Figures 317 (A6241), 318 (A8415), and 319 (A6240). These were said by Mungo Martin to be octopod tentacle suckers. Another informant said, however, "These are air bubbles," and a third stated, "These are sea anenomes eating." All of these identifications clearly point to Komokwa's undersea nature, and it is likely that one of the three is correct. A somewhat higher probability might be attached to the claim that they are suckers, since these are frequently clearly carved on halibut hooks, on which octopus was traditionally used as bait.

Fig. 308. Kwakiutl Komokwa mask from Sullivan Bay, with duck perched on head. Wood, with canvas neck and back of duck; black, red, green, white. Height of mask and duck: 34 in. MacMillan Purchase 1953. A4364

Fig. 309. (*Left*) Kwakiutl Komokwa mask from Smith Inlet, with loon perched on head. Wood; black, gray, red, green, white, orange. Height of mask and loon: 20½ in. MacMillan Purchase 1953. A6178. (*Right*) Kwakiutl Komokwa mask from Bella Bella, with rotating gulls on a starfish. Wood; red, black, white, green. Height: 17½ in. MacMillan Purchase 1951. A3634

Fig. 310. (*Above*) Kwakiutl Komokwa mask from Alert Bay, with a starfish with 9 curved 12-inch rays; said to have been last used around 1900. Wood with copper eyebrows; white, green, red, black, with orange rays. MacMillan Purchase 1953. A6164

Fig. 311. (*Right*) Kwakiutl Komokwa mask from Sullivan Bay, with duck on top of head. Wood; green, black, red. Height of mask and duck: 27¼ in. MacMillan Purchase 1951. A3686

Fig. 313. Kwakiutl Komokwa mask from Smith Inlet, said to have been made by Willie Seaweed in 1938. Wood; white, black, green, red. Height: 16 in. MacMillan Purchase 1953. A4289

Fig. 312. Kwakiutl Komokwa mask from Smith Inlet. Wood; black, brown, white, with red lips. Height: 12½ in. MacMillan Purchase 1953. A6351

Fig. 314. (*Left*) Kwakiutl Komokwa mask from Alert Bay. Wood and shredded cedar bark; white, black, green, red. Height: 12½ in. MacMillan Purchase 1952. A4242. (*Right*) Kwakiutl Komokwa mask from Smith Inlet. Wood; green, white, black, red. Height: 15 in. MacMillan Purchase 1953. A6177

Fig. 315. (*Left to right*) Kwakiutl Komokwa mask from Sullivan Bay. Wood; black, green, white, red. Height: 12 in. MacMillan Purchase 1951. A3681. Kwakiutl Komokwa mask from Sullivan Bay. Wood; gray, black, green, red. Height: 12 in. MacMillan Purchase 1951. A3683. Kwakiutl Komokwa mask from Gilford Island. Wood; red, green, black. Height: 11 in. MacMillan Purchase 1962. A8102

Fig. 316. (*Left*) Kwakiutl Komokwa mask from Blunden Harbour. Wood; green, red, black. Height: 11½ in. Museum Purchase 1953. A6239. (*Right*) Kwakiutl Komokwa mask from Alert Bay. Wood, cedar bark, and copper; red, green, white. Height: 13 in. MacMillan Purchase 1952. A4246

Fig. 317. (*Left*) Kwakiutl Komokwa mask from Blunden Harbour. Wood; red, white, green, black. Height: 20 in. Museum Purchase 1953. A5241. (*Right*) Kwakiutl Komokwa mask from Kingcome Inlet. Wood and shredded cedar bark; black, maroon, red, white, brown. Height: 12 in. MacMillan Purchase 1951. A3561

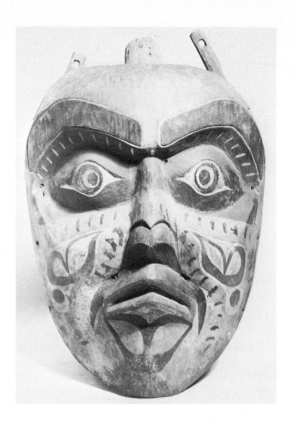

Fig. 318. (*Left*) Kwakiutl Komokwa mask from Quatsino, made in 1900. Wood; red, black, green. Height: 13½ in. MacMillan Purchase 1964. A8415. (*Right*) Kwakiutl Komokwa mask from Gilford Island. Wood; yellow, red, black. Height: 14 in. MacMillan Purchase 1952. A3822

Fig. 319. (*Left*) Kwakiutl Komokwa mask from Blunden Harbour. Wood; red, white, green, black. Height: 17 in. MacMillan Purchase 1953. A6240. (*Right*) Kwakiutl Komokwa mask from Sullivan Bay. Wood; black, green, white, red. Height: 11½ in. MacMillan Purchase 1951. A3682

Fish, Pugwis, and Killer Whale Masks

Fish masks (Pls. XXIV B, XXVIII B; Figs. 320-24) were sometimes highly naturalistic in representation, with self-explanatory features. In general, masks of sea creatures other than the killer whale had certain recognizable characteristics. Nose forms were either not prominent or flat. Usually there was a scalloped gill form around the cheeks or jaw, and sometimes even the forehead. Often the tail was slightly bifurcated to represent a fish tail, in contrast to the strongly bifurcated tail of the killer whale, or a fin symbol might appear as part of the facial design. There was a tendency to use white paint for facial coloring. Most of these masks had round eyes. Masks of the salmon (see Fig. 323), which was associated in the myths with twins, were always made in pairs, and these could be worn by any twin regardless of his inherited right.

In the case of Pugwis, or Man of the Sea, whom Boas calls Merman, the rounded contours of the face point downward to two large front teeth (Figs. 325, 326). Round eyes and gills are also characteristic.

The killer whale was an important character of Northwest Coast mythology, generally as a clan ancestor associated with sea beings, particularly Komokwa, sculpins, and loons. It was also associated with coppers, property disposition, and wealth. The killer whale was generally represented by masks so large that they might be called body masks, since they partially covered the body. When such a mask was worn it was necessary for the dancer to lean forward so as to bear the weight with his shoulder and back muscles, using the back of his arms to help support it. His hands were thus left free to manipulate the strings that moved the various appendages; his lower body and legs were concealed beneath a long cape of cedar bark fringe. This position and the covering of the dancer made it appear that the killer whale was floating or swimming whenever the dancer moved. In Tsetseka season the killer whales would arrive at the dance from the edge of the water as though they had just come up from the depths of the sea. Usually several killer whales swam in together, blowing and puffing.

Plates VII and VIII, and Figure 324 illustrate these body masks, complete with side fins, dorsal fins, and tails, all of which can be made to move sideways, back and forth, and up and down by pulling appropriate strings. In addition, three of the masks have movable lower jaws.

Fig. 320. (Left) Kwakiutl-style halibut mask from West Coast of Vancouver Island. Wood; black, red. Height: 14 in. MacMillan Purchase 1948, Rev. G. H. Raley Coll. A1750. (Right) Kwakiutl halibut mask from Alert Bay. Wood; black, red. Height: 13 in. Leon and Thea Koerner Foundation Grant 1957. A6801

Fig. 321. (Left) Kwakiutl Atlakim fish mask from Blunden Harbour. Wood and cedar bark; black, gray, silver, red, white. Height: 9½ in. MacMillan Purchase 1953. A6235. (Right) Kwakiutl Atlakim fish mask from Blunden Harbour. Wood and cedar bark; silver, black, red, orange. Height: 10 in. MacMillan Purchase 1953. A6215

Fig. 322. (*Left*) Kwakiutl bullhead fish mask from Sullivan Bay, part of the Atlakim series. Wood and cedar bark; red, green, black. Length: 17 in. MacMillan Purchase 1953. A6168. (*Right*) Kwakiutl "supernatural codfish" mask from Blunden Harbour. Wood and cedar bark, with copper ears; silver, gray, black, white, brown. Length: 15 in. MacMillan Purchase 1953. A6222

Fig. 323. (*Above*) Kwakiutl fish mask from Alert Bay. Wood; white, black, red. Height: 12 in. MacMillan Purchase 1953. A6167. (*Right, top to bottom*) Kwakiutl salmon mask from Village Island. Wood; red, orange, black, green. Height: 13 in. MacMillan Purchase 1952. A4155. Kwakiutl Atlakim salmon mask from Village Island. Wood and cedar bark; red, white, black. MacMillan Purchase 1952. A4161

Fig. 324. (*Above, left to right*) Kwakiutl fish mask from Gilford Island. Wood and cedar bark; brown, cream, black, green. Height: 12 in. Mac-Millan Purchase 1951. A3663. Inner face of Kwakiutl killer whale mask from Village Island. Wood; gray, white, black, green, red. Length: 16 in. MacMillan Purchase 1961. A7484. (*Right*) Kwakiutl killer whale mask from Bella Bella. Wood; green, red, black. Width: 4 ft. 7 in. Dr. G. E. Darby Valedictory Gift 1931. A1973. (*Below*) Kwakiutl killer whale mask from Kingcome Inlet, with movable fins, tail, and jaw. Wood; black, red, white, green. Length: 6 ft. 5 in. MacMillan Purchase 1953. A1596

Fig. 325. (*Left*) Kwakiutl Pugwis mask from Sullivan Bay. Wood; black, green, red, white. Height: 11 in. MacMillan Purchase 1953. A6303

Fig. 326. (*Below*) Kwakiutl Pugwis mask from Kingcome Inlet, with duck on top of head, made by Mungo Martin in 1911; cf. Boas 1908: Vol. V, Pl. XL, No. 4. Wood; gray, green, red, black, white. Height of mask and duck: 15½ in.; wingspread: 28 in. MacMillan Purchase 1951. A3659

Animal Masks

There were a number of birds, fish, and other animals that had no major role in the dances and no magic tricks, but were part of the clan myths and came in when these were re-enacted. The dancers who portrayed these performed mimetically, imitating the typical cries and methods of locomotion—flying, swimming, waddling, or rolling. Their masks were usually realistic representations.

The otters shown in Figures 327 and 328 were identified by Mungo Martin as land otters, distinguished from sea otters. The frog (Fig. 366, 367 [A8057]) was associated with coppers in various myth contexts. When the frog looked down into the water and saw the wealthy house of Komokwa and his wife, he was given the privilege of cutting the copper. Figure 366 has teeth of copper symbolic of this privilege.

There were several dog (Wawasleega) dances among the Kwakiutl. The mask shown in Figure 329 is the only one in the museum collection.

The deer (Fig. 330) had the character of being very sly and sharp. He often defeated enemies, such as wolves, not only by his wits but by his supernatural gifts. One of these mentioned in mythology was a "fog box" which, when opened, let out such a cloud of fog that pursuers were completely stopped.

There were two grizzly bear characters among the Kwakiutl. The Hamatsa grizzly bear (Nanes Bakbakwalanooksiwae), one of the high-ranking characters of the Hamatsa series, had no mask but painted his face red to symbolize a voracious bear mouth and wore a costume of bearskin and long wooden claws. Figure 338 illustrates a carved bear claw from Bella Coola, originally attached at the wrist to a bearskin costume. The Dluwalakha grizzly bear dancer wore not only a fur costume but also a mask. He was more of a comic buffoon, who was brought in during a lull in the proceedings and danced in a burly and comical way. A myth recounted by Boas mentions that the character Grizzly Bear was an excellent hunter because he had a powerful grizzly bear mask to put on when he wished to obtain game.

Bear masks (Fig. 331-37) were characterized by a certain massivity of head and muzzle carving. The muzzle was shorter and heavier than that of a wolf, with a square end. Teeth were usually carved in the jaw and were prominent, although short and not sharply pointed. Often no ears were indicated. The eye was generally a simple eye form, and the nostril was wide and flaring with a tendency to roundness. Bear masks were usually dark in color, brown or black. Often the back of the head was covered with a piece of black fur.

Among the Kwakiutl the Walasahakw dance was a group dance in which the dancers wore forehead masks and blankets. The wolf appeared in this dance as an ancestral myth figure, but generally had no attributes of fearsomeness. The forehead masks of wolves (Pl. XIX; Figs. 339-61) were held to the head either by a framework helmet made of twigs or, if they had very long muzzles, were braced at the back by a stick that was anchored across the chest or around the waist. There was also a Dloogwala dance which re-enacted the initiation of novices in the same spirit as that of the Nootka, and was probably borrowed from them. In northern Kwakiutl tribes a special supernatural wolf forced the members of the Nootlem society to re-enact wolf spirit possession and to behave in a violent fashion, as a "Dog Eating Society."

Among the Nootka the main ceremony was the wolf ritual, Klukwalla. This was the re-enactment by society members of the wolf initiation of their ancestor, who then introduced it to his family with its masks, songs, dances, and whistles, and taught them how to perform it.

The ceremony began with the blowing of wolf whistles outside the village. This was the signal for the novices to be kidnaped, hidden behind a concealed wall in the ceremonial house, and taught the appropriate performances. Among the Nootka the novices were children, and the initiation is said not to have been a terrifying one. It was a time of celebration in the village and included entertainment by buffoons and other comic characters.

The children were returned by the wolves, wearing new costumes of hemlock branches, and for several days displayed the songs, crests, and dances the wolves had taught them. Family crest masks were also worn. There was little display of spirit possession such as characterized Kwakiutl shaman dances. A potlatch completed the public ceremony.

All the children of the village were initiated at least once into this society. People of rank underwent the ceremony several times, using each time as the occasion for taking a new rank and name.

Nootka wolf masks (Figs. 362-65) were not carved like those of the Kwakiutl but were made in an irregular four-sided open box form held together at the fourth side at the back of the head by sticks, and worn on top of the head. Cedar bark was usually draped across the top and down the back of such masks.

Fig. 327. Kwakiutl land otter mask from Kingcome Inlet. Wood; black, white, brown. Length: 16 in. MacMillan Purchase 1953. A6207

Fig. 328. Kwakiutl land otter mask from Kingcome Inlet. Wood; black, white, brown. Length: 16 in. MacMillan Purchase 1953. A6208

Fig. 329. Kwakiutl dog mask from Turnour Island. Wood and cloth; green, black, red. Length: 15 in. MacMillan Purchase 1961. A7481

Fig. 330. (*Left*) Kwakiutl deer mask from Alert Bay. Wood and antlers; brown, black, green, white. Length: 16½ in. MacMillan Purchase 1954. A6359. (*Right*) Kwakiutl doe mask from Alert Bay. Wood; brown, blue, red, white, black. Length: 17 in. MacMillan Purchase 1951. A6104

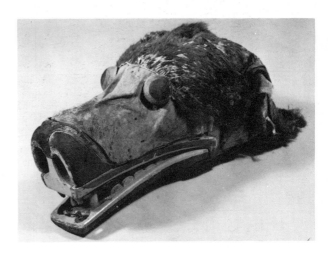

Fig. 331. (*Left*) Kwakiutl bear mask from Kingcome Inlet. Wood and bearskin; red, green, white, black. Length: 19 in. MacMillan Purchase 1953. A6192. (*Right*) Kwakiutl bear mask from Sullivan Bay. Wood, bearskin, and cardboard; orange, black. Length: 18 in. MacMillan Purchase 1952. A4238

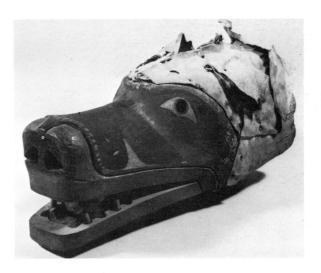

Fig. 332. (*Left*) Kwakiutl bear mask from Kingcome Inlet. Wood and copper; red, black, white, green. Length: 14 in. MacMillan Purchase 1953. A6152. (*Right*) Kwakiutl bear mask from Sullivan Bay. Wood and bearskin; red, green, black. Length: 19½ in. MacMillan Purchase 1952. A4239

Fig. 333. Kwakiutl bear mask from Alert Bay. Wood inlaid with abalone shell; black, white, red. Length: 21 in. MacMillan Purchase 1953. A3734

Fig. 334. Kwakiutl grizzly bear mask from Kingcome Inlet. Wood; black, red, white, green. Length: 17 in. MacMillan Purchase 1951. A3550

Fig. 335. Kwakiutl bear mask from Turnour Island. Wood and copper; red, black, green, white. Length: 14 in. MacMillan Purchase 1961. A7478

Fig. 336. Kwakiutl bear mask from Alert Bay. Wood, cedar bark, bearskin; white, black, red. Length: 10 in. Mac-Millan Purchase 1952. A4180

Fig. 337. (Left) Kwakiutl bear mask from Rivers Inlet, collected in 1914. Wood with commercial paint, copper nostrils, abalone shell eyes; brown, red, black. Length: 12½ in. MacMillan Purchase 1962. A8056. (Right) Kwakiutl bear mask from Bliss Landing. Wood; green, black. Height: 22 in. MacMillan Purchase 1948, Rev. G. H. Raley Coll. A1964

Fig. 338. Bella Coola bear claw, originally attached to bearskin costume. Alderwood with traces of blue paint. Length: 11 in. MacMillan Purchase 1963. A8371

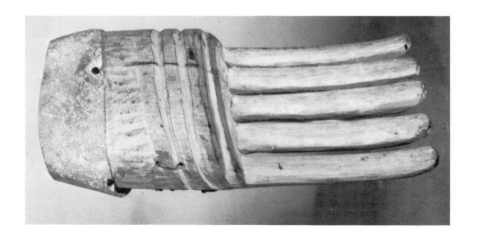

Fig. 339. Kwakiutl wolf mask from Gilford Island. Wood; red, green, white, black. Length: 20 in. MacMillan Purchase 1954. A6383

Fig. 340. Kwakiutl wolf mask from Campbell River. Wood; black, green, red, white. Length: 18 in. MacMillan Purchase 1951. A4022

Fig. 341. Kwakiutl wolf mask from Kingcome Inlet. Wood, cedar bark, cotton cloth, fur; black, white, orange, red. Length: 12½ in. MacMillan Purchase 1953. A6181

Fig. 342. Kwakiutl wolf mask from Turnour Island. Wood; red, yellow, green, white, black. Length: 18 in. Mac-Millan Purchase 1961. A7477

Fig. 343. Kwakiutl wolf mask from Turnour Island. Wood; orange, white, green, black. Length: 14 in. MacMillan Purchase 1961. A7480

Fig. 344. Kwakiutl wolf mask from Gilford Island. Wood; red, green, white, black. Length: 20 in. MacMillan Purchase 1953. A6130

Fig. 345. Kwakiutl wolf mask from Kingcome Inlet. Wood; red, black, green, white. Length: 15 in. MacMillan Purchase 1951. A6182

Fig. 346. Kwakiutl wolf mask from Sullivan Bay. Wood, skin, cedar bark; red, white, black. Length: 12½ in. MacMillan Purchase 1953. A4336

Fig. 347. Kwakiutl wolf mask from Kingcome Inlet. Wood; red, white, green, black. Length: 15½ in. MacMillan Purchase 1953. A6128

Fig. 348. Kwakiutl wolf mask from Gilford Island. Wood; red, green, white, black. Length: 20½ in. MacMillan Purchase 1953. A6129

Fig. 349. Kwakiutl wolf mask from Campbell River. Wood and cardboard; red, white, black, gray. Length: 17 in. MacMillan Purchase 1951. A4023

Fig. 350. Kwakiutl wolf mask from Alert Bay. Wood and cedar bark; red, white, black, green. Length: 19½ in. MacMillan Purchase 1952. A4241

Fig. 351. Kwakiutl wolf mask from Kingcome Inlet. Wood; red, black, green, white. Length: 16 in. MacMillan Purchase 1960. A4502

Fig. 352. Kwakiutl wolf mask from Kingcome Inlet. Wood; red, white, black, green. Length: 17 in. MacMillan Purchase 1960. A4503

Fig. 353. Kwakiutl wolf mask from Kingcome Inlet. Wood and skin; red, gray, white, black. Length: 28½ in. MacMillan Purchase 1960. A4498

Fig. 354. Kwakiutl wolf mask from Gilford Island. Wood; black, white, red. Length: 18 in. MacMillan Purchase 1952. A3809

Fig. 355. Kwakiutl wolf mask from Gilford Island. Wood; black, white, red. Length: 17 in. MacMillan Purchase 1952. A3810

Fig. 356. Kwakiutl wolf mask from Gilford Island. Wood; red, white, black. Length: 8 in. MacMillan Purchase 1954. A6378

Fig. 357. Kwakiutl wolf mask from King-come Inlet. Wood and skin, with glass eyes; red, white, green, black. Length: 14½ in. MacMillan Purchase 1951. A6087

Fig. 358. Kwakiutl wolf mask from Sullivan Bay. Wood; black, green, red, white. Length: 18 in. MacMillan Purchase 1951. A3685

Fig. 359. Kwakiutl wolf mask from Kingcome Inlet. Wood; red, black. Length: 18 in. MacMillan Purchase 1951. A3551

Fig. 360. Kwakiutl wolf mask from Gilford Island. Wood, copper, and cloth; red, green, black. Length: 10½ in. MacMillan Purchase 1954. A6376

Fig. 361. Kwakiutl wolf mask from Gilford Island. Wood and skin; red, black, green, white. Length: 34½ in. MacMillan Purchase 1952. A3817

Fig. 362. Nootka wolf mask from near Banfield, Vancouver Island. Wood with glass eyes; red, brown, white, black, blue. Length: 15 in. MacMillan Purchase 1952. A3712

Fig. 363. Nootka wolf mask, made after 1946. Wood and cedar bark; blue, red, white, black. Length: 15 in. MacMillan Purchase 1960. A4495

Fig. 364. Nootka wolf mask, made after 1946. Wood and cedar bark; black, red, green. Length: 15 in. MacMillan Purchase 1960. A4494

Fig. 365. (*Left*) Nootka wolf mask from Kyuquot. Wood; green, yellow, red, black. Length: 30 in. Mac-Millan Purchase 1961. A7862. (*Right*) Nootka wolf mask. Wood with tuft of twigs at top of head; yellow, white, black, red, green. Length: 24 in. MacMillan Purchase 1962. A8098

Fig. 366. Kwakiutl frog mask from Gilford Island. Wood, cedar bark, and copper; red, white, green, black. Length: 15 in. MacMillan Purchase 1953. A6319

Fig. 367. (*Left to right*) Bella Coola mountain goat mask, believed to be an early piece, possibly a child's mask to be used with a headpiece. Wood; white, blue, black. Height: 8½ in. MacMillan Purchase 1963. A8370. Bella Coola rabbit mask, said to be a scarce and early piece. Alderwood, probably originally covered with rabbit fur; traces of black paint around eyes and in mouth. Height: 11½ in. MacMillan Purchase 1963. A8365. Kwakiutl frog mask from Gilford Island. Wood; red, white, black, green. Height: 11 in. MacMillan Purchase 1962. A8057

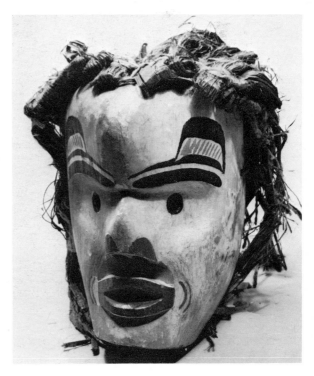

Fig. 368. (*Above*) Kwakiutl seal mask from Alert Bay. Wood; black, gray, white, blue, red. Length: 15½ in. MacMillan Purchase 1951. A6105. (*Right*) Kwakiutl squirrel or mouse mask from Kingcome Inlet. Wood and cedar bark; white, red, black. Height: 8½ in. MacMillan Purchase 1953. A6159

269

Bird Masks

Birds were very frequent in the Kwakiutl myths. Thunderbird and his younger brother Kolus were both ancestors of the Kwakiutl; each was the parent of many children who became chiefs of lineages.

Thunderbird was one of the supernatural birds of the myths. The flapping of his wings caused crashes of thunder, and lightning flashed from his eyes. He was so enormous that he fished for killer whales as though they were small fish, diving from the sky to seize them in his talons. The masks (Figs. 369, 371, 372) represent him with supernatural horns curving from his head. His costume was totally covered with feathers. The limited number of masks in the museum collection includes two that are painted with most unusual colors. Figure 369 is apple green, orange, white, and red; Figure 371 is a very pale blue, red, white, and black. Nowhere else in the collection are pale green and pale blue used.

Thunderbird's younger brother Kolus (Figs. 370, 373, 374), another supernatural ancestor of the Kwakiutl clan, was covered with heavy white down. According to the myth he had a tendency to perspire heavily because of his very hot covering. He was happy to remove this covering and became a man for a while (see pp. 21-22).

Characterized by a heavy, curved beak, the eagle mask (Pl. XXV; Figs. 375-80, 382) was generally worn with a coverall suit of feathers with large wings reaching from the shoulders to the wrists. These masks were generally fitted with mats on which white eagle feathers were sewn, worn to cover the head. Most of these coverings had been reduced to dust by moths before they were brought to the museum. There were no traditional colors for the eagles, which might be green, brown, or gray.

Another mythical bird was Khenkho, the so-called "supernatural crane." The masks in Figures 382 and 383 were identified by Bill Holm as being distinctive from either Raven, Hokhokw, or Crane, but very little is known about this character. Khenkho is characterized by his long narrow beak, ears, and elaborated nostrils.

Raven, the trickster, was a Northwest Coast culture hero who brought many benefits to mankind through his greed and curiosity, leaving a legacy of many inventions and tales of his picaresque adventures. Raven masks (Figs. 384-89) can be identified by a long, clear-cut beak, curved above but absolutely straight on its underside. The Hamatsa raven is different, much more elaborate, and with flared nostrils. In color the Hamatsa ravens are restricted to red, white, and black, with perhaps a touch of orange. Non-Hamatsa masks tend to be the same, with occasional touches of blue or green. They have no red cedar bark fringes and are, on the whole, less imaginative and not so skillfully carved as the Hamatsa raven masks.

Figure 390 (A1368) represents Raven as a human with symbolic face paintings, with perhaps some indication of sharpness and greed in his character.

Figures 388 (A8373) and 391 illustrate some non-Kwakiutl raven headdresses, which were fastened to a headband. Ribbons tied under the chin of the dancer held the headdress in place, and a cedar rope was fastened to a knot at the back of the blanket to anchor it.

Various sea birds were represented as part of the family myth characters: the merganser (usually named Diver by informants), loon, crane or heron, and seagull are those illustrated here. The loon, being associated with Komokwa and coppers, was the only one that was apparently of more than very minor significance.

Other bird masks worn by the Kwakiutl and other peoples included the grouse and the owl. The Nootka usually incorporated bird crests into headdresses worn on top of the head rather than wearing them as face masks. These headdresses, often characterized by a top fringe of sea lion whiskers or twigs and by parallel rows of carved feathers, were probably influenced by the northern headdresses.

Fig. 369. Kwakiutl Thunderbird mask from Gilford Island. Wood; orange, white, red, green. Length: 19 in. MacMillan Purchase 1951. A3771

Fig. 370. Kwakiutl Kolus mask from Smith Inlet. Wood; green, yellow, black, blue. Length: 16 in. Mac-Millan Purchase 1951. A4025

Fig. 371. Kwakiutl Thunderbird mask from Gilford Island, said to have been made by Jim Howard and used in 1918. Wood and feathers; blue, white, red, black. Length: 19 in. MacMillan Purchase 1953. A4304

Fig. 372. Kwakiutl Thunderbird mask from Sullivan Bay. Wood; green, black, red. Length: 19 in. MacMillan Purchase 1952. A4236

Fig. 373. Kwakiutl Kolus mask from Smith Inlet, made in 1938. Wood; orange, red, green, brown, white, black. Length: 17 in. MacMillan Purchase 1953. A4288

Fig. 374. Kwakiutl Kolus mask from King-come Inlet. Wood; green, white, red. Length: 22 in. MacMillan Purchase 1962. A4500

Fig. 375. Kwakiutl eagle mask from King-come Inlet. Wood; red, gray, black. Length: 17 in. MacMillan Purchase 1951. A3548

Fig. 376. Kwakiutl eagle mask from King-come Inlet. Wood; yellow, green, red, white, black. Length: 15 in. MacMillan Purchase 1953. A6199

Fig. 377. Kwakiutl eagle mask from King-come Inlet. Wood; green, brown. Length: 15 in. MacMillan Purchase 1954. A3416

Fig. 378. Kwakiutl eagle mask from Blunden Harbour, collected in 1927. Wood; gray, black, green, red, white. Length: 17 in. MacMillan Purchase 1952. A4324

Fig. 379. Kwakiutl eagle mask from Kingcome Inlet. Wood with feather thatch on top; green, red, gray, black, white. Length: 17 in. MacMillan Purchase 1953. A6180

Fig. 380. Tsimshian eagle mask from Skeena River. Wood; red, yellow, blue, black. Length: 12 in. MacMillan Purchase 1961. A7306

275

Fig. 381. (*Left*) Kwakiutl hawk mask from Gilford Island, Bella Coola style. Wood; yellow, green, red, black. Height: 16 in. MacMillan Purchase 1953. A6297. (*Right*) Bella Coola hawk mask. Wood and feathers; blue, red, white. Height: 16 in. Donated by Mrs. F. Sherbourne 1949. A1958

Fig. 382. (*Left*) Kwakiutl eagle mask from Gilford Island. Wood, mirror glass, and rubber band; blue, black. Height: 11½ in. MacMillan Purchase 1953. A4306. (*Above*) Kwakiutl Khenkho mask from Kingcome Inlet. Wood; black, red, white. Length: 33 in. MacMillan Purchase 1954. A6375

Fig. 383. (*Below*) Kwakiutl Khenkho mask from Alert Bay; cf. Boas 1908: Vol. V, Pl. XLI, Fig. 1. Wood and woolen cloth; black, gray, red. Length: 35 in. MacMillan Purchase 1961. A7883

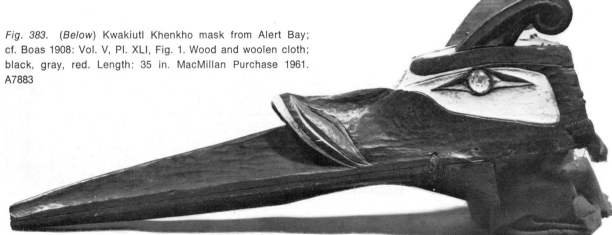

Fig. 384. Kwakiutl raven mask from Sullivan Bay. Wood; black, red, green, white. Length: 24 in. MacMillan Purchase 1952. A3784

Fig. 385. Kwakiutl raven mask from Bella Bella. Wood; red, black, green, white. Length: 21 in. MacMillan Purchase 1948, Rev. G. H. Raley Coll. A1743

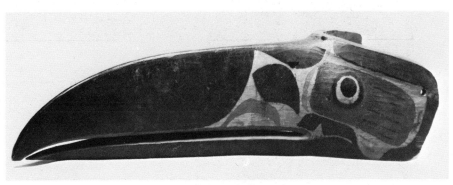

Fig. 386. Kwakiutl raven mask from Bella Bella. Wood; green, black, red. Length: 22 in. Museum Purchase 1947, Dr. G. E. Darby Coll. A7924

Fig. 387. Nootka raven mask from Ahousat. Wood; black, red. Length: 15 in. MacMillan Purchase 1962. A8234

Fig. 388. (*Left*) Nootka raven mask from Kyuquot. Wood; green, red, yellow, black. Length: 20 in. MacMillan Purchase 1961. A7863. (*Right*) Bella Coola raven headdress. Wood and cedar bark with mirror eyes; black, red, blue. Length: 15 in. MacMillan Purchase 1963. A8373

Fig. 389. Kwakiutl raven mask from Kingcome Inlet, said to be at least 100 years old. Wood; black, white, red. Length: 26½ in. MacMillan Purchase 1951. A3549

Fig. 390. (*Left*) Kwakiutl Atlakim grouse mask from Alert Bay, attributed to Willie Seaweed; said to be the first dancer to appear. Wood, cedar bark, and feathers; red, white, black, orange, brown. Height: 11 in. MacMillan Purchase 1951. A6088. (*Right*) Kwakiutl raven mask from Bella Bella. Wood and fur; black, green, red. Length: 11 in. Museum Purchase 1947, Dr. G. E. Darby Coll. A1368

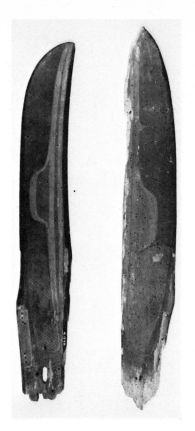
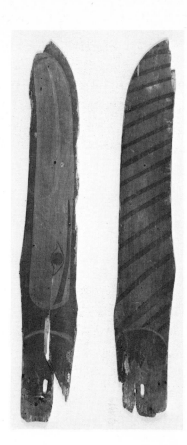

Fig. 391. Haida raven headdress from Clews Island. Wood; red, black. Length: 34 in. Burnett Coll. 1888. (Left to right) A1590, A1591, A1592, A1593

Fig. 392. (Top) Kwakiutl Atlakim bird mask from Village Island, made by Mungo Martin. Wood and cedar bark; black, white, red. Length: 7 ft. 5 in. MacMillan Purchase 1952. A4153. (Bottom) Kwakiutl Atlakim bird mask from Kingcome Inlet. Wood and cedar bark; black, white, red. Length: 5 ft. 5 in. MacMillan Purchase 1960. A4493

Insect Masks

The mosquito (Fig. 394), known as Scratcher, was one of a series of special characters who injected a comic interlude into the ceremony when they appeared. These clowns—Sneezer (see Atlakim mask in Fig. 142 [A6214]), Sleeper (Fig. 144 [A1967]), Laugher (Fig. 131), and so on—entered the dance house and exerted their power upon the house officials, causing them to scratch, sneeze, sleep, or laugh. When the people laughed too merrily, the heralds became annoyed and threw the same spell onto them; then all laughed helplessly until finally the heralds relented, releasing people from the spell, and threw it back to the instigators, who then departed.

Bees and wasps had the same function, intended to be amusing in the dances: with sharp-pointed sticks in their muzzles they flitted about, stinging people by touching them with their sharp barbs. Those who were stung were paid for their "damage" by special gifts during the potlatch.

The bumblebee masks (Fig. 396) from Kingcome Inlet are a complete set that belonged to one family. It consisted of one large and eight smaller masks, which were worn by children. Their dance was a mimetic one, indicative of flight and hovering. Cotton cloth covered the head of the dancer.

The wasp, as represented in a photograph by Curtis, was dressed in an over-all costume covered with short feathers.

Mosquitoes, gnats, and midges were said to be the flying sparks of the fire that consumed Bakbakwalanooksiwae when the ancestral hero burnt him up.

Fig. 393. Kwakiutl bumblebee mask from Kingcome Inlet. Wood; red, white, black. Height: 11½ in. MacMillan Purchase 1951. A3545

Fig. 394. Kwakiutl mosquito mask from Blunden Harbour. Wood and cedar bark; red, black. Height: 11 in.; length of stinger: 7½ in. MacMillan Purchase 1953. A6213

Fig. 395. Kwakiutl bumblebee mask from Alert Bay. Wood; red, white, black, green, brown. Length: 14 in. MacMillan Purchase 1953. A6336

Fig. 396. Kwakiutl bumblebee masks from Kingcome Inlet. Wood and cedar bark. (*Clockwise from top, left*) Made in 1938. Black, yellow, green, brown, white. Height: 8 in. MacMillan Purchase 1962. A8245. Black, yellow, red, green, white. Height: 9 in. MacMillan Purchase 1963. A8242. Yellow, black, green, orange, white. Height: 9 in. MacMillan Purchase 1962. A8238. Yellow, black, green, white, brown. Height: 7½ in. MacMillan Purchase 1962. A8243. Black, brown, yellow, green, white. Height: 7½ in. MacMillan Purchase 1962. A8241. Black, white, green, brown. Height 7½ in. MacMillan Purchase 1962. A8239. Black, white, yellow, orange, brown. Height: 8 in. MacMillan Purchase 1962. A8240. Yellow, black, green, white. Height: 8 in. MacMillan Purchase 1962. A8244. (*Center*) Black, red, green, brown, orange. Height: 12 in. MacMillan Purchase 1962. A8237

Natural Element Masks

The Kwakiutl incorporated natural elements—earthquake, sun, moon, echo, and others—into their Dluwulakha and family crest dances. These were especially important among the Bella Coola, whose Sisauk dancing society was entirely made up of these beings, and the concept may have been borrowed or received by marriage from them.

The two echo masks illustrated in Figures 408 and 409 are examples of Sopali, or dialogue masks, which carried on a light banter and humorous conversation with each other and with the spectators. See also Figure 402, another one of such a pair. These characteristically had a sun or a moon in one of its phases attached above the head.

Some of these Sopali masks, and all of the echo masks, were fitted with sets of wooden mouthpieces representing different characters (see Pl. XXVI; Figs. 407-10). A small basket fastened at the waist carried the extra pieces. Using the dance blanket as a concealment, the dancer lowered his head and secretly fitted in a new mouthpiece. This changed the character to represent the various stages of the myth.

The Nunalalahl, or weather headpiece (Figs. 402-5), was worn in a peaceful dance that could be done either by a man or by a woman.

Fig. 397. Kwakiutl sun mask. Wood; black, red, blue. Height: 11 in. Donated by Mrs. V. H. Clucas 1960. A7035

Fig. 398. Kwakiutl mask of raven in the sun, from Alert Bay, attributed to Willie Seaweed. Wood; white, orange, black. Diameter: 15 in. MacMillan Purchase 1953. A4511

Fig. 399. Bella Coola sun mask, collected between 1890 and 1910. Alderwood; green, red, black, white. Height, with rays: 12 in. MacMillan Purchase 1963. A8361

Fig. 400. Kwakiutl sun mask from Kingcome Inlet. Wood; green, white, black, brown, red. Height: 12 in.; length of rays: 6½ in. MacMillan Purchase 1952. A3788

Fig. 401. Kwakiutl mask of human face with moon above it, 1 of a pair from Sullivan Bay. Wood; red, black, green. Height, including moon: 18½ in. MacMillan Purchase 1952. A3782

Fig. 402. Kwakiutl weather headdress from Kingcome Inlet. Wood; white, black, red. Length: 21 in. Mac-Millan Purchase 1952. A3785

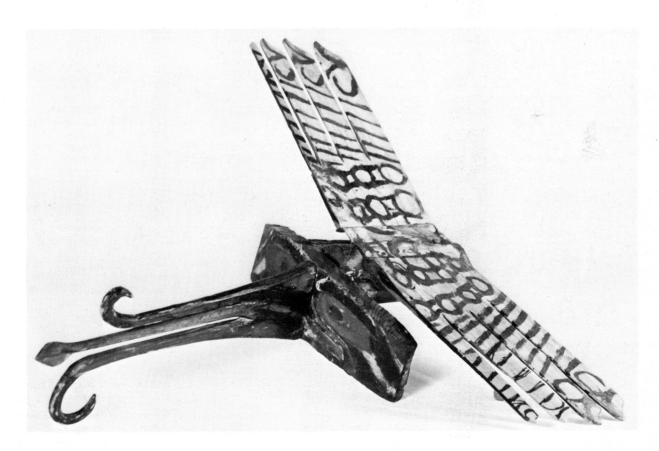

Fig. 403. Kwakiutl weather headdress from Kingcome Inlet. Wood and leather; black, white, red, green. Length: 18½ in. MacMillan Purchase 1952. A3786

Fig. 404. Kwakiutl weather headdress from Alert Bay. Wood; white, black, red. Length: 18 in. MacMillan Purchase 1953. A4270

Fig. 405. Kwakiutl weather headdress from Cape Mudge. Wood; yellow, orange, black, red. Length: 14 in. MacMillan Purchase 1962. A7984

Fig. 406. Kwakiutl earthquake mask from Kingcome Inlet, with movable visor, shown open and closed. Wood; white, black, green, red. Height: 14 in. MacMillan Purchase 1954. A6357

Fig. 407. Kwakiutl echo mask with interchangeable mouthpieces, from Bella Bella. Wood; black, red, white, green. Height: 13 in. Mouthpieces (*counterclockwise*): old man, echo, Tsonokwa, echo, bear, echo. MacMillan Purchase 1951. A3606

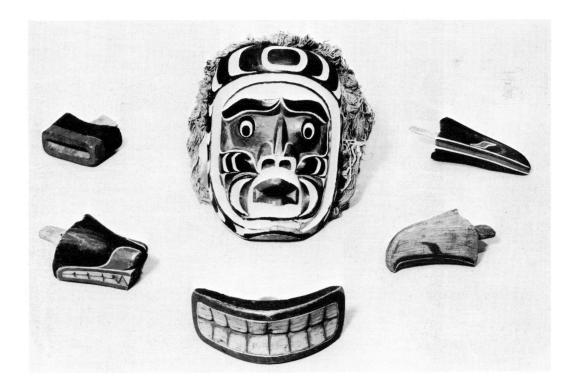

Fig. 408. Kwakiutl echo mask with interchangeable mouthpieces, from Alert Bay; made for Mrs. Charlie George, Sr., by her husband at the time of transfer of marriage privileges. Wood and hemp fiber; red, black, green, white. Height: 12 in. Mouthpieces (*left to right*): human, bear, human, eagle, raven. MacMillan Purchase 1953. A6243

Fig. 409. Kwakiutl echo mask from Alert Bay. The interchangeable mouthpieces are identical with those shown in Fig. 408. Wood and hemp fiber; red, black, green, white. Height: 12 in. MacMillan Purchase 1953. A6244

Fig. 410. Kwakiutl echo mask with interchangeable mouthpieces, from Kingcome Inlet. Wood; gray-black, red. Height: 14 in. Mouthpieces (*left to right*): teeth, lips. MacMillan Purchase 1952. A6031

Bookwus Masks

Bookwus, the Wild Man of the Woods, was a nonhuman character living in the woods. He ate ghost food and tried to persuade humans to eat it also, so that they would stay in the unreal forest world which he inhabited. He lived in an invisible house in the forest and attracted the spirits of the drowned to his home. Bookwus masks are illustrated in Figures 411-20. For a cockle-shell used as a clapper by Bookwus, see Figure 42 (A8050).

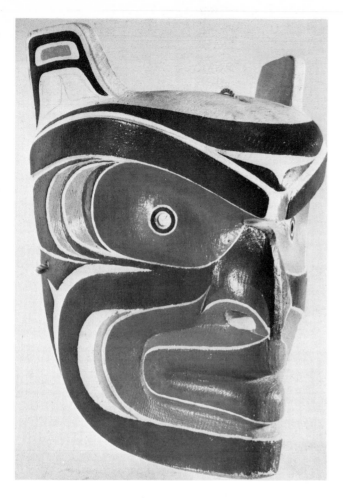

Fig. 411. Kwakiutl Bookwus mask from Alert Bay. Wood; black, white, gray, red, orange. Height: 11½ in. MacMillan Purchase 1953. A3483

Fig. 412. Kwakiutl Bookwus mask from Smith Inlet. Wood; black, red, gray, white. Height: 11½ in. MacMillan Purchase 1964. A8425

Fig. 413. (Left) Kwakiutl Bookwus mask from Smith Inlet. Wood; black, white, green, red. Height: 9 in. Mac-Millan Purchase 1953. A4287. (Right) Kwakiutl Bookwus mask from Smith Inlet. Wood and hemp fiber; red, black, gray, white. Height: 12 in. MacMillan Purchase 1953. A6176

Fig. 414. (Left) Kwakiutl Bookwus mask from Smith Inlet, said to be "an earlier mask." Wood with bottle caps for eyes; red, green, white. Height: 14 in. MacMillan Purchase 1953. A6175. (Right) Kwakiutl Bookwus mask from Smith Inlet. Wood; red, white, black. Height: 10½ in. MacMillan Purchase 1964. A8424

Fig. 415. (*Left*) Kwakiutl Bookwus mask from Gilford Island. Wood; white, red, black. Height: 10½ in. Mac-Millan Purchase 1953. A6482. (*Right*) Kwakiutl Bookwus mask from Smith Inlet. Wood; white, black, green, red. Height: 13 in. MacMillan Purchase 1961. A1493

Fig. 416. (*Left*) Kwakiutl Bookwus mask from Alert Bay, attributed to Willie Seaweed and said to have been last used in 1920. Wood and human hair; gray, red, yellow, orange, black, white. Height: 11 in. MacMillan Purchase 1953. A6242. (*Right*) Kwakiutl Bookwus mask from Kingcome Inlet. Wood and copper; green, black, white, red. Height: 14½ in. MacMillan Purchase 1960. A4501

Fig. 417. (Left) Kwakiutl Bookwus mask from Blunden Harbour. Wood and cedar bark; white, red, black. Height 10½ in. MacMillan Purchase 1953. A6220. (Right) Kwakiutl Bookwus mask from Blunden Harbour. Wood; black, red, green. Height: 14 in. MacMillan Purchase 1953. A4318

Fig. 418. (Left) Kwakiutl Bookwus mask from Smith Inlet. Wood; white, black, red, brown. Height: 11½ in. MacMillan Purchase 1953. A6353. (Right) Kwakiutl Bookwus mask from Blunden Harbour. Wood; orange, red, white, black. Height: 9½ in. MacMillan Purchase 1953. A6218

Fig. 419. (*Left*) Tsimshian Bookwus mask from Kitsegukla. Wood; black, red. Height: 10 in. MacMillan Purchase 1962. A7956. (*Right*) Kwakiutl Bookwus mask from Gilford Island, very similar to one illustrated in Curtis 1915: Vol. X, Pl. CLIX. Wood and fur; black. Height: 10½ in. MacMillan Purchase 1954. A6371

Fig. 420. (*Left to right*) Tsimshian Bookwus mask from Port Simpson. Unpainted wood with red lines on cheek. Height: 9 in. MacMillan Purchase 1965. A8540. Bella Coola Bookwus mask, collected between 1890 and 1910. Unpainted wood. Height: 9½ in. MacMillan Purchase 1963. A8376. Kwakiutl Bookwus mask from Gilford Island. Wood; gray, green, black. Height: 13½ in. MacMillan Purchase 1954. A6370

Kwekwe Masks

The Kwekwe mask originated with the Salish. Among these people it was an important crest mask worn by ritualists who inherited special powers and assisted at all life crises and social situations—birth, naming, marriage, and illness—by dancing masked, in groups of four. According to the myth, the mask's origin was from under the lake, and it was associated with earth-quakes and healing.

The Kwakiutl received the Kwekwe from the Comox by gift. After having decided to wage war to get this dance and mask, they were invited in as guests of the Comox and freely given the dance and the box of associated gear.

The Salish Kwekwe masks were generally painted in two colors—red and blue, red and white, or red and black. The unpainted ones shown in Figures 424 (A6813), 425 (A6546), and 426 (A6812) were commissioned by the museum from Andrew Charles of Musqueam, a senior member of the Kwekwe dancers and an excellent carver. They are copies of older ones (see Fig. 425 [A6811]) from Musqueam which are now in the museum, and were left unpainted in order to show the details of their carving.

The Kwekwe mask was usually supplemented by a brightly colored cloth frill extending from its circumference. Swan quills and feather tufts were attached at the top of the mask and bobbed up and down during the dance. The costume traditionally worn with the mask was a tunic of cloth extending nearly to the knee, covered with feathers that were attached upside down by the point of the quill so that they swayed with the movements of the dancer's body. Leggings of eagle down (later of goat's wool) were fastened at the knee and ankle by deer hoof rattle gaiters. Pecten shell rattles, made of groups of four shells strung on a withe, were always part of this dance.

The masks in Plate XXXI, from Friendly Cove, are interesting examples of a further variation on the Kwekwe theme. These are Nootka adaptations of a Kwekwe mask, and have unusually elaborate carvings. Their owner called them "welcome" masks.

Fig. 422. Kwakiutl Kwekwe mask from Turnour Island. Wood; natural, brown, black. Height: 13 in. MacMillan Purchase 1962. A7983

Fig. 421. Kwakiutl Kwekwe mask from Gilford Island, attributed to Willie Seaweed. Wood; white, black, red, green. Height: 13 in. MacMillan Purchase 1952. A4095

Fig. 423. (*Left*) Coast Salish Kwekwe mask from Musqueam Reserve. Wood; red, white, blue. Height: 17 in. Museum Purchase 1954. A6475. (*Right*) Kwakiutl Kwekwe mask from Blunden Harbour. Wood and cedar bark; red, black, white. Height: 10½ in. Museum Purchase 1952. A6216

Fig. 424. (*Left*) Coast Salish Kwekwe mask from Musqueam Reserve, 4 generations old. Wood; blue, red, white. Height: 19 in. Museum Purchase 1954. A6473. (*Right*) Coast Salish Kwekwe mask from Musqueam Reserve, carved by Andrew Charles. Unpainted wood. Height: 21 in. Museum Commission 1954. A6813

Fig. 425. (*Left*) Coast Salish Kwekwe mask from Musqueam Reserve, carved by Andrew Charles. Unpainted wood. Height: 17 in. Museum Purchase 1954. A6546. (*Right*) Coast Salish Kwekwe mask from Musqueam Reserve, 4 generations old. Wood; brown, red. Height: 16 in. Museum Purchase 1954. A6811

Fig. 426. (*Left to right*) Coast Salish Kwekwe mask from Musqueam Reserve, carved by Andrew Charles. Unpainted wood. Height: 21½ in. Museum Commission 1954. A6812. Coast Salish Kwekwe mask from Musqueam Reserve. Wood; red, white, blue. Height: 19 in. Museum Purchase 1954. A6474. Coast Salish Kwekwe mask from Musqueam Reserve. Wood; red, black. Height: 21 in. MacMillan Purchase 1954. A6116

Speaker Masks

The dignitary who was the official speaker for the chief on public occasions might or might not wear a mask. Recent practice in the Alert Bay region has been to omit the mask. Speakers wearing masks were illustrated by Boas (1895:627, Fig. 194) in seven examples which are very much like many in this collection. Masks like these were also worn by a group of people hired by the host to come up at the end of a potlatch and "officially" thank him for his munificence.

These masks (Figs. 427-38) are similar in style to the ones called "Gamblers' Masks" by Samuel Barrett in his notes (Ritzenthaler and Parsons 1966) although no details are added (see Pls. 25, 26, 27, 28).

Another group of masks included those worn by guests who portrayed "people in the crowd" at a potlatch, forming a link between the speaker and the invited guests.

Fig. 428. Kwakiutl speaker mask from Bella Bella. Wood; natural, blue, black. Height: 11 in. Museum Purchase 1947, Dr. G. E. Darby Coll. A7943

Fig. 427. Kwakiutl speaker mask from Alert Bay. Wood; red, black. Height: 8¾ in. Leon and Thea Koerner Foundation Grant 1957. A6632

Fig. 429. (*Left*) Kwakiutl speaker mask from Sullivan Bay. Wood; black, orange. Height: 9½ in. MacMillan Purchase 1952. A3777. (*Right*) Kwakiutl speaker mask from Sullivan Bay. Wood; red, black. Height: 10 in. MacMillan Purchase 1952. A4177

Fig. 430. (*Left*) Kwakiutl speaker mask from Sullivan Bay. Wood; red, black. Height: 8¼ in. MacMillan Purchase 1952. A4261 (*Right*) Kwakiutl speaker mask from Sullivan Bay. Wood; black, red. Height: 9½ in. MacMillan Purchase 1952. A3776

Fig. 431. (Left) Kwakiutl speaker mask from Alert Bay. Wood; orange, black. Height: 8½ in. Leon and Thea Koerner Foundation Grant 1957. A6629. (Right) Kwakiutl speaker mask from Alert Bay. Wood; orange, black. Height: 10 in. Leon and Thea Koerner Foundation Grant 1959. A6633

Fig. 432. (Left) Kwakiutl speaker mask from Alert Bay. Wood; orange, black. Height: 8 in. Leon and Thea Koerner Foundation Grant 1959. A6628. (Right) Kwakiutl speaker mask from Alert Bay. Wood; orange, black. Height: 10 in. Leon and Thea Koerner Foundation Grant 1959. A6631

Fig. 433. (*Left*) Kwakiutl speaker mask from Sullivan Bay. Wood; white, black, red. Height: 12¼ in. MacMillan Purchase 1951. A3679

Fig. 434. (*Below, left to right*) Kwakiutl speaker mask from Blunden Harbour. Wood; red, white, black. Height: 12 in. Museum Purchase 1951. A6238. Kwakiutl speaker mask from Alert Bay. Wood; green, orange, red, white, black. Height: 9¾ in. MacMillan Purchase 1952. A4247. Kwakiutl speaker mask from Blunden Harbour. Wood; white, black, red. Height: 9½ in. MacMillan Purchase 1953. A4319

Fig. 435. (Left) Kwakiutl speaker mask from Alert Bay, originally with "a moon coming out of the forehead," now missing. Wood; white, black, red. Height: 11 in. MacMillan Purchase 1951. A6110a. (Right) Kwakiutl speaker mask from Alert Bay. Wood and cloth: gray, brown, black. Height: 10½ in. MacMillan Purchase 1951. A6110c

Fig. 436. (Left) Kwakiutl speaker mask from Sullivan Bay. Wood; red, black. Height: 10¼ in. MacMillan Purchase 1952. A4178. (Right) Kwakiutl speaker mask from Alert Bay. Wood; orange, blue, black. Height: 10¼ in. Leon and Thea Koerner Foundation Grant 1959. A6630

Fig. 437. (*Left*) Kwakiutl speaker mask from Alert Bay. Wood; brown, gray, black. Height: 11¼ in. MacMillan Purchase 1951. A6110b. (*Right*) Kwakiutl speaker mask from Sullivan Bay. Wood; red, black. Height: 9½ in. MacMillan Purchase 1952. A4174

Fig. 438. (*Left*) Kwakiutl speaker mask from Sullivan Bay. Wood; red, black. Height: 10 in. MacMillan Purchase 1952. A3727. (*Right*) Kwakiutl speaker mask from Blunden Harbour. Wood; red, white, black. Height: 12 in. MacMillan Purchase 1953. A4320

Human Face Masks

This category (Figs. 439-53) is an unsatisfactory one from the standpoint of identification. Aside from the simple fact that they are human faces, they may have very little in common. The problem of identification of Kwakiutl masks, which are so tied to locality and to family privilege within one area, is an extremely difficult one. Boas noted this on his first field trip, when he tried to obtain identifications from photographs of masks he had seen in German museums. Within a region in which several tribal groups visit and communicate, there is usually somebody who can recognize the group's family masks. If the masks are not familiar, however—perhaps because they represent a privilege seldom used by a family that has many—then they may pass unnoticed. None of the masks shown in this section has been recognized or satisfactorily identified by anyone.

There are, however, leads to the possible identification of some of them. The woman portrayed in Plate XXVIII (A3586) is almost certainly the wife of Komokwa, and arrived with the mask of Komokwa illustrated in Plate XX, along with the echo mask shown in Plate XXVI. These three masks are all certainly from the hand of the same very gifted carver. It seems very likely that Figure 439, a "ridicule" mask, which was listed in Raley's notes as being from Kyuquot, was not in fact made there although it certainly could have been obtained there. It has a strong, intense dramatic style that is lacking in the masks of that area. Furthermore, because it is black all over, it should in my opinion be placed among the northern Kwakiutl, where it also fits stylistically (see p. 62 on the use of black paint).

The face in Figure 446 (A4182) represents a comic white man character in one of the small satiric skits that served as side comedies during the potlatch celebrations, as described by Boas (1895:558, 562-63). Figure 449 (A8055) is also probably of this nature.

Figure 443 (A4185) represents very accurately the face of a dancer possessed by a spirit, and it is possible that the same state is represented by the Tsimshian mask in Figure 441 (A7368).

The Nootka masks (Figs. 451-53) have not been identified further. Most of them were collected without notes other than provenience by Dr. Raley, but two facts may be kept in mind concerning them: most Nootka masks were made in pairs, representing one male, one female; and a great many of them were meant to be comical buffoons or clowns. The Nootka stressed the comic element in their winter dance, even the Klukwalla wolf dance being associated with jokes and playfulness.

The paired Nootka masks were carved for each important character, and two dancers wore these and danced simultaneously. Over the years many such pairs have been separated, and one of the masks has been lost before the other reached the museum. In the museum's collection, the following pairs are still intact: the wolf masks of Figures 363 and 364; the grouse headdresses of Figures 238 and 239; and the "human face" masks of Figures 451 (A3713, A3714), 452 (A1959, A1960), and 453 (A1962, A1963). It will be noted that these Nootka masks are quite massive in style, and simple to the point of crudity.

Fig. 439. Kwakiutl human face "ridicule" mask from Kyuquot. Wood; black. Height: 12 in.
MacMillan Purchase 1948, Rev. G. H. Raley Coll. A3155

Fig. 440. (Left) Nootka human face mask from West Coast of Vancouver Island. Wood; green, black, yellow, red, white. Height: 12½ in. MacMillan Purchase 1948, Rev. G. H. Raley Coll. A1961

Fig. 441. (Below, left to right) Tsimshian mask of woman's face from Skeena River. Wood; black, red. Height: 9 in. MacMillan Purchase 1961. A7313. Tsimshian human face mask from Skeena River. Natural wood with black and red paint. Height: 9 in. MacMillan Purchase 1961. A7309. Tsimshian human face mask from Skeena River. Wood; red, blue, black. Height: 10½ in. MacMillan Purchase 1961. A7368

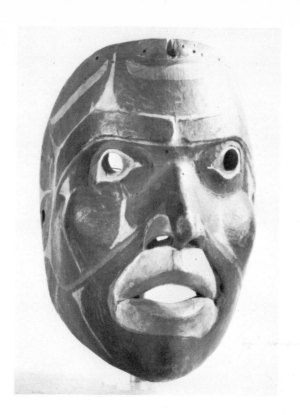

Fig. 442. (*Left*) Bella Coola human face mask, an early mask said to have been "killed" in a dance by the dagger shown in Fig. 165 (A8363). Alderwood; green, gray, black. Height: 10 in. MacMillan Purchase 1963. A8362. (*Right*) Kwakiutl human face mask from Sullivan Bay. Wood and copper; light gray, dark gray, red. Height: 12¾ in. MacMillan Purchase 1951. A3684

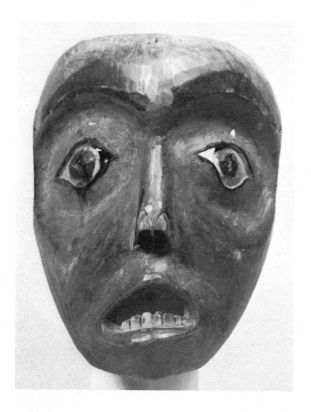
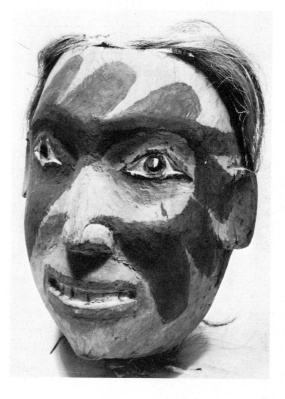

Fig. 443. (*Left*) Kwakiutl human face mask, attributed to Charlie George. Wood; brown, black. Height: 8 in. Museum Purchase 1951. A4185. (*Right*) Haida human face mask from Queen Charlotte Islands. Wood and horse-hair; green, red, white. Height: 9 in. MacMillan Purchase 1960, Rev. W. E. Collison Coll. A7069

Fig. 444. (*Left*) Tsimshian human face mask from Skeena River. Unpainted wood. Height: 10½ in. MacMillan Purchase 1961. A7314. (*Right*) Bella Coola human face mask from Kimsquit, representing Death. Wood; black. Height: 11 in. MacMillan Purchase 1948, Rev. G. H. Raley Coll. A1749

Fig. 445. (*Left*) Tsimshian human face mask from Skeena River. Natural wood with green, black, and red paint. Height: 9½ in. MacMillan Purchase 1961. A7308. (*Right*) Nootka human face mask from West Coast of Vancouver Island. Wood; green, red, black, orange. Height: 11 in. MacMillan Purchase 1948, Rev. G. H. Raley Coll. A1793

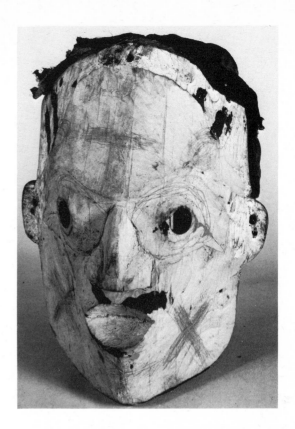

Fig. 446. (*Left*) Kwakiutl human face mask from Alert Bay, representing a white man. Wood, cedar bark, and horsehair; red, white, black. Height: 11 in. MacMillan Purchase 1952. A4182. (*Right*) Unfinished Bella Coola human face mask. Unpainted wood. Height: 10½ in. MacMillan Purchase 1963. A8369

Fig. 447. (*Left*) Kwakiutl human face mask from Alert Bay. Wood and cedar bark; red, black, white. Height: 7½ in. MacMillan Purchase 1953. A6342. (*Right*) Kwakiutl human face mask from Alert Bay. Wood and cedar bark; red, white, black. Height: 7 in. MacMillan Purchase 1953. A6343

Fig. 448. Kwakiutl twin human face masks from Bella Bella. Unpainted wood. Height 10 in. MacMillan Purchase 1948, Rev. G. H. Raley Coll. A1732

Fig. 449. (*Left to right*) Kwakiutl human face mask from Sullivan Bay. Wood; green, black, brownish-red. Height: 10 in. MacMillan Purchase 1952. A4262. Kwakiutl human face mask from Alert Bay, over 100 years old. Wood; green, red, black. Height: 11½ in. MacMillan Purchase 1951. A4020. Kwakiutl human face mask from Quatsino. Wood; green and red with black moss decoration. Height: 12 in. MacMillan Purchase 1962. A8055

Fig. 450. (Left) Tsim-shian human face mask from Kitsegukla; the bird on top of the head twirls when a string is pulled. Wood and bearskin; brown, black, white. Height: 14 in. MacMillan Purchase 1962. A7957. (Right) Bella Coola human face mask. Un-painted wood with white teeth and X burnt on cheek. Height: 10½ in. MacMillan Purchase 1963. A8368

Fig. 451. (Left to right) Nootka human face mask from Ucluelet. Unpainted wood. Height: 10½ in. MacMillan Purchase 1948, Rev. G. H. Raley Coll. A6815. Nootka human face mask from Banfield, representing a male buffoon. Wood; red, yellow, black, white, blue. Height: 14½ in. Museum Purchase 1952. A3713. Nootka human face mask from Banfield, representing a female buffoon. Wood; red, yellow, blue, white. Height: 15½ in. Museum Purchase 1952. A3714

Fig. 452. (*Left*) Nootka human face mask from West Coast of Vancouver Island. Wood; red, black. Height: 12½ in. MacMillan Purchase 1948, Rev. G. H. Raley Coll. A1959. (*Right*) Nootka human face mask from West Coast of Vancouver Island. Wood; black, red. Height: 10¼ in. MacMillan Purchase 1948, Rev. G. H. Raley Coll. A1960

Fig. 453. (*Left to right*) Nootka human face mask from West Coast of Vancouver Island. Wood; yellow, red, black, green. Height: 14 in. MacMillan Purchase 1948, Rev. G. H. Raley Coll. A1962. Nootka human face mask from West Coast of Vancouver Island. Wood; yellow, white, black, green, red. Height: 13¾ in. MacMillan Purchase 1948, Rev. G. H. Raley Coll. A1963. Nootka human face mask from Ucluelet. Wood decorated with black paint. Height: 14½ in. MacMillan Purchase 1948, Rev. G. H. Raley Coll. A6814

Complex Masks

Two kinds of masks involving multiple identity were developed by the Northwest Coast Indians. One of these, the mask with interchangeable mouthpieces, allowed the dancer to change from one character to another by
inserting one of a number of distinctive mouthpieces which he kept concealed under his blanket. This kind of mask is illustrated by the echo masks
shown in Plate XXVI and Figures 407-10.

Even more dramatic were the transformation masks, an amazing combination of an imaginative conception with technical ingenuity. These masks,
which reached their highest development among the Kwakiutl, carried out
the very essence of Kwakiutl mythology by revealing the dual nature of a
mythological creature. The story of the founding of the Walas gens by the
mythological bird Kolus, recounted by Curtis (1915:137), contains an example
of the kind of transformation that was strikingly depicted through the use of
these masks (see pp. 21-22).

Carefully carved and balanced on hinges, the mask was intricately
strung. At the climactic moment of the dance, the dancing, the music, and
the beat of the batons all changed tempo, speeding up just before the transformation and then halting while it occurred. When certain strings were
pulled by the dancer, the external shell of the mask split, usually into four
sections, sometimes into two. These pieces of the external covering continued to separate until the inner character was revealed, suspended in their
center.

Four Kwakiutl transformation masks, and one Nootka example, are shown in Figures 454-58. In each case the mask is shown both as it appears when it is closed and with the outer part pulled open to reveal the human or other ancestor being into which the bird or animal is transforming itself.

Fig. 454. Kwakiutl complex wolf-man mask from Alert Bay, shown closed (*above*) and open (*below*). Wood and cedar bark; green, brown, red, black, white. Length: 16 in. MacMillan Purchase 1954. A6373

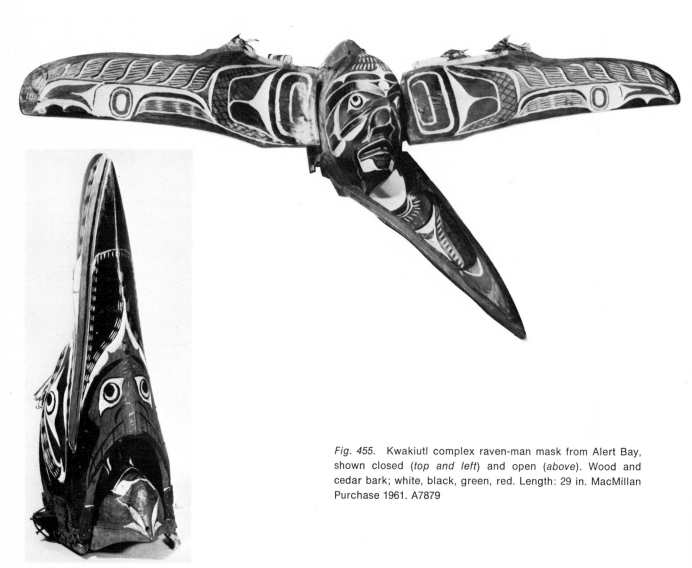

Fig. 455. Kwakiutl complex raven-man mask from Alert Bay, shown closed (*top and left*) and open (*above*). Wood and cedar bark; white, black, green, red. Length: 29 in. MacMillan Purchase 1961. A7879

Fig. 456. Kwakiutl complex raven-Kolus mask from Alert Bay, attributed to Charlie George, Sr.; shown closed (*above*) and open (*below*). Wood, cedar bark, leather, and metal; black, white, red, green. Length: 23 in. Mac-Millan Purchase 1953. A6256

Fig. 457. Kwakiutl complex raven-man mask from Kingcome Inlet, shown closed (*top*) and open (*left*). Wood and cedar bark; white, black, green, red. Length: 3 ft. MacMillan Purchase 1960. A4497

Fig. 458. Nootka complex wolf-eagle mask from Ahousat, shown closed (*below*) and open (*left*). Wood and feathers; black, green, yellow. Length: 19 in. MacMillan Purchase 1962. A7968

Kerfed Boxes, Dishes, and Cradles

The kerfed box of the Northwest Coast (Pl. XXI; Figs. 459-74) was a triumph of woodworking technology.

A cedar board was split from the log and smoothed to the desired thickness. Three equidistant parallel lines were grooved at right angles to the long edge so that when the board was steamed over a period of time it could be bent along the grooves to right angles. Then, after application of more steam and pressure, the first and fourth sides were drawn together, and their edges were sewn invisibly with cedar rootlets.

A groove was cut neatly along one long edge of the board on the inside so that a bottom board could be fitted into it tightly. Holes were drilled and pegs were inserted to hold the bottom in place. Usually a cover was made by cutting a square piece from a block of wood so that it fitted the top of the box. On many boxes a back "lip" of wood was left standing upright across the rear edge of the cover to make it easier to lift and replace the lid.

Such a box, well made, was watertight. These boxes were used as vessels for storing water or fish oil, for cooking with water and hot stones, and for storage of foodstuffs and household gear. Boxes for domestic use were attractively finished by the grooving of "fluted" patterns along the front and sides.

There were also boxes of ceremonial importance, finely carved and beautifully painted with family crests, which were used for the storage of the most valuable treasures of the family and were prized as gifts in potlatch

325

giving. The myths contain many references to "boxes of treasure" acquired from supernatural sources. The box of whistles was of this nature, symbolizing the family crest privileges that were transferred to the bride's husband during the marriage ceremony.

Kerfed boxes were also used as drums, which were suspended from the rafters in front of the drum beater. The kerfed box in a larger size was used as a coffin.

Some of the food dishes used in ceremonial entertainment were kerfed and completed in the same fashion as the boxes (Pl. XXX; Figs. 472, 474, 475). Many of these, unlike the boxes, had convexly curved sides, and they were always finely carved or painted. Of many sizes, they were used for serving food or to hold the fish oil into which fish was dipped.

Most dishes were made of wood, but the one shown in Figure 472 (A7056) is of baleen. Some of the finest were unpainted. These were regarded as family heirlooms and had crest names which were recited when the dishes were brought in.

Ordinary cradles were woven as basketry and were regarded as temporary and expendable. Others, however, intended to be ceremonial and permanent, were made by the same technique as boxes (Figs. 476, 477) and were adorned with the crest carvings of the child for whom they were intended.

Fig. 459. (*Left*) Tsimshian storage box from Aiyansh. Wood: black, red. Height: 26 in. MacMillan Purchase 1962. A8228. (*Right*) Kwakiutl storage box from Kitamaat. Wood; black, red. Height: 23 in. MacMillan Purchase 1948, Rev. G. H. Raley Coll. A6571

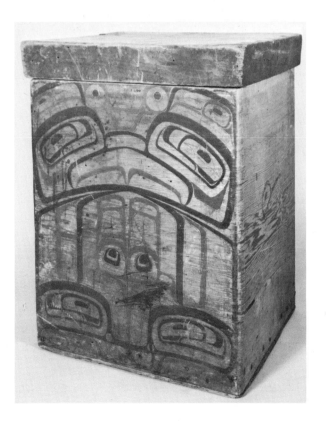

Fig. 460. (*Left*) Haida storage box with lid from Queen Charlotte Islands, collected before 1911. Wood; black, red. Height with lid: 29 in. Frank Burnett Coll. 1927. A400. (*Right*) Kwakiutl storage box with lid from Kitamaat. Wood; black, red. Height with lid: 22 in. MacMillan Purchase 1948, Rev. G. H. Raley Coll. A4382

Fig. 461. (*Left*) Haida storage box with lid from Queen Charlotte Islands, collected before 1911. Cedarwood; black, red. Height with lid: 27 in. Frank Burnett Coll. 1927. A399. (*Right*) Kwakiutl storage box with lid from Kitamaat. Wood; black, red. Height with lid: 19½ in. MacMillan Purchase 1948, Rev. G. H. Raley Coll. A4383

Fig. 462. (*Left*) Tsimshian storage box from Kispiox. Wood; black, red. Height with lid: 24 in. MacMillan Purchase 1948, Rev. G. H. Raley Coll. A6568. (*Right*) Tlingit storage box with lid from Prince of Wales Island, collected before 1900. Wood; black, red. Height with lid: 26 in. MacMillan Purchase 1961. A7450

Fig. 463. (Left) Kwakiutl storage box from Kitamaat. Wood; black, red. Height: 24 in. MacMillan Purchase 1948, Rev. G. H. Raley Coll. A3576. (Right) Kwakiutl storage box from Kitamaat. Cedarwood; black, red. Height: 27 in. MacMillan Purchase 1948, Rev. G. H. Raley Coll. A3582

Fig. 464. (Left) Tsimshian storage box with lid from Port Simpson. Wood; black, red. Height with lid: 25 in. MacMillan Purchase 1965. A8539. (Right) Tsimshian storage box with lid from Kitsegukla. Wood; black, red. Height with lid: 26 in. MacMillan Purchase 1962. A8229

Fig. 465. (*Left*) Tsimshian storage box with lid from Kitsegukla. Wood; black, red. Height with lid: 20½ in. Mac-Millan Purchase 1962. A7960. (*Right*) Kwakiutl storage box with lid from Kitamaat. Cedarwood; black, red. Height with lid: 24 in. MacMillan Purchase 1948, Rev. G. H. Raley Coll. A3578

Fig. 466. (*Left*) Tsimshian storage box with lid from Port Simpson. Wood and shell; black, red. Height with lid: 23 in. MacMillan Purchase 1962. A8227. (*Above*) Haida storage box with lid. Wood; black, red. Length: 31 in. MacMillan Special Grant 1962. A8211

Fig. 467. (Above) Kwakiutl storage box from Kitamaat, with carved raven on lid. Wood; black, red. Length: 11¼ in. MacMillan Purchase 1948, Rev. G. H. Raley Coll. A1571. (Right) Kwakiutl storage box with lid from Kitamaat. Wood; red, black. Height with lid: 9 in. MacMillan Purchase 1948, Rev. G. H. Raley Coll. A6563

Fig. 468. (Left) Kwakiutl storage box with lid from Kitamaat. Wood and shells; black, red. Height with lid: 21 in. MacMillan Purchase 1948, Rev. G. H. Raley Coll. A6572. (Right) Kwakiutl model box and lid, with rope in position, from Fort Rupert; collected in 1885. Wood with cedar bark rope; black, red. Height with lid: 7 in. MacMillan Purchase 1963. A8390

Fig. 469. (Left) Kwakiutl storage box with lid from Bella Bella. Wood; white, black, red. Height with lid: 13 in. MacMillan Purchase 1948, Rev. G. H. Raley Coll. A8335. (Right) Kwakiutl storage box with lid from Allison Harbour, with ropes in position. Unpainted cedarwood and cedar ropes. Height with lid: 20½ in. MacMillan Purchase 1953. A6321

Fig. 470. Kwakiutl food box from Bella Bella. Wood and shells; black, red. Length: 21 in. Museum Purchase 1947, Dr. G. E. Darby Coll. A1722

Fig. 471. Kwakiutl oil box from Bella Bella. Unpainted wood and operculum shells. Length: 6 in. Museum Purchase 1947, Dr. G. E. Darby Coll. A1944

Fig. 472. (Right) Haida oil box from Queen Charlotte Islands, collected in 1864. Unpainted wood and copper pegs. Length: 4 in. Leon and Thea Koerner Foundation Grant 1960. A7944. (Below, left to right) Haida oil dish from Queen Charlotte Islands. Baleen. Length: 8 in. MacMillan Purchase 1960, Rev. W. E. Collison Coll. A7056. Tsimshian food box from Kitkatlah. Unpainted wood and shells. Length: 15½ in. MacMillan Purchase 1948, Rev. G. H. Raley Coll. A1737

Fig. 473. (*Left*) Kwakiutl grease box from Kitlope. Unpainted wood. Height: 8½ in. MacMillan Purchase 1948, Rev. G. H. Raley Coll. A1625. (*Right*) Tlingit food storage box from Prince of Wales Island, collected in 1900. Wood; black, red. Length: 18½ in. Museum Purchase 1961. A7448

Fig. 474. (*Above, left to right*) Kwakiutl oil box from North Vancouver Island. Unpainted wood and shells. Length: 19 in. MacMillan Purchase 1951. A3563. Haida food dish from Queen Charlotte Islands. Cedarwood; black, red. Length: 18 in. MacMillan Purchase 1948, Rev. G. H. Raley Coll. A3392. (*Left*) Haida-style feast dish, collected before 1890. Unpainted wood. Length: 16½ in. MacMillan Purchase 1961. A7549

Fig. 475. Tsimshian food dish from Telegraph Creek. Wood and shells; black, red. Length: 15 in. Museum Purchase 1952. A4135

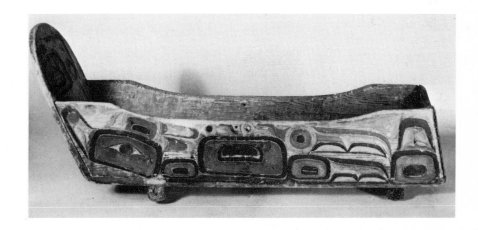

Fig. 476. Kwakiutl cradle from Fort Rupert, collected in 1885. Wood; black, red, green. Length: 30 in. MacMillan Purchase 1963. A8388

Fig. 477. Kwakiutl cradle from Kitamaat. Wood; black, red. Length: 3 ft. 3 in. MacMillan Purchase 1948, Rev. G. H. Raley Coll. A6519

Canoes and Paddles

The canoe of the Northwest Coast was essential and basic to the whole way of life, and some of the most skilled craftsmanship and complex technology were devoted to its production.

Illustrated here are examples of the typical northern canoe, which was different and distinct from the famous Nootka canoe. It was characterized by a high, projecting bow and stern and carefully rounded sides. Made in many sizes, up to sixty feet in length, these canoes were used for fishing, for trade, for visits, or for war. Important ones were carved or painted with family crest figures on the prow.

The canoes shown in Figures 478-82 are small ones—models of their large counterparts. Although they are finely made, finished, and painted, they reflect a different kind of craftsmanship from the real ones they represent. There was no need to expand these by the use of hot water and pressure. The large canoes, which were made of wood softened with hot water and shaped under pressure, were the product of a specialist, who directed other laborers at many stages and took over the work himself at all points where delicacy of judgment was required. These model canoes were carved by skilled carvers, not necessarily canoe specialists. They were made for several possible purposes. Small canoes were sometimes shown as representation, or tokens, of large ones in potlatch gift giving. Others were made as toys, and still others as "supernatural treasure" used in a winter dance. Many were made for sale to tourists.

The model canoes carved by Charles Edenshaw illustrate several stages of Haida canoe development: Figure 481 shows an early form; Figure 482 is the "classic" Haida canoe; and Plate XXXII B illustrates the cedar mat sail and mast that were used after the arrival of sailing ships.

The safety of the canoe party depended on a strong, well-made paddle. Considerable knowledge and technique were involved in selecting the wood and cutting, shaping, and smoothing the paddle. The crest designs painted on them, usually in red and black, represent a high development of symbolic abstraction.

The Haida paddle shown in Figure 484 (A7526), larger than the others, was used by the steersman.

Fig. 478. Model canoe from Bella Coola with figure of a seated man; wolf motif. Wood; blue, red, black. Length: 31 in. Museum Gift, Frank Burnett Coll. 1927. A401

Fig. 479. Kwakiutl model canoe from Fort Rupert, carved by Mungo Martin, with 2 seated figures, 1 holding a harpoon; killer whale motif. Cedar bark; green, black, yellow, red, purple. Length: 16 in. Museum Purchase 1950. A4259

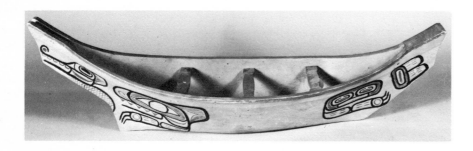

Fig. 480. Haida model canoe from Queen Charlotte Islands, carved by Charles Edenshaw. Wood; blue, green, black, red. Length: 30 in. MacMillan Purchase 1960, Rev. W. E. Collison Coll. A7097

Fig. 481. Haida model canoe, old type, from Queen Charlotte Islands, carved by Charles Edenshaw. Wood; red, black. Length: 31 in. MacMillan Purchase 1960, Rev. W. E. Collison Coll. A7096

Fig. 482. Haida model canoe, later type, from Queen Charlotte Islands, carved by Charles Edenshaw. Wood; green, blue, red, black. Length: 31 in. MacMillan Purchase 1960, Rev. W. E. Collison Coll. A7098

Fig. 483. (*Left to right*) Kwakiutl canoe paddle from Kitamaat. Wood; red, black. Length: 5 ft. 2 in. MacMillan Purchase 1948, Rev. G. H. Raley Coll. A1492. Kwakiutl canoe paddle from Kitamaat. Wood; black, red. Length: 4 ft. 5½ in. MacMillan Purchase 1948, Rev. G. H. Raley Coll. A1598. Kwakiutl woman's canoe paddle from Kitamaat. Wood; black design. Length: 3 ft. 7 in. MacMillan Purchase 1948, Rev. G. H. Raley Coll. A1548. Kwakiutl canoe paddle from Kitamaat. Wood; black design. Length: 4 ft. 8 in. MacMillan Purchase 1948, Rev. G. H. Raley Coll.

Fig. 484. (Left to right) Haida steering paddle from Queen Charlotte Islands, collected before 1880. Wood; black design. Length: 5 ft. 9 in. MacMillan Purchase 1961. A7526. Tsimshian canoe paddle from Kitsegukla. Wood; black, yellow, brown. Length: 5 ft. 6 in. MacMillan Purchase 1948, Rev. G. H. Raley Coll. A1550. Tsimshian canoe paddle from Nass River. Wood; black, brown. Length: 5 ft. 4 in. MacMillan Purchase 1948, Rev. G. H. Raley Coll. A1539. Tsimshian-style canoe paddle, collected before 1880. Wood; black design. Length: 5 ft. 2 in. MacMillan Purchase 1961. A7523

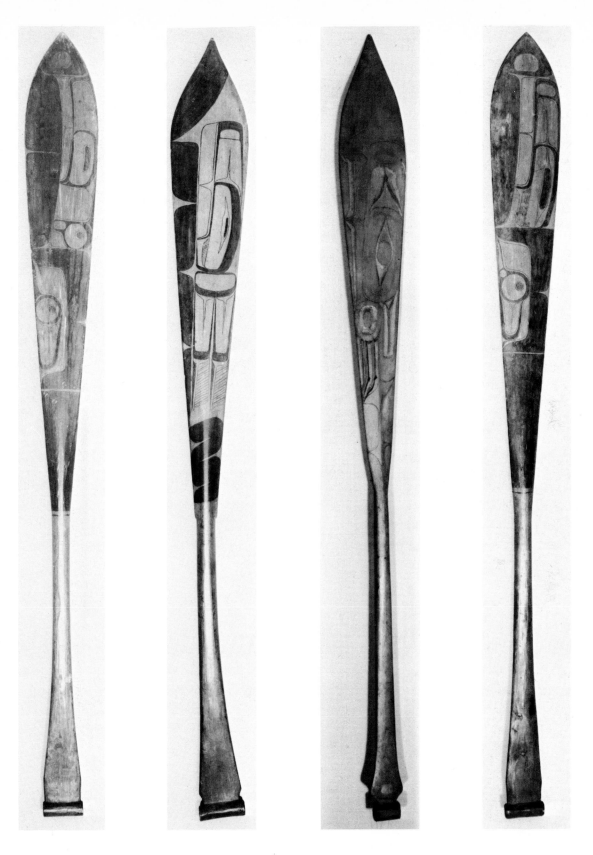

Fig. 485. (*Left to right*) Haida canoe paddle from Queen Charlotte Islands, collected before 1880. Wood; black design. Length: 5 ft. 3 in. MacMillan Purchase 1961. A7520. Tsimshian-style canoe paddle, collected before 1880. Wood; black design. Length: 5 ft. 2 in. MacMillan Purchase 1961. A7521. Tsimshian canoe paddle from Nass River. Unpainted wood. Length: 5 ft. 7 in. MacMillan Purchase 1948, Rev. G. H. Raley Coll. A1547. Haida canoe paddle from Queen Charlotte Islands, collected before 1880. Wood; black design. Length: 5 ft. MacMillan Purchase 1961. A7518

Fig. 486. (*Left to right*) Haida canoe paddle from Queen Charlotte Islands, collected before 1880. Wood; black design. Length: 5 ft. 4 in. MacMillan Purchase 1961. A7522. Canoe paddle, probably Tsimshian, collected before 1880. Wood; red, black. Length: 5 ft. 4 in. MacMillan Purchase 1961. A7525. Haida canoe paddle from Queen Charlotte Islands, collected before 1880. Wood; black design. Length: 5 ft. MacMillan Purchase 1961. A7517. Coast Salish canoe paddle from Comox, with eagle design. Wood; green, black, white, red. Length: 5 ft. 5 in. MacMillan Purchase 1953. A1599a. Coast Salish canoe paddle from Comox, with double-headed snake design. Wood; black, red, white. Length: 5 ft. 5 in. MacMillan Purchase 1953. A1599b

Totem Poles, House Posts, and Mortuary Poles

The tall, spectacular carved totem pole reached its peak in the latter half of the nineteenth century, by which time most tribes had adopted the practice of placing a family crest in front of the lineage house as a declaration of heraldry. Such a pole could not be erected without a potlatch, and its erection was the validation of the claims to the crests shown upon it. The figures on the pole were the ancestral persons of myth and lineage in their symbolic crest forms. The myths were recounted as the pole was put up with all of the ritual and protocol that accompanied important occasions.

Totem poles were carved by professionals who were commissioned to make them and who directed a number of men in the whole process of locating, felling, trimming, and carving the tree. The specialist and his assistants were paid at the potlatch subsequently given.

The pole was raised into place in front of the house by groups of men with a series of levers, rollers, and multiple riggings, and was set into a deep pit. Once established it was left to stand until it weathered into decomposition and collapsed. Since it could not be erected again without another ceremony, it was usually left when it fell.

There were several other kinds of pole carvings bearing family crests.

The house posts that supported the massive rafters inside the cedar plank houses were often carved with ancestral figures (Figs. 492-95). Such house posts were named. These carvings were sometimes made separately and were merely facings to the structural posts. The figures on these pillars represented one or more ancestral beings.

Other poles of major importance to the lineage house were the memorial pole and the door pole. The memorial pole was erected near the house in memory of a deceased chief, in the course of a series of mourning ceremonies. Such poles sometimes held the large boxes in which the body of the chief was interred (see Fig. 495 [A7093] for a model of a Haida memorial pole).

The door pole was a tall carved totem pole placed in front of the house in such a way that one of the ground-level figures contained the entrance door to the house.

Many of the poles shown in Figures 487-91 are model totem poles, first created in response to a demand by the tourist trade for a portable product of this region during the last decades of the nineteenth century. Because they were made by fine carvers, these models are worthy of the traditions that went into the development of this unique art form.

Not illustrated here are the massive totem poles and house posts which comprise the collection of the Totem Pole Park of the University of British Columbia.

Fig. 487. Kwakiutl totem pole from Bella Bella, with detail at right. Wood; black. Height: 10 ft. 10 in. MacMillan Purchase 1948, Rev. G. H. Raley Coll. A6543

Fig. 488. (*Left to right*) Haida model totem pole from Skidegate. Wood; brown, black. Height: 34 in. Mac-Millan Purchase 1948, Rev. G. H. Raley Coll. A1700. Haida model totem pole from Skidegate. Wood; black. Height: 17½ in. MacMillan Purchase 1948, Rev. G. H. Raley Coll. A1664. Haida model totem pole from Queen Charlotte Islands. Wood; brown, black. Height: 35 in. MacMillan Purchase 1948, Rev. G. H. Raley Coll. A1705

Fig. 489. (Left) Haida model totem pole from Queen Charlotte Islands, with detail *(center)*. Wood; brown. Height: 25½ in. MacMillan Purchase 1948, Rev. G. H. Raley Coll. A1703

Fig. 490. (Right). Haida model totem pole from Masset. Unpainted wood. Height: 31¼ in. MacMillan Purchase 1948, Rev. G. H. Raley Coll. A1707

Fig. 491. (*Left to right*) Haida model totem pole from Queen Charlotte Islands, carved by John Cross. Wood; brown, red, black, white. Height: 3 ft. 1 in. MacMillan Special Grant 1960, Rev. W. E. Collison Coll. A7088. Haida model totem pole from Skidegate. Wood; black. Height: 25 in. MacMillan Purchase 1948, Rev. G. H. Raley Coll. A1704. Tsimshian totem pole from Nass River. Unpainted wood with touches of black. Length: 7 ft. 4 in. MacMillan Special Grant 1962. A8212. (*Right, top*) Haida model totem pole from Masset. Unpainted wood. Height: 21 in. MacMillan Purchase 1948, Rev. G. H. Raley Coll. A1701. (*Bottom*) Haida model totem pole from Masset. Unpainted wood. Height: 21½ in. MacMillan Purchase 1948, Rev. G. H. Raley Coll. A1702

Fig. 492. Kwakiutl human figure house post from Kitamaat. Wood; black. Height:
5 ft. 2 in. MacMillan Purchase 1948, Rev. G. H. Raley Coll. A1779

Fig. 493. Kwakiutl human figure house post from Kitamaat. Wood; black. Height:
5 ft. 9 in. MacMillan Purchase 1948, Rev. G. H. Raley Coll. A1778

Fig. 494. Kwakiutl bear house post from Kitamaat, with details of paw (*right, top*) and ear (*right, bottom*). Wood; black. Height: 6 ft. 3 in. MacMillan Purchase 1948, Rev. G. H. Raley Coll. A1790

Fig. 495. (*Left*) Kwakiutl beaver house post from Kitamaat. Wood; black. Height: 5 ft. 3 in. MacMillan Purchase 1948, Rev. G. H. Raley Coll. A1789. (*Right, top*) Haida model memorial pole with bear carving, from Queen Charlotte Islands, carved by Charles Edenshaw. Wood; red, green, black. Height: 17 in. MacMillan Purchase 1960, Rev. W. E. Collison Coll. A7093. (*Bottom*) Kwakiutl carving of human face, part of a house post, from Campbell River. Wood; white, black, green, red. Width: 21¼ in. MacMillan Purchase 1951. A4026

Fig. 496. Tsimshian house front boards from Port Simpson, 2 of 26 wooden planks, 7-10 ft. length, painted red and black. MacMillan Purchase 1948, Rev. G. H. Raley Coll. A6558

Fig. 497. Salish house post from Duncan, with 4 supernatural otters. Height: 8 ft. Donated by Office of Indian Affairs 1950. A1725

Human and Animal Carvings

A number of other types of carvings were made by the Kwakiutl and by other peoples of the Northwest Coast. Portraits of chiefs were sometimes carved as commemorative figures in recognition of an outstanding potlatch or some great deed. Such a carving might be placed on a tall pole, on the front roof gable, or in front of the chief's house on a special occasion (Fig. 501). Among the Kwakiutl, portraiture was often used more directly for illusion. A substitute head, for example, might serve to illustrate magical decapitation.

Ridicule figures were carved for the purpose of shaming a rival who had failed in boastful claims or had fallen short of meeting a social challenge. Such figures were often represented as emaciated beggars, and were sometimes seated at the fireside at a potlatch. Emmons (1914:64) recounts the revenge of an Indian chief of Graham Island who, after being fined by the court, had a portrait figure made of the judge and argued with it. Boas (1895-366) recounts a quarrel between a man and his father-in-law. When the marriage exchange gifts failed to follow the expected satisfactory agreement, the young man showed his contempt for his father-in-law by having a carving of his wife made, a chain put around the neck of the effigy, and the figure "drowned" with all due ceremony. This reflected adversely on her family's ability to meet their commitments.

Welcome figures were placed in front of a house or on the beach in attitudes expressing a welcome to visitors arriving by sea. Curtis (1915: 141) describes a post at Nimpkish, carved before 1865, which represented

354

the chief's scout gazing out over the water to watch for canoes arriving with wedding proposals for him.

As we have already seen, the Kwakiutl often used carvings to create an illusion, as in the case of the novice arriving in a canoe who apparently drowned when the canoe overturned (Curtis 1915:161). Swanton (1905:160) mentions a black whale built by the Haida which was large enough to hold ten novices inside.

Examples of some of these human figures are shown in Figures 498-504.

Some miscellaneous animal carvings, and implements decorated with crest designs, are illustrated in Figures 505-20. It should be noted that many tools and implements of domestic use were made in a decorative form which had no relation to ceremony or ritual. The craftsman probably put in the extra work for his own pleasure.

Fig. 498. Coast Salish grave figures of mourning man (*left*) and woman (*right*) from Sardis. Wood; white, brown. MacMillan Purchase 1948, Rev. G. H. Raley Coll. (*Left*) Height: 5 ft. 6 in. A1780. (*Right*) Height: 5 ft. 3 in. A1781

Fig. 499. (*Left*) Kwakiutl ancestor figure from Alert Bay. Wood: brown, black, red. Height: 4 ft. 10 in. Mac-Millan Purchase 1948, Rev. G. H. Raley Coll. A1800. (*Right*) Kwakiutl grave effigy from old village near Kita-maat. Unpainted wood. Height: 23 in. MacMillan Purchase 1948, Rev. G. H. Raley Coll. A1799

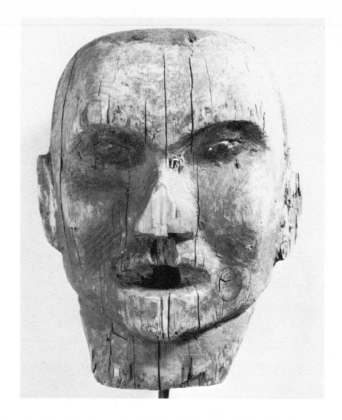

Fig. 500. (*Left*) Kwakiutl grave effigy from Kitamaat. Unpainted wood. Height: 11 in. MacMillan Purchase 1948, Rev. G. H. Raley Coll. A3688. (*Right*) Tsimshian ceremonial carving of human head from Aiyansh. Wood; red, black. Height: 9 in. MacMillan Purchase 1962. A8232

Fig. 501. (*Left*) Kwakiutl carving of a human head from a pole outside a house at Kingcome Inlet. Wood; red, black. Height: 9½ in. MacMillan Purchase 1953. A6153. (*Right*) Haida carving of seated chief from Queen Charlotte Islands. Wood; black, red. Height: 9½ in. MacMillan Purchase 1960, Rev. W. E. Collison Coll. A7106

Fig. 502. (*Left*) Bella Coola carving of a man seated in a canoe (see Fig. 478). Wood; red, blue, black. Height: 7 in. Frank Burnett Coll. 1927. A401a. (*Right*) Kwakiutl effigy from the grave of a chief at Kitamaat. Wood; brown, black. Height: 11 in. MacMillan Purchase 1948, Rev. G. H. Raley Coll. A1706

Fig. 503. Coast Salish carving of Indian, from North Vancouver Reserve, carved by D. Williams in 1951. Varnished wood. Height: 14½ in. Museum Purchase 1951. A4187

Fig. 504. Coast Salish carving of Indian agent from North Vancouver Reserve, carved by D. Williams. Varnished wood. Height: 14 in. Museum Purchase 1951. A4186

Fig. 505. (Left) Tsimshian carved angel from Port Simpson, made by Freddie Alexei in 1886. This was used in a church as a baptismal font, but was said to have been removed because it frightened the children. Wood; blue-gray, black, white. Height: 34 in. MacMillan Purchase 1948, Rev. G. H. Raley Coll. A1776. (Right) Kwakiutl carving of a bear with a fish in its paws. Wood; black. Height: 3 ft. 1½ in. Museum Gift 1950. A6533

Fig. 506. (Above) Salish carving of bear's head from Coquitlam. Wood; black, red. Length: 9 in. Frank Burnett Coll. 1927. A408. (Right) Haida carving of sea bear from Queen Charlotte Islands, collected in 1889. Unpainted wood. Length: 12 in. Mac-Millan Purchase 1948, Rev. G. H. Raley Coll. A6437

Fig. 507. (*Above*) Kwakiutl wolf carving from Campbell River. Wood; blue, red, white. Length: 10 in. MacMillan Purchase 1962. A8286. (*Right*) Kwakiutl carving of hawk from Alert Bay. Varnished wood; black, red. Height: 10½ in. Gift of Mrs. F. G. Sherbourne 1948. A1712

Fig. 508. (*Above, left*) Kwakiutl carving of crane's head from Gilford Island, presumably part of a mask. Wood; black, red. Length: 17 in. MacMillan Purchase 1952. A3436. (*Right*) Salish carving of duck from the top of a totem pole outside a house in Comox. Unpainted wood. Length: 4 ft. 3 in. MacMillan Purchase 1962. A7981

Fig. 509. Kwakiutl killer whale carving from Sullivan Bay. Wood; black, red, blue, white. Length: 12 in. MacMillan Purchase 1953. A4340

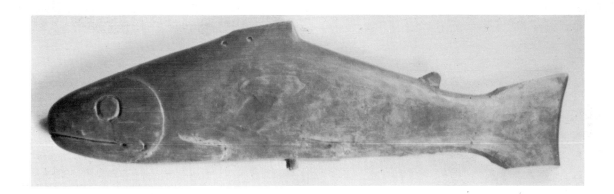

Fig. 510. Kwakiutl fish-man charm from Kitamaat; 2 views. Wood; black. Height: 8 in. MacMillan Purchase 1948, Rev. G. H. Raley Coll. A3439

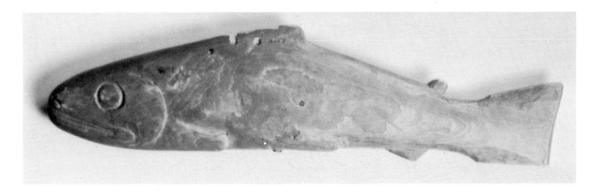

Fig. 511. 2 Tsimshian carved wooden fish from Port Essington, probably from 2 sides of a mask. Wood; brown. Frank Burnett Coll. 1927. (*Top*) Length: 14½ in. A153. (*Bottom*) Length: 15 in. A152

Fig. 512. Prehistoric club in the form of a ball and bird, from the North Arm of the Fraser River. Wood. Length: 14½ in. MacMillan Purchase 1964. A8548

Fig. 514. (Left to right) Kwakiutl wolf-shaped club from Kitamaat. Wood. Length: 12 in. MacMillan Purchase 1962. A7958. Kwakiutl club from Gilford Island, carved in the shape of a hand holding a stone. Wood. Length: 14½ in. MacMillan Purchase 1952. A4115. Kwakiutl net float in the shape of a sea otter. Unpainted wood. Length: 17½ in. MacMillan Purchase 1948, Rev. G. H. Raley Coll. A3437

Fig. 513. (Left to right) Kwakiutl club. Wood. Length: 12 in. MacMillan Special Grant 1962. A8076. Kwakiutl fish club from Bella Bella. Wood. Length: 16 in. MacMillan Purchase 1948, Rev. G. H. Raley Coll. A1481. Tsimshian war club in the shape of a human figure, from Metlakatla. Wood. Length: 20½ in. MacMillan Purchase 1948, Rev. G. H. Raley Coll. A1482

Fig. 515. (Left) Coast Salish bird-shaped mat creaser from Vancouver Island. Wood. Length: 6 in. Museum Purchase 1948. A3519. (Above) Kwakiutl duck-shaped net float from Kingcome Inlet. Wood; black, white. Length: 20 in. MacMillan Purchase 1953. A6198

Fig. 516. (Left) Tsimshian canoe bailer from Nass River, the handle carved with a crane's head design. Wood. Length: 15 in. MacMillan Purchase 1951. A6191. (Right) Kwakiutl carving of man and animal from Bella Bella, probably the handle of an implement. Wood; red, black. Length: 7½ in. Frank Burnett Coll. 1927. A131

Fig. 517. (Left) Prehistoric spear thrower in the form of an animal and a human head, dredged up from the mouth of the Skagit River; described in Taylor and Caldwell 1953. Unpainted wood. Length: 15½ in. MacMillan Purchase 1959. A7021 (Right) Haida halibut hook from Queen Charlotte Islands. Wood, fiber, and ivory. Length: 12 in. MacMillan Special Grant 1960, Rev. W. E. Collison Coll. A7112

Fig. 518. (Left) Kwakiutl halibut hook. Wood and commercial nail. Length: 11 in. MacMillan Purchase 1948, Rev. G. H. Raley Coll. A3438. (Right) Haida halibut hook from Queen Charlotte Islands, with carved octopus tentacles and otters. Wood and iron nail. Length: 10½ in. Frank Burnett Coll. 1927. A136

Fig. 519. Coast Salish spindle whorl from Comox. Wood. Diameter: 9½ in. Gift of Mrs. F. L. Beecher 1952. A4323

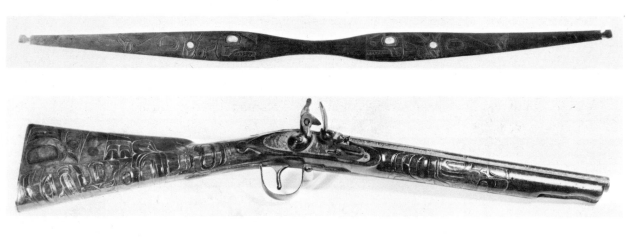

Fig. 520. (*Top to bottom*) Tsimshian bow from Hartley Bay. Wood with abalone shell inlay. Length: 3 ft. 8 in. Gift of Mr. Thomas Wallace. A6838. Haida carved Parker and Field flintlock trade musket from Skidegate. The muzzle has been shortened and carved with a crest animal. Length: 32½ in. MacMillan Purchase 1948, Rev. G. H. Raley Coll. A1584. (*Left*) Tsimshian incised drawing on a whale's vertebra with inlaid abalone shell, from Port Simpson. Width: 7 in. Gift of Miss Fanta Tait 1965. A8534

Soul Catchers

These small carved objects (Figs. 521-23) were not connected with the pot-latch or the dancing societies but were part of the shaman's gear, and were used by him as an important property in his performances. A small box carved with magical symbols, the soul catcher was carried by the shaman when he pursued the soul of an ailing patient under his care. Usually at twilight, the soul, visible only to the shaman, fluttered toward the horizon. With the stopper removed from his magic box, the shaman followed it, beguiling it with incantations. When he succeeded in approaching it, he popped it into the box, replaced the stopper, and returned it to the patient, who then recovered.

Fig. 521. Kwakiutl soul catcher from Kit-lope, a finely carved Sisiutl with a movable head on the center figure. Unpainted wood. Length: 6½ in. MacMillan Purchase 1948, Rev. G. H. Raley Coll. A1774

Fig. 522. Nootka soul catcher from Vancouver Island, collected before 1890. Bone center piece, wooden legs and eagle figurine; black, white, green. Length: 23 in. MacMillan Purchase 1961. A7542

Fig. 523. Kwakiutl soul catcher from Kitamaat, killer whale design, purchased by Rev. Raley in 1895. Wood; black, brown. Length: 8 in. MacMillan Purchase 1948, Rev. G. H. Raley Coll. A4258

Stonework

Before the introduction of metal to the Northwest Coast, stone was used for tools of all types (see Figs. 3-5). Thereafter it continued to be used for heavy hammers, mawls, and pile drivers (Figs. 525, 530, 533), sometimes carved with human or animal designs. It was also employed for beads and for stone bowls (Figs. 524, 526-29, 531), which were used for a variety of purposes, such as the grinding of paint colors and, among the Haida, the mixing of tobacco and lime. Clubs were also made of stone (Figs. 524, 534, 537), and there was widespread trade in the blades that were made from the nephrite found in the Fraser River area (Fig. 2).

The southern Kwakiutl did not, to any significant degree, engage in stonework.

Fig. 524. (Left to right) Kwakiutl stone carving of mother and child from Bella Bella. Height: 5½ in. Museum Purchase 1947, Dr. G. E. Darby Coll. A1352. Salish soapstone carving of a seated human figure in a bowl, part of a shaman's bowl from Patricia Bay. Height: 7½ in. MacMillan Purchase 1962. A11507c. Haida stone club in the shape of a human head with abalone shell inlay, from Queen Charlotte Islands. Length: 7½ in. MacMillan Purchase 1960, Rev. W. E. Collison Coll. A7150

Fig. 525. (Left) Salish stone carving of human head from Comox. Height: 7½ in. Gift of William Douglas 1950. A1636. (Right) Kwakiutl black stone pile driver with incised human face, from Kitamaat. Width: 10 in. MacMillan Purchase 1948, Rev. G. H. Raley Coll. A4483

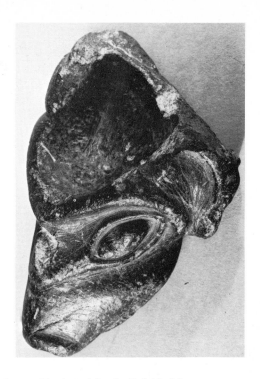

Fig. 526. (*Left*) Haida carving of a face in carbonaceous shale, from Queen Charlotte Islands. Height: 9 in. MacMillan Purchase 1960, Rev. W. E. Collison Coll. A7147. (*Right*) Salish soapstone bowl from Patricia Bay, in the shape of the head and forelegs of an animal. Length: 6 in. MacMillan Purchase 1962. A11536c

Fig. 527. (*Left*) Kwakiutl stone carving of whale and eagle from Bella Bella. Length: 10 in. Museum Purchase 1947, Dr. G. E. Darby Coll. A1131. (*Right*) Bella Coola fish-shaped stone bowl colored inside with red ocher. Length: 5½ in. Gift of Bert Robson 1950. A6550

Fig. 528. (*Left*) Haida frog-shaped stone mortar bowl from Queen Charlotte Islands, with red painted design. Width: 8 in. MacMillan Purchase 1960, Rev. W. E. Collison Coll. A7076. (*Right*) Haida stone mortar bowl from Queen Charlotte Islands, with anthropomorphic design. Height: 9½ in. MacMillan Purchase 1960, Rev. W. E. Collison Coll. A7077

Fig. 529. (*Left*) Kwakiutl stone bowl from Port Hardy, with 9 knobs around the base. Diameter: 12 in. Mac-Millan Purchase 1962. A11693c. (*Right*) Kwakiutl stone medicine bowl from Bella Bella, with bird design. Length: 6 in. Dr. G. E. Darby 1931 Alumni Valedictory Gift. A1353

Fig. 530. Kwakiutl stone hammer from Kitamaat, with frog design. Width: 3½ in. Mac-Millan Purchase 1948, Rev. G. H. Raley Coll. A3002

Fig. 531. Kwakiutl skull-shaped stone mortar dish from Bella Bella. Width: 3½ in. Museum Purchase 1947, Dr. G. E. Darby Coll. A3484

Fig. 532. (Left) Haida stone carving of a frog's head from Queen Charlotte Islands. Width: 6 in. MacMillan Purchase 1960, Rev. W. E. Collison Coll. A7153. (Right) Tsimshian stone pile driver from Nass River. Length: 10½ in. MacMillan Purchase 1948, Rev. G. H. Raley Coll. A6438

Fig. 533. (Left) Bella Coola stone pile driver, a stone slab with grooves for 4 fingers and thumb. Length: 15½ in. Mac-Millan Purchase 1959. A7025. (Right) Bella Coola stone pile driver with thumbholes. Length: 13½ in. Gift of Bert Robson 1949. A4010

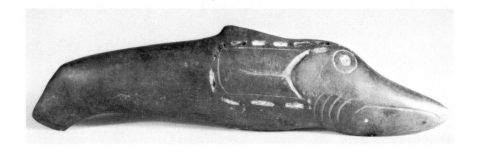

Fig. 534. Haida stone club in the shape of a killer whale with abalone shell inlay, from Queen Charlotte Islands. Length: 12 in. MacMillan Purchase 1960, Rev. W. E. Collison Coll. A7148

Fig. 535. Haida stone fish carving from Queen Charlotte Islands. Length: 6½ in. MacMillan Purchase 1960, Rev. W. E. Collison Coll. A7152

Fig. 536. Tsimshian stone carving in the shape of a killer whale, from Khutzeymatleen Inlet. Length: 12¼ in. Gift of A. Henuset 1953. A4256

Fig. 537. Kwakiutl stone club from Vancouver Island. Length: 9½ in. MacMillan Purchase 1962. A8285

374

PART III
Appendixes, Glossary, Bibliography, Index

APPENDIX I

Style and Attributions

Within the many variations in traditional form, individual carvers attempted to create stylistic variation and a personal mark. Again and again, informants noted a distinctive individual style. Willie Seaweed was mentioned frequently as having strong detailed outlines as his trademark. Mungo Martin early in his career carved an oblong, rather clumsy eye space (Figs. 54, 57). Such details are identifiable in carvings of both known and unknown carvers. Comments of many craftsmen and observers included: "You want to show you're smarter than anyone else, so you make it different"; "He always put something different on his carving."

It will be noted, looking at any of the categories of masks, how very different the variations are. The salient features of Hamatsa Galokwudzuwis (Figs. 80-109) are a short broad beak, with some treatment of the curving, plus prominent flared nostrils. Within this basic tradition are dozens of individual styles.

It is less surprising to have some carvers clearly identified by stylistic traits than to have several serious and knowledgeable informants give conflicting identifications. It has even happened, occasionally, that a carver failed to recognize his own work from photographs of it. The presumably correct identification was made by other informants, with convincing citation of time and place. Sometimes it was recalled that several people had worked together, as in a Renaissance *atélier,* to produce the single carving.

It is true that a carver who was a specialist might forget a commissioned carving, for such men were in much demand and might produce many pieces in a long lifetime. Some masks were carved "between sunrise and sunset," as T. F. McIlwraith notes, and Curtis (1948:II, 54) records that two days were taken for a carver to carve many of the dance masks for a winter dance. However, in spite of this large output, most carvers did recognize their own style of carving, particularly in a mask carved for someone for a dance that had a special association, clearly remembered; the artist who failed to note one of his works would be the exception.

The most helpful Kwakiutl informants were Mungo Martin and Dan Cranmer, both of them careful students of their own culture, anxious to pass on their knowledge and have it recorded. I have relied very heavily on identifications, interpretations, and comments from these two fine men. There were also many others seriously interested and concerned about accuracy. Their names are given in the list at the end of this section.

In a few instances statements of different informants at different times and places led to conflicts of identification. Individual motives gave rise to peculiar errors. One man identified nine out of ten items as having been carved by his father, even when everyone else identified them differently. Some outstanding masks that would seem to be distinctive and easy to recognize were attributed to as many as five carvers. In such a case the conflict in attributions is recorded in detail in the catalogue files of the museum, along with any serious remarks offered by way of identification.

Informants tended to be more in accord when placing the carvings in a time sequence. People remembered vividly the occasion for which the items had been made, and how old they themselves were at the time. This was true for both men and women of all ages. "I was at that potlatch for ———— at ———— when I was twelve, and I saw it then." And, of course, those who had participated as dancers were even more likely to remember how old they and their relatives had been. They also remembered clearly life crisis rites of their whole family, such as puberty announcements and first-name potlatches for children, or the time a novice was initiated.

Not all the informants who were questioned were equally serious or well informed. Some casual informants, not always the younger ones, but perhaps less interested, made such comments as, "You can tell they are not swans. The neck is not long enough," about a set of headdresses identified by the owner as a swan (Fig. 228); or (of the Merman, Fig. 326), "This is a beaver. You can tell by his large teeth." (This particular mask was carefully identified by others and has been documented by Boas as Merman.)

Prerogatives of the Kwakiutl are very much tied to place. Most Kwakiutl informants were likely to remember the place of origin of a privilege ("from the Heiltsuk at the marriage of ——— with ——— of ———"). It was also noted that some island families tended to accumulate privileges pertaining to sea beings of one kind of another (see Pl. XXVIII B; Figs. 23, 306, 315 [A8102], 324 [A3663], which are all from Gilford Island).

The close association of these ceremonial materials with vivid and meaningful events sometimes led to an extraordinarily clear recollection of details. Thus one informant noted that a certain dish (Fig. 252) was given to the D—— family in 1924 at the same time as the skull (Fig. 122 [A6160]), which was to be worn on a neck ring as a Komunokas privilege. This concern with the importance of the details of the material culture undoubtedly helped to make the Kwakiutl culture so viable, its products almost endless, and their uses so imaginative.

Following is a list of Kwakiutl informants, with each person's village and approximate age at the time of identifying the various objects.

Mrs. Moses Alfred, Alert Bay, 72

Mrs. Agnes Cranmer, Alert Bay, 55

Chief Dan Cranmer, Alert Bay, 62-72

James Dick, Kingcome Inlet, 66

Charlie George, Jr., Nahwahto, 59

Mrs. Dick Hawkins, Kingcome Inlet, 73

Tommy Hunt, Fort Rupert, 60

Chief Tom Johnson, Fort Rupert, 80

Chief Mungo Martin, Fort Rupert, 70-80

Mrs. James Roberts, Alert Bay, 76

Chief Bill Snow, Gilford Island, 64

Joe Seaweed, Blunden Harbour, 56

Willie Seaweed, Blunden Harbour, 93

Jim Sewid, Alert Bay, 53

Peter Smith, Turnour Island, 68

Billy Sandy Willie, Kingcome Inlet, 75
Dick Willie, Quatsino, 76

The canons of tradition and style in Kwakiutl carving and painting can best be examined by studying the masks of the Hamatsa. For at least one hundred and thirty years, these cannibal birds have been carved by the southern Kwakiutl, and they are represented here by one hundred examples.

This frequent repetition might have resulted in a rigid standardization of appearance. A study of them in detail, however, shows that there is great individual variation in both carving and painting to the point where every mask is unique even although general Northwest Coast tradition, tribal and local style, and the characteristic marks of the individual craftsmen are likely to be represented on them all.

Each bird has a basic form: Raven has a beak that relates it to other ravens; Hokhokw has a very special long narrow beak; Crooked Beak has the fantastic protuberance or frill coming from the forehead. (The original form from which this was derived is open to conjecture: it has some similarity to the heavy prominence surmounting the beaks of the puffin, the scoter, and the rhinoceros auklet, all of which were known to the Kwakiutl.) The basic coloring of these masks was also determined by tradition: black was the main color and possibly the color of the earlier northern forms (p. 62), white was used to accent the eyes or details of carving, and red was introduced to emphasize the flaring nostrils and lips.

Within the general framework set by the form, each mask is a fresh and individual creation. Even the structural form of the various features in their total balance and proportion can vary with the individual choice of the carver.

This series of masks shares one basic element, virtuosity of wood carving. They illustrate (and were undoubtedly part of the evidence for) the remark of Boas (1927:25) that artistry began when absolute technical competence had been mastered. The Hamatsa carvers had become virtuosos for whom wood carving had few limitations. The wood became plastic in their hands, and planes and lines swelled, curved, and tapered, delicately or boldly.

Besides this technological virtuosity, all of these masks shared the general form dictated by tradition: head, beak, eye, brow, and nostril. A further traditional element was the use of "space fillers," the design elements of various forms, used to fill space and to tie the various parts of the over-all design togther. These fillers included parallel tapering lines, parallel "bracket" lines, claw designs, scalloped edges, and ovoid "front head' form, and a long delicate feather-shaped line.

It becomes necessary to refer to the masks themselves in order to see how individual artists chose and selected details.

The following pages list the Kwakiutl artists named and recognized within the southern Kwakiutl region, with the masks identified as theirs.

If we turn to the works of the fine carver, Willie Seaweed, it is possible to select and compare any chosen feature—an eye form, space fillers, a nostril—of the masks carved by him.

Informants noted particularly that the nostril form was "always" carved by Willie Seaweed in a characteristic fashion. Figure 93, Crooked Beak, can offer an example. It is a nostril of parallel curves, with tapering lines joining at the bottom curve, the whole accentuated by a convex ridge. Yet other examples of nostrils carved by him show not one but several forms, and unique individual manifestations of them (cf. Pl. IV A; Figs. 76, 77). In each of these the nostrils are different from those of the others.

Turning from the detail to the whole mask, and looking again at the same Seaweed carvings, it can be seen that an over-all style relates all of these masks to one another. They all show a precision, a flair, and a perfection of finish that is part of the "Willie Seaweed style." The work of other carvers shows a similar differentiation of the single piece within the craftsman's distinctive style.

It is probably this distinctive over-all style that informants recognized when they looked at the masks. Feeling the need to be specific in describing the work, they chose a feature which seemed, because of some familiarity, to be "typical" carving.

One more carver may serve to offer another illustration of this same point.

Charlie George, Sr., carved the three masks shown in Figures 69, 90, and 101. There is not much similarity of detail in the actual features. Nostril, eye, head, and face each has a different presentation, and yet the choice of space fillers and their organization in the whole form makes an over-all impact that conveys the carver's style. This impact was felt by all the informants who had been familiar with his works.

A continuing interest in material culture on the part of the Kwakiutl led them to be concerned about identifying their familiar carvings. Seventeen carvers have been identified among the southern Kwakiutl creators of the work illustrated in this volume, and there are many others who were not named by any informant. The time span covered was at least eighty years or three long generations.

Following is a list of carvers and the objects attributed to each, together with the carver's village and the dates of birth and death when known.

John Davis, Nahwahto, 1869-1939: Hamatsa raven mask (Fig. 49)

Charlie George, Sr., Nahwahto, 1889- , and Charlie George, Jr., Nahwahto, 1910-   (because it was often impossible to ascertain from the informants whether the father or the son was the carver referred to, their works are listed together here): Hamatsa raven masks (Figs. 69, 70), Hokhokw mask (Fig. 79), Crooked-Beak masks (Figs. 88, 90, 91, 95, 96, 100, 101, 103), human face masks (Figs. 408, 443 [A4185]), complex mask (Fig. 456)

Chief George, Nahwahto, 1873-1949: Hamatsa raven masks (Figs. 47, 53), Crooked-Beak mask (Fig. 97)

Dick Hawkins, Kingcome Inlet, 1896-1957: Hamatsa raven masks (Figs. 46 [A3815], 51, 61), Crooked-Beak mask (Fig. 102), ceremonial skull (Fig. 122 [A6160]), Sisiutl headdress (Fig. 126 [A3604])

Jim Howard: Hamatsa multiple mask (Fig. 110), Hamatsa head ring (Fig. 111 [A6377]), Crooked-Beak headpiece (Fig. 111 [A3664]), Thunderbird mask (Fig. 371)

Charlie James, Fort Rupert, 1876-1948: Hamatsa multiple mask (Pl. IV B), Sisiutl feast dish (Fig. 251), feast dish (Fig. 259)

Jack James: Hamatsa raven mask (Fig. 56), Hokhokw mask (Pl. III B)

Joe Johnny: Crooked-Beak mask (Fig. 99)

Mungo Martin, Fort Rupert, 1880-1962: Hamatsa raven masks (Pl. III A; Figs. 54, 57, 62), Hokhokw mask (Fig. 74), Hamatsa multiple mask, made with Willie Seaweed (Pl. V A), Chilkat pattern board (Fig. 185), Pugwis mask Fig. 326), Atlakim bird mask (Fig. 392 [A4153]), model canoe (Fig. 479)

Johnny Nolie: Hamatsa raven mask (Fig. 58)

Dick Price, 1880-1936: Solatlala rattles (Fig. 38), Hamatsa raven mask (Fig. 50), Hokhokw masks (Figs. 73, 75), Crooked-Beak masks (Figs. 81, 85), multiple mask (Pl. V B), Sisiutl headdress (Fig. 126 [A3790])

Willie Seaweed, Nahwahto, 1873- : Hamatsa raven masks (Figs. 46 [A6121], 52, 59, 60), Hokhokw masks (Figs. 76, 77), Crooked-Beak masks (Pl. IV A; Figs. 83, 87, 93), multiple mask, made with Mungo Martin (Pl. V A), Noohlmahl mask (Fig. 117), Atlakim masks (Figs. 133, 390), Atlakim masks, made with Joe Seaweed (Figs. 135-39), Tsonokwa mask (Fig. 146 [A6271]), Thunderbird headdress (Fig. 233), Komokwa mask (Fig. 313), Atlakim grouse mask (Fig. 390 [A6088]), raven in the sun mask (Fig. 398), Bookwus mask (Fig. 416 [A6242]), Kwekwe mask (Fig. 421)

Joe Seaweed, Nahwahto, 1910- : Atlakim masks, made with Willie Seaweed (Figs. 135-39)

Arthur Shaughnessy, Alert Bay, 1884-1945: ceremonial curtains (Figs. 10, 12), Hamatsa raven mask (Fig. 65), sun mask (Pl. XXIII)

Frank Walker: power boards (Fig. 130 [A3797, A3798])

George Walkus: Atlakim "Sneezer" mask (Fig. 142 [A6214])

Tom Wamiss, Kingcome Inlet: Crooked-Beak mask (Fig. 82)

A list of non-Kwakiutl carvers follows.

Freddie Alexei, Tsimshian, Port Simpson: carved angel (Fig. 505 [A1776])

Andrew Charles, Salish, Musqueam Reserve, 1897-1961: Kwekwe masks (Figs. 424 [A6813], 425 [A6546], 426 [A6812])

John Cross, Haida, Skidegate, 1850-1939: model totem pole (Fig. 491 [A7088])

Charles Edenshaw, Haida, Port Simpson, 1839-1924: silver bracelets (Figs. 240 [A8094], 241 [A8093]), walking sticks (Fig. 243), oil dish (Fig. 274 [A7054]), model canoes (Pl. XXXII B; Figs. 480-82), model memorial pole (Fig. 495 [A7093])

Bill Reid, Haida, 1920-   : silver bracelets (Figs. 240 [A1500], 241 [A8412]), gold bracelet (Fig. 240 [A1501])

D. Williams, Salish: carved Indian (Fig. 503), Indian agent (Fig. 504)

APPENDIX II

A Potlatch at Alert Bay in 1966, Reported by Mrs. Dan Cranmer

The Tseka season in recent years is much shorter than in earlier times, and the following is an example of a fairly recent potlatch of Chief Tom Johnson of Fort Rupert at which time his marriage exchange with Mary Hunt was completed.

In the afternoon Chief Johnson received from his wife quantities of goods as well as privileges. This signified the completion of the marriage exchange. Later in the evening came the time *kwekhula* when there was "plain dancing" (the *kwekhula* was just women's dancing at four different times in the same evening). There were just small gifts given at this time. Then the Hamatsa appeared seizing those who were to become dancers. All those Hamatsa present at the gathering *hwasuleehl* (jumping up and uttering Hamatsa cries). Those seized by the Hamatsa were taken out of the house presumably into the woods. This ended the first day's activities.

The next day Peter Smith gathered the people in the village together *(kapekw)*. This function was an important one and was always performed by the same person who inherits it. When the people were assembled in the house those who could *yeylakwula* (chanting with no accompaniment) were given rattles and began to chant as they walked slowly from the back of the house to the door. (It is important to turn before leaving the front of the house and also when reaching the door.) They were followed by the rest of the people to the graveyard where the novices were waiting. Some of those in the procession were dancing. In the meantime the Hamatsa *hwasuleehl* while their attendants tried to capture them. The procession returned to the house, and the spectators took their seats. After the spectators were seated the dancers (Danum) waited outside until the Hamatsa entered first. The novices all wore fresh hemlock branch head rings. Some also wore hemlock branch skirts. The Hamatsa circled the fire, went behind the curtain, and appeared above it. This happened four times before the Hamatsa disappeared again. The novices then entered the house, turned, and *tsahkeed* (moving with short, quick steps), turned again, and went behind the screen, entering from the right. There they stayed till evening. In the evening a large rope or band of red cedar bark was brought in, and a relative of the person giving the potlatch was in the center. Six attendants held the band around the relative, and all walked slowly around the fire from the door to the front of the house, turning in the proper manner. They stopped in front of the curtain at which time the cedar bark cutter (Tosa) appeared. The Tosa was always a member of the Hamatsa society, and his duties as cutter were inherited. His face was painted black, and he wore a plain black blanket. He circled the fire four times, raised his knife four times, turning each time in the correct manner before cutting through the cedar bark uttering the Hamatsa cry. The bark was cut with a special knife, and four cuts were made. The wide strips of bark were then torn up into smaller strips and distributed to those gathered.

This was followed by the sprinkling of eagle down on the heads of those who now wore the cedar bark bands. Those gathered were now said to have "gone through" *(lakhsa)*. Tseka names were now used, there was very little talking. Everyone spoke in whispers.

The fourth night the *kikilnila* began. One person from each of the villages represented was given a red cedar bark head ring. He left his seat and went out of the house, coming back in, turning and moving with small quick steps to the front of the house where he faced the singers and began to dance. Each dancer received a gift from the chief giving the potlatch. Dancers of different societies may *hwasuleehl,* and their song is sung. The last dancer in this series is Lulotlalahl, who with Raven entices the Hamatsa back into the house. (The Hamatsa had disappeared at the beginning of *kwekhula* and now reappears at *kikilnila*.) All the Hamatsa *hwasuleehl* together. The novice Hamatsa appears and disappears again four times. The *kikilnila* is finished.

The next day *kimya* begins. Efforts are made to tame the Hamatsa, and his attendants finally succeed. In the evening the novices discarded their hemlock branch head rings and skirts and put on the regalia of their particular dances. They then performed their dances. Four times the singers *kwekhula* the dancers.

Sometime after midnight Tom Omhid performed the ceremony of *kwasa* (to bathe). A small ring of cedar bark in the shape of a human figure was passed over the head of each dancer four times. He then stepped through the ring symbolizing a bathtub *(kanayoo).* Tom Omhid chanted as this ritual was performed. All novices who had entered their societies at this potlatch went through this ritual. Omhid then picked up the *kanayoo,* circled the fire four times chanting as he went. After completing the fourth circle he put the *kanayoo* into the fire and when it was burning carried it outside and hung it on a pole in front of the house. This signified the end of the novice's performance at Tom Johnson's potlatch. Some of the novices received new names. Then everything was given away.

APPENDIX III

An Eye-Witness Account
of the Hamatsa Ritual

(From Curtis 1915: 179-82)

"Now from the secret room comes the sound of many whistles of different pitch, high and low, blowing notes short and long, and through all rings the hoarse, thrilling cry of hamatsa: *hap! hap! hap!* Six or eight attendants appear with their backs to the people. Their robes are fastened at the neck and tied back at the waist, so that only the back and the chest are covered, and beneath the robe each has a whistle so placed that by bending the neck he can reach it with his mouth. They keep the hamatsa hidden as long as they can, but usually he soon breaks through their line, and they run after him, trying to keep around him, and some holding him by the hemlock neck-ring as if they were restraining a wild beast. After dancing for a moment on his *yûtsu* blankets he moves along stooping, sliding ahead one foot then the other. When he comes to the rear, as also when he reaches the front of the room, he always pivots on the left foot, but seldom does this elsewhere. He extends one arm, palm upward, then the other. He advances on certain lines which have been secretly marked out on the floor, and those who have been previously warned by the initiator that hamatsa will bite them sit where these lines touch the edge of the open space, so that hamatsa can easily reach them. Generally they sit out in front of the others, but with a few spectators scattered near and perhaps even in front of them, so as not to be too conspicuous. As the hamatsa dances, his attendants occasionally whisper to him the position of the next person to be bitten. It is necessary to restrict the number of those bitten, since each one must be paid. Usually a large canoe of two hundred blankets is the price, the amount depending on the rank of the bitten one. The hamatsa usually bites two or three men as soon as he comes out of the secret room.

"At the end of the first four songs, while the singers beat on the boards, the hamatsa, still stooping low, runs rapidly around the room with his arms outstretched on either side, palms downward and hands trembling slightly, as he simulates great strength. The attendants run behind, two holding his upper arms and the others grasping the hemlock neck-ring. After encircling the fire twice, he suddenly throws off the hemlock ring, wristlets, and anklets, and runs about the fire twice and still more rapidly, and finally he dashes behind the *máwihl* at the left side, while the attendants go around at the right.

"As soon as he has disappeared, the cry of *hap! hap! hap!* ceases, and the people hear the cry of the raven, *ḵô! ḵô! ḵô!* and the sound of raven's mandibles clapping together. Two of the singers begin to chant slowly, and there appears a man—supposedly hamatsa—wearing *ḵwáhiwiwi hámsiwi,* the mask of *Ḵwáhqaqalhóhsiwi.* He faces the *máwihl,* and dances by step-ping high without moving from his place. At the end of the song he leaps suddenly into the air and squats down simultaneously with the ending of the song. The singers abruptly accelerate their beating to a rapid tempo, and the raven masker goes through various motions, while squatting on the floor and holding in his hands the strings that control the beak. Thus he is unable to aid his movements with his hands, and as his performance at times amounts almost to contortions while he squats or actually sits flat on the floor with a ponderous, unwieldy mask on his head and his hands occupied with the strings, his task is not a light one. Only a very strong man can under-take it. As the singing proceeds, he leaps to his feet, the beak flies open and claps shut, and he cries *hap! hap! hap! ḵô ḵô! ḵô!* to indicate that he is both hamatsa and raven. Then begins another song with the slow, measured beat-ing, and the raven masker moves toward the door of the house, stepping high and timing his arrival at the front of the room with the end of this song, so that just after arriving there he again leaps into the air and drops to the floor as the song ends. Again the tempo becomes rapid, and the raven repeats his dance. When the next song is begun, he returns to the right, rear corner and dances. At the end of this fourth song he rushes behind the *máwihl,* and simultaneously out dashes the hamatsa from the other side, with his *hap! hap! hap! ḳô ḳô! ḳô!* while the attendants pursue him. He crouches and runs rapidly round the fire four times, while the singers beat rapidly without singing. He constantly utters his cries, and his attendants hold him as before, as if to restrain him with great effort. After the fourth circuit they dash again behind the *máwihl*.

"Immediately is heard the cry, *hap, hap, hap! hawuwuwuwuwuwuwuwu!** and there is the noise of a great beak clapping shut. Then comes out another man wearing the mask of *Kalóqŭtsuis (kalóqiwihámsiwi)* and performs to the same songs and in the same manner as the raven masker.

"After this masker has withdrawn, hamatsa comes again, this time with *hap! hap! hap! hô hô! hô!* He performs just like the other two maskers. When he retires, hamatsa comes out, stark naked since throwing off the hemlock, and runs stooping around the fire four times, while the initiator rises and calls to the attendants, "Hold him down!" They leap upon him and bring him to the ground, making a great show of having to exert strength, and hamatsa acts like a wild animal. When finally they have mastered him, they hold him there, and an old hamatsa, stark naked, takes a five-foot staff and calls for an old cedar-bark blanket, which he rolls and ties to one end of the rod, like a mop. This staff is the 'tamer of the man-eater with fire.' He brings the roll close to the fire, and the singers begin to beat without singing. He swings slowly about, counter-clockwise, and when his back is to the fire the singers give a loud, abrupt stroke and he leaps into the air. He turns on around and again holds the mat near the fire. This act is repeated four times, and the last time the roll is actually put into the fire and lighted. It burns slowly, and he walks with it around the room. When he approaches hamatsa, the strokes of the batons become more violent. He waves the blazing mat four times over hamatsa and the attendants, continuing the fourth motion in a swing completely around the circle, and when his back is turned to hamatsa the singers give a loud rap and he leaps into the air. He turns on around, and repeats his motions. Every time the blazing mat is waved over him and the sparks fall on his bare back, hamatsa cries *hap! hap! hap!* The attendants crouch around him with bowed heads. When for the fourth time the old

---

* This resembles the sound made when one shivers and utters the exclamation expressive of coldness.

hamatsa turns away from the group, and the singers beat loudly, he throws the staff with its burning mat carelessly toward the door. Any one who happens to be struck receives something for the damage, usually a large canoe, from the man giving the ceremony. Sometimes the initiate still wears his hemlock rings, in which case the old hamatsa tears them off and casts them into the fire.

"The initiator now calls again to the attendants to hold the hamatsa down, and a woman of high rank brings a robe, usually a bearskin and preferably that of a grizzly-bear, which she belts around the initiate's waist. Then she puts on him the red cedar-bark ornaments: the wristlets *(tsitsihĪtsani)* and the anklets *(tsitsihĪtsitseĕ)*, consisting of four superimposed rings, the ends of the bands flowing free; the neck-ring *(yóhawi)*, a large, thick rope of cedar splints wrapped spirally with reddened cedar-bark cord; and the headband *(yúhwu̧hi)*, consisting of three rings, one above the other, each succeeding one being slightly larger and hence jutting out beyond the one below it. Then tallow is rubbed on his face, and one of the attendants crushes charcoal in his palms and powders the hamatsa's face until it is black. Another announces, 'It is finished.' The hamatsa seems now very weak. All the supernatural strength is apparently gone from him. The singers begin to sing in slow tempo, and he rises and dances quietly. Women engaged by the initiator rise in their places and perform their gesture dances. When the song ends he crouches while the attendants stand about him. Another song is begun, and hamatsa rises again and dances very quietly, while the attendants whistle less loudly. Twelve songs are repeated in this way, and each time hamatsa becomes more tranquil and the whistles more subdued. As the last song nears the end, he walks into the secret room.

"Then the speaker, for the giver of the dance, distributes miscellaneous gifts, such as canoes and guns, but not blankets, to the singers and those who have been engaged to perform in various capacities, and the people depart."

Northwest Coast Collections in the Museum of Anthropology, University of British Columbia

Mrs. G. H. W. Ashwell Collection, 15 baskets, gift of Mrs. Galt, 1954

Mrs. F. L. Beecher Collection, approximately 50 items, gift, 1950

R. O. Brooks, 50 items, MacMillan Purchase, 1950

Mrs. G. O. Buchanan Collection, 10 items, gift of Mrs. G. S. Scholfield, 1960

Mr. J. M. Buchanan Collection, 300 items, gift, 1948

Mr. Frank Burnett Collection, 270 items, gift, 1927

A. J. Buttimer Memorial Collection, 200 baskets, gift, 1935

Cadwallader Collection, Fort Rupert, 20 items, collected 1885-1948, MacMillan Purchase, 1963

Mr. F. Carson, 60 items, gift, 1957

D. Clayton Collection, 20 items, Bella Coola, collected 1890-1910, MacMillan Purchase, 1963

Rev. W. E. Collison, 150 items, mostly from Queen Charlotte Islands, collected between 1889 and 1925, MacMillan Purchase, 1960. William Edwin Collison was born in 1874 at Kinkolith, son of the pioneer missionary, W. H. Collison, who began the collection. In 1899 W. E. Collison was appointed to the Anglican Church at Masset, and in 1911 to Port Simpson. In 1920 he was appointed Indian Agent for the Nass River District, with headquarters in Prince Rupert. He left that post in 1925 and died in 1948.

Edith Bevan Cross Collection, 230 items, MacMillan Purchase, 1962

R. A. Cummings, 440 items, archeological materials, gift, 1936

Mrs. J. Cuzen, 7 items, gift, 1958

Thomas F. Daly, 30 items, Museum Purchase, 1959

Dr. and Mrs. G. E. Darby, 50 items, Valedictory Gift, Class of 1931; 20 items, Museum Purchase, 1947; loan, 1949. Dr. George E. Darby was medical missionary for the United Church of Canada at Bella Bella from 1912 until 1959. From 1959, he was Coordinator of Medical Hospitals and Mission Work for the United Church of Canada. His collection was gathered between 1912 and 1959 at Bella Bella.

Mr. G. Morton Fergusson, 4 items, Tsimshian, 1957

Mrs. Grace M. Frost, Skidegate, Queen Charlotte Islands, 30 items, MacMillan Purchase, 1964

Fyfe Smith Family Collection, 70 items, gift, 1957

Mr. Wilhelm Helmer Collection, 70 items, Nootka and Tsimshian, MacMillan Purchase, 1960-64

Leon and Thea Koerner Foundation grants, approximately 150 items, 1950-65

Dr. Walter C. Koerner, purchase grants for 10 major items, 1957-66, 8 gifts also given to Museum by Dr. Koerner

Dr. and Mrs. Hunter C. Lewis, 7 items, gift, 1966

Mr. M. MacKay, 70 items, northern tribes, collected before 1948, MacMillan Purchase 1959

H. R. MacMillan, Special Grant. The major part of these Museum materials was purchased through a series of annual grants given to the Museum by Dr. MacMillan for this purpose. From 1950 to 1964, these made possible direct purchases from Indian families. In addition, Dr. MacMillan made special purchases of major collections, such as the Raley and Collison collections, and others.

Mr. Ed Meade, 100 items, first-hand collections of various groups, MacMillan Purchase, 1955-65

Miscellaneous sources, 2,000 items, MacMillan Purchase, 1950-65

R. H. Nichols Collection, 20 items, Salish, Museum Purchase, 1958-61

Rev. G. H. Raley, approximately 1,000 items, mostly from the northern Kwakiutl area, collected between 1893 and 1914, MacMillan Purchase, 1948. George H. Raley was born in Barnsley, England, in 1864, and came to Canada in 1882. In 1893 he was appointed the Methodist missionary to Kitamaat. Here he published and printed a periodical, *Na-Na-Kwa* ("Dawn of the West Coast") from 1898 on. In 1906 he went to

Port Simpson. From 1904 until 1914 he was superintendent of the Port
Simpson District, which included all the area north of Alert Bay. In 1914
he left this region and became principal of the Coqualeetza Residential
School, retiring in 1934. He died in 1958.

Bill Reid Collection, 20 items, drawings, tools, and Haida materials

Bert Robson, 150 items, Bella Coola and Lytton, gifts, 1950-60

Mr. William Rowe through Mr. George Ades, 60 items, Salish, collected 1881,
MacMillan Purchase, 1961

Dr. F. G. Sherbourne, 6 items, Bella Coola, gift, 1948

Mr. and Mrs. Sidney Garfield Smith, 5 items, collected 1912, gift, 1960

G. Stevenson, 6 items, Haida, collected 1880, Museum Purchase, 1952

Mr. T. R. Stock, 25 items, collected 1920-30, MacMillan Purchase, 1961

Barbara Sulley Collection, 92 items, 1949

Mr. John Spotteswood Tait, 12 items, collected 1897, gift of Miss Fanta
Tait, 1965

Mr. Thomas Wallace, 4 items, Tsimshian, 1957

Mr. B. H. Weare, 21 items carved by Charlie James of Alert Bay, ca. 1910,
gift of Lanning family, 1961

Mrs. Vera Webb, Prince Rupert, 30 items, MacMillan Purchase, 1950-65

Mrs. A. C. Whitley, 76 items, collected before 1910, MacMillan Purchase,
1964

Mrs. W. C. Woodward, 10 items, gift, 1951

Glossary

This glossary contains the Kwakiutl words found in the text and captions, listed alphabetically according to the spelling used in this book. Wherever possible, each entry includes a literal translation of the term as well as a brief description of its meaning as used. Most of the words are derived from the Fort Rupert dialect of Kwakiutl. Some northern Kwakiutl words that have been borrowed by the southern tribes are also included.

ALK. "Blood"; a chief's speaker or herald.

AMHALAYT (Tsimshian). A special type of forehead mask consisting of a wooden frontal piece attached to a crown of upright sea-lion whiskers and a trailer of ermine skins.

ATLAKIM. A generic term referring to a series of dances and their associated masks.

BAKBAKWALANOOKSIWAE. "The first one to eat man at the mouth of the river"; initiating spirit of the Hamatsa dancers.

BAKOOS. "Profane, secular"; a season; the period from March to November during which Kwakiutl social organization was based on lineage and rank.

BOOKWUS. A mythological figure, known also as the Woodman, Wild Man of the Woods.

DANUM. The initiated troop of dancers.

DLOOGWI. The supernatural treasure of dancers, e.g., the Tokwit frog, used as a stage prop.

DLOOGWALA. The wolf dance series of the Nootka, their main series, also pronounced Klukwalla.

DLUWALAKHA. "Once more come down"; a word used by the northern Kwakiutl for a dancing series. The spirits who come down grant special supernatural privileges and treasures to their dancers. Used among the southern Kwakiutl for the dancing series not initiated by the violent spirits.

DUNTSIK. A Sisiutl spirit board conjured up from the ground in the Tokwit performances.

GAKHULA. An Intruder who introduces the Tsetseka season.

GAKHULAGUMHL. The mask of Gakhula, the Intruder.

GALOKWUDZUWIS. One of the three bird-monster guises of the Hamatsa dancer, the "Crooked Beak."

GEEKUMHL. A chief's mask; used to describe a Tsonokwa mask worn when cutting the copper.

GISUKSTOLA. Ceremonial box lid used in the marriage-privilege transfer ceremony.

GWISPECK. An official staff of office of the Sparrows.

HAMATSA. "Cannibal"; the name of the highest ranking Kwakiutl dancing society and its members; also used for the novice being initiated into the dance order.

HAMSHAMTSUS. "Eater on the ground"; the name of an earlier Kwakiutl dancing society and its members; also a character in the Hamatsa ritual.

HAMSPEK. Tethering pole of the cannibal dancer, against which he tested his supernatural strength.

HAYLEEKILAHL. "Embodiment of the personation of healing; the Healer"; a character in the War Spirit dance and the Hamatsa, who has the supernatural power of restoring to life.

HETLIWEY. A light forehead mask.

HOKHOKW. "Long-beaked"; one of the three bird-monster guises of the Hamatsa dancer.

HOTLULITI. "Obeyed by All"; the director of ceremonies in each winter dancing order, in its own house.

HWASULEEHL. A dancer gets excited in the house.

KANAYOO. A cedar bark ring made in the shape of a man and used in the ceremonial bathing of a new Hamatsa.

KAPEKW. Assembly at the beginning of the winter dances.

KHENKHO. A mythological bird, similar to a crane, with flaring upright nostrils and a downcurved beak.

KIKILNILA. Dancing to bring back the novices who have disappeared.

KIMYA. Surrounding and capturing the new Hamatsa.

KINKALATLALA. Bakbakwalanooksiwae's female slave, also known as Heyleegistey, who helps to tame the Hamatsa.

KLASILA. Four-day carnival time preceding the Tsetseka season.

KLUKWALLA. The main wolf dance of the Nootka, also pronounced Dloogwala.

KOLUS. A bird creature, younger brother of Thunderbird, covered with thick white down.

KOMOKWA. "The wealthy one"; known also as King or Chief of the Sea and Protector of Seals. This mythological character is nearly always associated with wealth and coppers.

KOMUNOKAS. "Rich woman"; Bakbakwalanooksiwae's female servant.

KOOSIOOT. A Bella Coola winter dancing society.

KULA. A culture hero said to have been the first to capture a whale.

KWAKWAKWALANOOKSIWAE. "The raven at the mouth of the river"; the Hamatsa raven, one of the three bird-monster guises of the Hamatsa dancer, distinguished from the clan raven.

KWASA. Ceremonial bathing of a newly initiated dancer.

KWEKHULA. Women's dance, not sacred but for entertainment.

KWEKWE. This character, who is supposed to cause earthquakes, was borrowed—complete with associated paraphernalia—from the neighboring Coast Salish Indians.

LAKHSA. Those who were initiated "in the house of Bakbakwalanooksiwae."

LULOTLALAHL. "Embodiment of ghosts"; one of the dancers in the War Spirit dance.

MAMAKA. "Thrower"; the name of a character in the War Spirit dancing society.

MATUM. The flyer, who bears the supernatural quartz crystal in the War Spirit dance.

MAWIHL. "Screen"; a ceremonial curtain or board used as a partition to form the dressing room for dancers at the rear of the house.

MITLA. In the North this is the name of a particular dancing society and its members. In the South it is a character in the War Spirit dance, portrayed by both men and women.

NANES BAKBAKWALANOOKSIWAE. The Hamatsa grizzly bear; one of the winter dancers in the Hamatsa series.

NENOLU. A mimic in the Atlakim series.

NOOHLMAHL. "Fool dancer"; one of a group of dancers in the Hamatsa series who act as police.

NOONSISTALAHL. "Fire thrower"; a character in the Hamatsa series who is obsessed with fire.

NOOTLEM. In the North, a word used for a dance series; the Dog-eating society. In the South, a word used to indicate "nonsacred."

NOOTLEMGEELA. "Making foolish," or "sleight-of-hand"; a character sometimes represented by Dloogwi puppets.

NUNALALAHL. "Weather"; forehead mask.

POTLATCH (Chinook). "To give"; the Northwest Coast social institution of feasting and distributing goods to validate social claims.

PUGWIS. Sea being, Merman.

SISAUK. A Bella Coola ceremonial season.

SISIUTL. The fabulous double-headed serpent, an important Kwakiutl mythological character, especially important to warriors and War Spirits dancers.

SOLATLALA. The Hamatsa's attendant, traditionally a Heleega (healer).

SOPALI. Dialogue mask, of echo or moon beings.

TAKIUMI. "Holding the Upper Part"; the official in charge of the distribution of gifts at the potlatch.

TANIS (northern Kwakiutl). "Cannibal"; the northern Kwakiutl "house name" for the Hamatsa.

TCHENES. Hair ornaments.

TLAKWAKILAYOKWA. "Born to be Copper Maker Woman"; wife of Komokwa; also a high-ranking title for women.

TOKWIT (Wikeno). "To walk"; the female war spirit dancer and associated magical tricks and devices.

TOSA. One who cuts the ceremonial cedar bark used in the winter dances and distributed to all present.

TSAHKEED. Dancing with short fast steps.

TSEKA. Winter ceremony, singular form.

TSETSEKA. From the Heiltsuk word for "shaman"; the winter dances which took place during the period from November to March and during which the social organization of the Kwakiutl people was based on membership in the dancing societies rather than on clan affiliations. The word implies "secret" and "sacred."

TSONOKWA. A family of giants, especially a wild woman of the woods who plays several important roles.

WALASAHAKW. A wolf dance series among the Kwakiutl.

WAWASLEEGA. "Chief dog" mask and dancer.

WIKHSA. Those who were initiated but not by Bakbakwalanooksiwae.

WINALAGILIS. "Making war all over the earth"; the patron spirit of the winter dance (Tsetseka) season, initiator of all so-called "war" dancers.

YATHLA. A large ceremonial cradle used for a naming ceremony in connection with the copper.

YEYLAKWULA. Singing one's sacred song.

YUKWEEWAE. A dancer's headdress with a carved frontal piece of crest design.

Bibliography

Allen, Rosemary

1954   "The Potlatch and Social Equilibrium," a paper presented to the 5th Alaskan Science Conference, *Davidson Journal of Anthropology.*

Barbeau, Marius

1912   "The Bearing of the Heraldry of the Indians of the Northwest Coast of America upon their Social Organization," *Man,* Vol. XII.

Barnett, Homer G.

1938   "The Nature of the Potlatch," *American Anthropologist,* N.S. Vol. X, pp. 349-58.

1942   "The Southern Extent of Totem Pole Carving," *Pacific Northwest Quarterly,* Vol. XXXIII, pp. 379-89.

Boas, Franz

1890   *On the Use of Masks and Head Ornaments on the North West Coast of America.* (Internationales Archiv für Ethnographie.) Leiden.

1895   *The Social Organization and Secret Societies of the Kwakiutl Indians.* (United States National Museum Report.)

1898   *Facial Paintings of the Indians of Northern British Columbia.* (American Museum of Natural History Memoir, Vol. II, No. 1.)

Boas, Franz, with George Hunt

 1902–5 *Kwakiutl Texts.* (Memoirs of the American Museum of Natural History, Vol. I.)

 1909 *The Kwakiutl of Vancouver Island.* Memoirs of the American Museum of Natural History, Vol. VIII, No. 2.)

 1910 *Kwakiutl Tales.* (Columbia University Contributions to Anthropology, Vol. II.)

 1920 "The Social Organization of the Kwakiutl," *American Anthropologist*, N.S., Vol. XXII, No. 2.

 1921 *Ethnology of the Kwakiutl.* (Annual Report of the Bureau of American Ethnology, Vol. XXXV, pp. 43-1481.)

 1927 *Primitive Art.* Oslo.

Bolles, T. Dix

 1893 "Chinese Relics in Alaska," *Proceedings of the United States National Museum,* Vol. XV, pp. 221-22.

Codere, Helen

 1950 *Fighting with Property: A Study of Kwakiutl Potlatching and Warfare 1792-1930.* (Monographs of the American Ethnological Society, No. 18.) Reissued by the University of Washington Press, Seattle, 1966.

 1956 "The Amiable Side of Kwakiutl Life," *American Anthropologist,* Vol. LVIII, pp. 334-51.

 1959 "The Understanding of the Kwakiutl," in *The Anthropology of Franz Boas*, edited by Walter Goldschmidt. San Francisco, Calif.

Curtis, Edward S.

 1915 *The North American Indian.* Vol. X and Folio. Norwood.

Dall, William Healey

 1881–82 *On Masks, Labrets, and Certain Aboriginal Customs.* Annual Report of the Bureau of American Ethnology, Vol. III, pp. 67-202.

de Laguna, Frederica

 1963 "Obituary on Mungo Martin," *American Anthropologist,* Vol. LXV, No. 4, pp. 894-96.

Drucker, Philip

1939   "Rank, Wealth and Kinship in North West Coast Society,"
            American Anthropologist, N.S., Vol. XLI, pp. 55-65.

1940   "Kwakiutl Dancing Societies," *Anthropological Records,*
            Vol. II, pp. 201-30. University of California.

1948   "The Antiquity of the North West Coast Totem Pole,"
            Journal of Washington Academy of Sciences, Vol. XXXVIII,
            pp. 389-97.

1950   "Culture Element Distribution of North West Coast," *An-
            thropological Records*, Vol. IX, p. 3. University of Cali-
            fornia.

1955   *Indians of the Northwest Coast.* (American Museum of
            Natural History, Anthropological Handbook No. 10.) New
            York.

1965   *Cultures of the North Pacific Coast.* San Francisco, Calif.

Duff, Wilson

1956   "Prehistoric Stone Sculpture of the Fraser River and Gulf
            of Georgia," *Anthropology in B.C.,* No. 5, p. 15.

1960   *The Killerwhale Copper: A Chief's Memorial to His Son.*
            Provincial Museum of Natural History and Anthropology,
            Victoria, B.C.

1964   *The Indian History of British Columbia.* Vol. I, *The Impact
            of the White Man.* (Provincial Museum of Natural History
            and Anthropology, Victoria, B.C., Anthropological Memoir
            No. 5.)

Emmons, George T.

1907   *The Chilkat Blanket.* (Memoirs of the American Museum of
            Natural History, Vol. III, pp. 329-400.)

1914   "Portraiture among the North Pacific Tribes," *American
            Anthropologist,* N.S., Vol. XVI, pp. 59-67.

Feder, Norman, and Edward Malin

1964   *Art of the North West Coast.* Denver Museum of Art.

Ford, Clellan S.

1941   *Smoke from Their Fires.* New Haven, Conn.

Galpin, F. W.

1902–3   "The Whistles and Reed Instruments of the American Indians of the North West Coast," *Proceedings of the Musical Association,* London, pp. 115-36.

Garfield, Viola E., *et al.*

1951   *The Tsimshian: Their Arts and Music.* (Publications of the American Ethnological Society, Vol. XVIII.) Reissued by the University of Washington Press, Seattle, as *The Tsimshian Indians and Their Arts,* 1966.

1955   "Making a Bird or Chief's Rattle," *Davidson Journal of Anthropology,* No. 1, pp. 155-64.

1956   "Antecedents of Totem Pole Carving," *Proceedings of Alaskan Sciences Conference,* Washington.

Goddard, Earl Pliny

1945   *Indians of the Northwest Coast.* 2nd ed. (American Museum of Natural History, Anthropological Handbook No. 10.) New York.

Goldman, Irving

1937   "The Kwakiutl Indians of Vancouver Island," in *Cooperation and Competition among Primitive Peoples,* edited by Margaret Mead. New York.

Gunther, Erna

1951   *Indians of the Northwest Coast.* Taylor Museum and Seattle Art Museum, Colorado Springs and Seattle.

1962   *Northwest Coast Indian Art.* Seattle World's Fair Exhibition, Seattle, Washington.

Haeberlin, H. K.

1918   "Principles of Esthetic Form in the Art of the North Pacific Coast," *American Anthropologist,* N.S., Vol. XX, pp. 258-64.

Harner, J. Michael

1965   *Art of the North West Coast.* Lowie Museum of Anthropology, University of California, Berkeley.

Holm, Bill

1961   "Carving a Kwakiutl Canoe," *The Beaver,* Summer.

1965   *Northwest Coast Indian Art.* University of Washington Press, Seattle.

Hawthorn, Audrey

1952   "Mungo Martin: Totem Pole Carver," *The Beaver,* March.

1956   *People of the Potlatch.* Vancouver Art Gallery and University of British Columbia, Vancouver.

1961   *Kwakiutl Art: The Paintings of Chief Henry Speck.* B.C. Indian Designs, Vancouver.

1963   "A Living Haida Craft," *The Beaver,* Summer.

1964   "Mungo Martin: Artist and Craftsman," *The Beaver,* Summer.

Hawthorn, Harry B.

1961   "The Artist in Tribal Society: The North West Coast," in *The Artist in Tribal Society,* edited by Marion Smith. London.

Jenness, Diamond

1960   *The Indians of Canada.* 5th ed. (National Museum of Canada, Anthropology Series No. 15.) Ottawa.

Keithahn, Edward L.

1964   "The Origin of the Chief's Copper," *Anthropological Papers of the University of Alaska*, Vol. XII, No. 2, pp. 59-78.

Kroeber, A. L.

1923   "American Culture and the North West Coast," *American Anthropologist,* N.S., Vol. XXV, No. 1.

Leechman, D.

1942   "Abalone Shells from Monterey," *American Anthropologist,* N.S., Vol. XLIV, pp. 159-62.

Lévi-Strauss, Claude

1963   *Structural Anthropology,* chap. xiii. New York.

Lopatin, Ivar

1945   *Social Life and Religion of the Indians in Kitimat, British Columbia.* (University of Southern California Social Science Series, Vol. XXVI, No. 1.)

McFeat, Thomas R., ed.

1966   *Indians of the North Pacific Coast.* Toronto. U.S. edition, University of Washington Press, Seattle, 1967.

McIlwraith, Thomas F.

1948   *The Bella Coola Indians.* 2 vols. Toronto.

Murdock, George Peter

1934   *Our Primitive Contemporaries.* New York.

Nesbitt, James K.

1954   "Potlatch in the Park," *The Beaver,* March.

Niblack, Albert P.

1888   *The Coast Indians of Southern Alaska and Northern British Columbia.* (United States National Museum Report.)

Olson, Robert L.

1935   *Indians of the Northwest Coast.* (American Museum of Natural History, Vol. XXXV.)

1940   "The Social Organization of the Haisla," *Anthropological Records,* Vol. II, pp. 169-200.

1950   "Black Market Prerogatives among the Northern Kwakiutl," *Publication of the Kroeber Anthropological Society,* Vol. I, pp. 78-80.

1954   "Social Life of the Owikeno Kwakiutl," *Anthropological Records,* Vol. XIV, pp. 213-59.

1955   "Notes on the Bella Bella Kwakiutl," *Anthropological Records,* Vol. XIV, pp. 319-48.

Read, C. H.

1891   "An Account of a Collection of Ethnographic Specimens Formed during Vancouver's Voyages," *Journal of the Anthropological Institute,* Vol. XXI, pp. 99-108.

Ritzenthaler, Robert E., and Lee A. Parsons, eds.

1966   *Masks of the Northwest Coast.* (Milwaukee Museum Publications in Primitive Art, No. 2.)

Rowe, John Howland

1962   *Chavin Art.* Museum of Primitive Art, New York.

Sapir, E.

1915   "Social Organization of the West Coast Tribes," *Proceed-*

ings and Transactions of the Royal Society of Canada, Ser. 3, Vol. IX, pp. 355-74.

Smith, Marion

1955   "Continuity in Culture Contact." *Man,* Vol. LV, pp. 100-5.

1956   "The Cultural Development of the North West Coast," *Southwestern Journal of Anthropology,* Vol. XII, pp. 272-94.

Swanton, John R.

1904   "The Development of the Clan System of Secret Societies among the Northwest Coast Tribes," *American Anthropologist,* N.S., Vol. VI, pp. 477-85.

1905   *The Haida of the Queen Charlotte Islands.* Vol. V, *Jessup Expedition to the North West Coast.* American Museum of Natural History, New York.

Stott, Margaret

1966   "The Southern Kwakiutl Copper: A Study Based on the George Hunt Manuscript." Unpublished graduating essay, University of British Columbia.

Waite, Deborah

1966   "Kwakiutl Transformation Masks," in *The Many Faces of Primitive Art,* edited by Douglas Fraser. Englewood Cliffs, N.J.

Waterman, T. T.

1923   "Some Conundrums in North West Coast Art," *American Anthropologist,* Vol. XXV, pp. 435-51.

Index

Alaska, 14, 202

Alderwood, 9

Alert Bay: potlatch at, described, 384-86; mentioned, ix, x, 28, 35, 73, 379

Alexei, Freddie, 383

Alfred, Mrs. Moses, 379

Alk. *See* Speaker

Ancestral myths. *See* Mythology

Angels, 72, 383

Aprons, ceremonial, 57, 174

Atlakim dance series, 46, 57; costumes for, 57, 168; characters of, 138-39

Atlakim masks, 138-39, 280, 382, 383

Attributions, 13-14, 381-83

Bakbakwalanooksiwae, 46, 51, 280

Bakoos: defined, 33; mentioned, 34, 77

Barrett, Samuel, 302

Baskets, 234

Batons: use of, 43-44, 47, 59, 77, 95

Beads, 202, 369

Bear, 19; Hamatsa grizzly, 41, 47, 51, 123-24, 390; masks of, 253-54

Bella Bella, viii, 27, 72, 239

Bella Coola, vii; style of carving, 11; dancing societies, 49; natural element masks, 283

Bella Coola River, 4

Birds: supernatural, 22; masks of, 271. *See also* Hamatsa: bird-monster masks; *and under names of individual birds*

Blankets, 14; used in dances, 42; as unit of wealth, 26, 30, 239, 388. *See also* Button cloaks

Blunden Harbour, 379

Boas, Franz: on dancing societies, 46, quoted, 48; quoted on Atlakim dancers, 138-39; on speaker masks, 302; on problems of identification, 309; on carving, 380; mentioned, xi, 34, 58, 310

Bolles, Lieut. T. Dix, 61

Bookwus: masks of, 291, 383

Boxes, 21, 23; construction and uses, 325-26

Bracelets, 383. *See also* Jewelry

Buffoons: in dances, 41; masks of, 310. *See also* Noohlmahl

Bumblebee: masks of, 62, 280

Button cloaks, 59, 173

Cannibalism: and Hamatsa ritual, 51

Canoe paddles, 337

Canoes: construction of, 336; model, 336, 382, 383

Carvers: Kwakiutl, 381-83; non-Kwakiutl, 383

Carving, 8; techniques and tools of, 9-10, 14; stylistic analysis of, 10-12, 62, 63, 377-82; dating of, 63

Cedar, 9, 14

Cedar bark, 4, 14; in Hamatsa ritual, 40, 44, 52, 53, 96, 116-17, 382, 385; for war spirit dancers' costumes, 54; for Atlakim costumes, 57; in Bakoos season, 116; for non-Hamatsa head and neck rings, 168; on Nootka wolf masks, 255

Charles, Andrew, 297, 383

Chiefs' headdresses, 191

Chief's seat. *See* Seat, chief's

Chilkat: blankets, 173; pattern board, 382

Clappers, 59, 78; used by Bookwus, 291

Cloaks, 59, 173

Clothing, 173-74. *See also* Costumes; Hats

Collison, Rev. W. E., viii

Colors: in Northwest Coast painting, 11, 60, 62

Comox, 23, 297

Complex masks, 319-20, 382

Cook, Capt. James, 61

Copper ceremony: accompanying potlatch, 27; described, 30-31; and Tsonokwa, 152-53; ceremonial daggers used in, 163

Coppers, 44, 68; described, 30, 158; as symbol of wealth, 30-32; rattles, 79; and Komokwa, 239; and frogs, 253

Cosmetics, 44, 53, 203

Costumes: Atlakim, 57, 168; Hamatsa, 116; for Kwekwe dance, 297-98; Sisiutl design on, 133; non-Hamatsa, 168; of bears, 254. *See also* Blankets; Cedar bark; Clothing; Hemlock

Cowichan River, 4

Crabs, 73

Cradles, 326; ceremonial, 158

Crane: masks of, 271. *See also* Khenkho

Cranmer, Chief Dan, ix, x, 28, 379; on attributions, 378

Cranmer, Mrs. Dan, 379; describes potlatch, 384-86

Crooked-Beak (Galokwudzuwis), 51, 138, 139; masks of, 62, 96; styles of masks, 377

Cross, John, 383

Curtain, ceremonial. *See Mawihl*

Curtis, Edward S.: quoted on inheritance of myth, 21-22; quoted on titles of rank, 22; quoted on display of masks, 34-35; quoted on Tokwit dancer, 37-38; on theatrical illusion, 42; on dancing societies, 46, 47-48; on Hamatsa cannibalism, 51; on hats, 184; on carving, 378; describes Hamatsa ritual, 387-90; mentioned, xi, 40, 59, 354, 355

Dancing, 4; in winter ceremonies, 22; accompanying potlatch, 27; in Hamatsa ritual, 37, 52, 95, 388-90; in war spirit ritual, 37; described, 39

Dancing societies: Kwakiutl, 46-48; other, 49

Darby, Dr. G. H., viii

Davis, John, 382

Death mask, 62

Deer: masks of, 253

Dick, James, 379

Dishes. *See* Feast dishes

Display board: for potlatch, 236

Dloogwala dance, 254

Dloogwi (supernatural treasure), 22, 46, 58, 72-73

Dluwalakha dances and masks, 41-42, 46, 58-59, 239, 283

Dog: masks of, 253. *See also* Nootlem

Door poles, 344

Drucker, Philip: describes Dluwalakha dance, 41-42, 58-59; on dancing societies, 46; on Hamatsa cannibalism, 51; quoted on *dloogwi*, 72; mentioned, 35, 127

Drums, 77, 326

Duff, Wilson, xi

Duntsik (power board), 55, 133, 383

Eagle: feast dishes, 11-12; down, 44, 385; masks of, 62-63, 270-71; costume of, 270-71

Earthquake masks, 283

Echo: masks of, 11, 59

Edenshaw, Charles, 337, 383

Emmons, George T., 354

Feast dishes, 27, 48, 133, 215-16, 326, 382, 383

Feasts, 27, 34, 215

Fish, 3, 215; masks of, 247-48

Food. *See* Feasts

Fools. *See* Buffoons

Fort Langley, 27

Fort Rupert, vii, x, 27, 379, 382, 384

Fort Simpson, 27

Fort Victoria, 27

Fraser River, 4, 369

Friendly Cove, 298

Frog: masks of, 253

Gakhula (Intruder), 35; masks of, 92

Galokwudzuwis. *See* Crooked-Beak

"Gamblers' masks," 302

Geekumhl, 153

George, Charlie, Jr., 379, 382

George, Charlie, Sr., 381-82

George, Chief, 382

Ghost dancers, 54, 55-56; masks of, 129

Gilford Island, 379

Graham Island, 354

Grave effigies, 62

Grouse: masks of, 271; headdresses, 310

Gwispeck, 207

Haida, vii, 4; style of carving, 11; potlatch, 25, 49; shamans, 49; dancing societies, 49; hats, 184; canoe, 337

Hairpins. *See* Jewelry

Haisla, 50

Halibut hooks, 240

Hamatsa: dancers, 37, 40, 46, 116; ritual, 45, 50-53, 384-86, described by Curtis, 387-90; society, 46; dance, acquisition of, 50; whistles, 51; initiation, 51-53; rattles, 79; bird-monster masks, 95-96, 380-82, 383; associated with skulls, 129; grizzly bear, 253-54; mentioned, 55. *See also* Cedar bark: in Hamatsa ritual; Head and neck rings: Hamatsa
Hamatsa raven. *See* Raven, Hamatsa
Hamshamtsus, 51
Hamspek, 52
Hats, 184-85
Hawkins, Dick, 382
Hawkins, Mrs. Dick, 379
Hayleekilahl, 55
Head and neck rings: Hamatsa, 116-17; non-Hamatsa, 168
Headdresses, chiefs', 191; helmet, 197
Heiltsuk, 50, 73, 379
Helmet headdresses, 197
Hemlock, 9; branches, in Hamatsa ritual, 51-52, 385-86, 388, 390; in war spirit dancer's costume, 54
Heron: on headdress, 197; masks of, 271
Hetliwey, 116
Hokhokw, 47, 138, 139; masks of, 96
Holm, Bill, xi, 13, 271
House posts, 13, 62, 343-44
Howard, Jim, 382
Hudson's Bay Co., 27; blankets, *see* Blankets
Human face masks, 62, 309-10, 382
Hunt, Mary, 384
Hunt, Tommy, 379

Iconography, 11, 13, 23
Identification: problems of, 309. *See also* Attributions
Informants: listed, 379-80
Inheritance, 4, 19-20, 21-23; of rank, 43
Initiation ceremonies, 23; in Tsetseka season, 36-38; of Hamatsa, 50, 51-53; in Nootka wolf ritual, 254-55
Insects: masks of, 280
Intruder. *See* Gakhula

James, Charlie, 382
James, Jack, 382
Jewelry, 14, 202-3. *See also* Beads; Bracelets
Johnny, Joe, 382
Johnson, Chief Tom, 379, 384, 386

Kerfed boxes, 325
Khenkho: masks of, 271

Khutzeymatleen Inlet, 4
Killer whales, 40, 48; masks of, 247-48
Kimsquit, 62
Kingcome Inlet, 379, 380, 382
Kinkalatlala, 42, 51, 116, 129
Kitamaat, viii, 13, 62
Kitlope, 50, 61, 62, 63, 127
Klasila: defined and described, 34-35; masks in, 59; mentioned, 46, 57, 90, 168
Klemklemalitz, 4
Klukwalla ritual, 254, 310
Koerner, Dr. Walter C., viii
Koerner Foundation, viii
Kolus, 59, 319; myth and masks of, 22, 270
Komokwa, 19, 32, 59; masks of, 11, 240, 309, 383; described, 239-40; and killer whale, 247; and frog, 253
Komokwa's wife, 32, 239-40; masks of, 11, 240, 309
Komunokas, 51, 116
Koosioot, 49
Koskimo, 90
Kwakwakwalanooksiwae. *See* Raven, Hamatsa
Kwekwe: masks of, 12, 297-98, 383; dance, 23, 49, 78; myth and ritual of, 297-98
Kyuquot, 62, 309

Ladles, 62, 215, 226. *See also* Spoons
Lakhsa, 52, 385
Loon, 239, 247, 271

McIlwraith, T. F., 378
MacMillan, Dr. H. R., viii
Mamaka, 54-55
Maple, 9
Marriage: and transfer of privileges, 23. *See also* Privileges
Martin, Chief Mungo, vii-ix, 240, 253, 379, 382; carving style of, 377; on attributions, 378
Martin, Mrs. Mungo, viii, ix
Masks: Dluwalakha, 34; mourning, 34, 90; construction of, 60, 95-96, 247-48; craftsmanship of, 60-61; attributions and dating, 61-62; transformation, 319-20. *See also under individual characters*
Mats, 234
Matum, 55
Mawihl (ceremonial curtain), 14, 41, 52, 67-68, 383
Memorial poles, 344
Merganser: masks of, 271
Merman. *See* Pugwis
Mitla: dancing order, 37; character, 37, 42, 46, 47, 55, 78

Moon: in Dluwalakha dance, 58-59; masks of, 59, 283
Mosquitoes: masks of, 280
Mourning masks, 34, 90
Museum of Anthropology, U.B.C., vii-xi
Musqueam Reserve, 4, 297, 383
Mythology, 4, 19-20, 21-24, 51, 54-56, 59, 66-67, 133, 152, 168, 239, 270-71, 291, 297. *See also under names of mythological characters*

Nahwahto, 379, 382
Nanes Bakbakwalanooksiwae. *See* Bear: Hamatsa grizzly
Nass River, 4
National Museum of Canada, 28
Necklaces. *See* Jewelry
Neck rings. *See* Head and neck rings
Nimpkish, 354
Nolie, Johnny, 383
Noohlmahl, 51, 53; masks of, 123, 383
Noonsistatahl, 51, 55
Nootka, vii, 4, 62; style of carving, 12; wolf ritual, 49, 254-55; masks, 61, 271, 310, 319; hats, 184; feast dish, 215; canoe, 336
Nootlem: society, 37, 254; defined, 58
Nootlemgeela, 72
North Vancouver Reserve, 4
Northwest Coast Indians, vii, 3-4. *See also under individual tribes*
Nunalalahl, 283

Octopus, 239, 240
Oil dishes. *See* Feast dishes
Olson, Robert L.: quoted on buffoons, 41; mentioned, 35, 127
Omhid, Tom, 386
Orthography, ix, xi
Otter: masks of, 253
Owl: masks of, 271

Paddles, canoe, 337
Painting: characteristics of, 12-13
Paints and brushes, 12, 14, 67, 369
Patricia Bay, 4
Port Simpson, 383
Potlatch, ix-x, 4, 23; defined and described, 25-29; banning of, 28; Haida, 49; and Tsonokwa, 152; and coppers, 158; and ceremonial hats, 185; baskets and mats as gifts at, 234; miscellaneous properties, 236; in Nootka wolf ritual, 255; totem poles and, 343; at Alert Bay, described, 384-86
Power board. *See Duntsik*
Price, Dick, 383

Prince Rupert, 4
Privileges, 4, 19-20, 22; transfer of, 77
Property. *See* Inheritance; Potlatch
Pugwis (Merman): masks of, 247-48, 379, 382
Puppets, 72-73

Quatsino, 380
Queen Charlotte Islands, 4

Raley, Rev. G. R., viii, 61, 62, 309
Rank, 4, 39; titles of, 21, 22; in dancing societies, 43-45. *See also* Inheritance
Rattles, 78-79, 158, 298
Raven, 19, 67, 73, 138, 139; myths and masks of, 271, 383. *See also* Raven, Hamatsa
Raven, Hamatsa, 51, 271, 385, 388; masks of, 62, 96. *See also* Raven
Red cedar, 3-4, 9. *See also* Cedar bark
Reid, Bill, 383
Religion. *See* Mythology
Ridicule carvings, 354; masks, 62, 309
Roberts, Mrs. James, 379

Salish, iv, 4; style of carving, 12; dances of, 49; and Kwekwe ritual, 49, 297; cloaks, 173; hats, 184
Salmon: on head rings, 168; masks of, 247
Scow, Chief Bill, 379
Sculpin, 239, 247
Sea bear, 19
Sea birds: masks of, 271
Seals, 239; dancing order, 37, 38, 117
Sea raven, 19
Seat, chief's, 63
Seaweed, Joe, 379, 383
Seaweed, Willie, 379, 383; carving style of, 377, 381
Sewid, Jim, 379
Shamans, 47; Haida, 49; rattles, 79; neck ring, 117; staff, 207
Shaughnessy, Arthur, 383
Sisauk, 49, 283
Sisiutl, 19, 68, 152; headdresses, 54, 382, 383; bow, 55, 163; staff, 55; described, 133; feast dishes, 215, 382
Skidegate, viii, 383
Skulls, ceremonial, 54, 96, 129, 382
Slaves, 4, 22, 23, 163
Smith, Peter, 380, 384
Soapberry spoons, 226
Solatlala rattles, 79, 383
Sonahed, 62
Songs, 4, 34, 43
Sopali masks, 283
Soul catchers, 62

Sparrows: dancing order, 37, 38, 47, 48, 55
Speaker (Alk): role of, 43; masks of, 302
Speakers' staffs, 43, 62
Spoons, 48, 215, 226. *See also* Ladles
Staffs, ceremonial, 43, 62, 207
Stonework, 369
Style. *See under* Carving; Painting
Sullivan Bay, 11, 12
Sun: masks of, 59, 283, 383
Swan, 58-59; headdress, 378-79
Swanton, John R., 355

Tanis masks, 61, 62, 127
Tattooing, 203
Technology, 8 ff.
Templates: for painting, 12
Theatrical devices, 39-40, 41, 42, 55
Thunderbird, 19, 22, 59, 67; masks of, 60, 270, 382; described, 270; headdress, 383
Tlingit, vii, 4
Tokwit: dancers, x, 37-38, 41, 55, 72; box, 73; cradle, 73
Tools, 9; for carving, 9-10; decoration of, 355; stone, 369
Totem Pole Park, 344
Totem poles, vii, 4, 21, 62, 383; meaning and construction of, 343-44
Transformation masks, 59, 319-20
Treasure: boxes for, 326; model canoes as, 336. *See also Dloogwi*
Tsetseka, 23, 34, 35, 46, 77; defined, 33; described, 36; staging of, 39-42
Tsimshian, vii, 4; style of carving, 11; dancing societies, 49
Tsonokwa, 19, 47; masks and character of, 92, 152-53
Turnour Island, 380

Vancouver, B.C., 4
Vancouver Island, 4
Victoria, B.C., ix, 4

Walasahakw dance, 254
Walker, Frank, 383
Walking sticks, 383
Walkus, George, 383
Wamiss, Tom, 383
War spirit dancers, 37, 47, 54-56. *See also* Winalagilis
Washington State, 4
Wasp, 22
Weapons: ceremonial, 163; stone, 369
Weather: supernatural embodiment of, 22; headpiece, 283
Weaving, 4, 8. *See also* Baskets; Chilkat blankets; Cradles; Hats
Webster, Gloria, x
Welcome figures, 354; masks, *see under* Kwekwe
West Saanich, 4
Whale: feast of, 215; carving of, 355. *See also* Killer whales
Whistles, 23, 35, 42, 77-78; Hamatsa, 51, 78, 387, 390; at potlatch, 236; in Nootka wolf ritual, 254
Wigs, 59
Wikhsa, 52
Wild Man of the Woods. *See* Bookwus
Williams, D., 383
Willie, Billy Sandy, 380
Willie, Dick, 380
Winalagilis, 46, 54, 129; and Sisiutl, 133. *See also* War spirit dancers
Wolf: masks of, 11, 62, 63, 254-55, 310; dance, 49
Wood: kinds used by carvers, 9

Xaihais, 62
X-ray painting, 12

Yellow cedar, 9
Yew, 9